IELTS

GENERAL TRAINING

READINGS FOR EXAM PRACTICE

SUDIPTO MUKHERJEE
MBA

KIRANPREET KAUR MAKKAR
DGO

Published by: **Makkar Publishing House**

SCF 15, Phase-7, Mohali, Punjab - 160062

M: 9646044322, 9872461083

www.makkarielts.com | ravielts@gmail.com

Makkar Publishing House

Reprint 2022

First published in India in 2019 by **makkarIELTS**

Written by: Sudipto Mukherjee, Kiranpreet Kaur Makkar

Cover Illustration: Amrit Pal Singh

Cover Page Image Courtesy: Alex Iby

Printed By: Chandigarh Publishing House, Sector 41, Chandigarh

Passages for reading tests have been sourced from the internet and their sources are acknowledged.

ISBN: 978-93-5351-900-1

About the Author

Sudipto Mukherjee has a remarkable academic record, standing first in the All India NDA entrance examination and later in his MBA course at FMS, Delhi and was accorded gold medals on both occasions. He has served in the Armed Forces; in the Corporate field, he has worked for the Tata Group amongst others, and has also been the CEO of an MNC. He teaches English in a government school as a social service and has also been coaching IELTS aspirants for some time.

INDEX

GENERAL INTRODUCTION

The Reading Test comprises of 40 questions in all and each correct answer carries 1 mark. Each test has five parts, or passages; the kind of answer required for each part may be different. The total time allotted for the Reading Test is 60 minutes.

Given below are the kinds of questions generally asked, though one can never say if a different kind may not be introduced in the future.

1. **A passage is given and your responses are required as TRUE/FALSE/or NOT GIVEN.**

THE ABACUS

Abacus, plural abaci or abacuses, is a calculating device, probably of Babylonian origin, that was long important in commerce. It is the ancestor of the modern calculating machine and computer. The earliest "abacus" likely was a board or slab on which a Babylonian spread sand so he could trace letters for general writing purposes. The word abacus is probably derived, through its Greek form abakos, from a Semitic word such as the Hebrew ibeq ("to wipe the dust"; noun abaq, "dust"). As the abacus came to be used solely for counting and computing, its form was changed and improved. The sand ("dust") surface is thought to have evolved into the board marked with lines and equipped with counters whose positions indicated numerical values—i.e., ones, tens, hundreds, and so on. In the Roman abacus the board was given grooves to facilitate moving the counters in the proper files. Another form, common today, has the counters strung on wires.

The abacus, generally in the form of a large calculating board, was in universal use in Europe in the Middle Ages, as well as in the Arab world and in Asia. It reached Japan in the 16th century. The introduction of the Hindu-Arabic notation, with its place value and zero, gradually replaced the abacus, though it was still widely used in Europe as late as the 17th century and survives today in the Middle East, China and Japan; an expert practitioner can compete against many modern mechanical calculating machines.

Questions

Do the following statements agree with the information given in the text?

Write:

TRUE	If the statement agrees with the information
FALSE	If the statement contradicts the information
NOT GIVEN	If there is no information on this

1. The Abacus might have originated in Babylon. T ✓

2. An expert on the Abacus can calculate faster on it than on a calculator. NG ✓

3. The abacus was used sparsely in the Middle Ages in Europe. F ✓

4. The Abacus has been replaced with calculators and is no longer in use. F ✓

(4)

2. **The next type of question is similar to the first, but responses to the questions are asked in the form of YES/NO/NOT GIVEN.**

If we took the same passage on Abacus, the TRUE answers would be YES, FALSE would be NO and the NOT GIVEN would remain as is.

3. **The third type of question requires a short answer, comprising of two or three words, and/or a number; the specific requirement is spelt out in the question.**

TRAVELLING TO GOA

Goa is a popular tourist destination, and a road or train journey is an inexpensive way to get there. There are two common routes which people take for a Mumbai to Goa road trip and it is upon you to decide which route would suit you better. The train options are summarized below.

A convenient and inexpensive way of getting from Mumbai to Goa is by train, via the Konkan Railway. It's much more comfortable than the bus and the scenery is more spectacular. If you take an overnight train, you'll be there the next morning. The average travel time is 12 hours. Book early though, as space fills up fast.
The fastest train from Mumbai to Goa is the new 22119 Mumbai CST – Karmali Tejas Express "luxury" semi-high speed train, which completes the trip in 8.5 hours. It commenced operating in May 2017 and runs during the day. The train departs CST station in Mumbai at 5 a.m. You can have a choice of a veg or non-veg breakfast, which is served on the train. It reaches Karmali in north Goa after several halts, including Ratnagiri and Kudal, at 1.30 p.m., just in time for lunch at Goa itself. The train usually runs five days a week -- Tuesday, Wednesday, Friday, Saturday, and Sunday. However, its frequency reduces the three days a week (Monday, Wednesday, and Saturday) during the monsoon season, from June until October.

Questions

Fill in the blanks in the sentences below using **NOT MORE THAN THREE WORDS AND/OR NUMBERS** from the text above.

1. If you travel to Goa by train, you will find it ...convenient and inexpensive ~~way~~. ✓

2. In order to ensure you get a reservation, you should ...book early... ✓

3. The fastest train from Mumbai to Goa made its first run in ...8.5 hours... ✗

4. The halts of Train No.22119 from Mumbai CST to Karmali in North Goa include ...Ratnagiri and ~~Kundal~~ Kudal. ✓

(3)

4. Another type of question requires matching a statement to a part of the text.

7 KINDS OF MONKEYS THAT ARE KEPT AS PETS

Many people keep monkeys as pets, and children no doubt fancy having one too. The most common types of monkeys kept as pets are:

3 ***A.* Capuchin**

Capuchins are primates and are often seen in movies and on television. They are famous for their small size and mischievous nature. They are highly intelligent, territorial and will live up to 40 years in captivity. That's 40 years of diapers, in case you didn't realize they don't learn to use the toilet.

2 ***B.* Chimpanzee**

The chimpanzee is the largest primate typically found as a pet. It isn't actually a monkey, but rather is an ape. Chimps are also often seen in movies and on television. Reports of chimps attacking their owners and other people, even killing them, are common. Chimpanzees are large and strong, and males especially are very aggressive. They can live for 60 years and more. These are not household pets.

4 ***C.* Macaque**

Macaques are smaller primates and can live up to 30 years, needing diaper changes all that time. They need large, secure cages so they don't get lost in your house or run outside and climb up electric poles, which is often the outcome. Even though these are smaller primates, they still require extremely large enclosures, at least 30 feet square. Even some zoos don't provide primates with the appropriate amount of space.

5 ***D.* Tamarin**

Tamarins are tiny primates that weigh less than a pound but will live about 15 years in captivity. They can still deliver a nasty bite despite their small mouths and need very secure cages with tiny bar spacing; if not, they will escape or get stuck in the bars.

***E.* Squirrel Monkey**

These are very acrobatic monkeys. They live up to 25 years, use their tails to hang on branches, and need a lot of space (as does any primate). They will also wear diapers their entire life and eat a variety of foods.

F. Marmoset

Similar to the tamarins in size and housing requirements, marmosets are teeny-tiny primates. They are quick and not suited to handling since they don't sit still in your lap.

G. Guenon

These are little primates weigh in at about 10 pounds and live about 25 years in captivity. Guenons, like all primates, are very high maintenance. There are almost two dozen species of guenons, with the green monkey, vervet, and grivet being possibly the most popular in captivity. They thrive in large groups; therefore one by itself is not suited to live in a house of humans.

Questions

For which type of pet monkey are the following statements true? Write A – G against each statement. You may use any letter only once. Any statement may have more than one answer.

1. If you have this type of a monkey as your pet, you should keep more than one of them. G
2. This primate is not actually a monkey. B
3. Keep this one as a pet and you will be changing its diapers for four decades. A
4. These types need very secure cages with tiny bar spacing, otherwise they may escape and end up on top of electric poles. C
5. They may be small, but beware of their bite. D

5. **There is a type of question where you will need to pick an appropriate word from a list of given words to fill in a sentence.**
Make sure you choose the most appropriate word given its context in the passage.

THE UNITED NATIONS AND SECURITY IN A NUCLEAR-WEAPON-FREE WORLD

The following is an extract of the address of the Secretary-General of the United Nations to the East-West Institute on the above subject.

It is a great pleasure to welcome you all to the United Nations. I salute the East-West Institute and its partner non-governmental groups for organizing this event on weapons of mass destruction and disarmament. This is one of the gravest challenges facing international peace and security. So I thank the East-West Institute for its timely and important new global initiative to build consensus. Under the leadership of George Russell and Martti Ahtisaari, the East-West Institute is challenging each of us to rethink our international security priorities in order to get things moving again. You know, as we do, that we need specific actions, not just words. As your slogan so aptly puts it, you are a "think and do tank".

One of my priorities as Secretary-General is to promote global goods and remedies to challenges that do not respect borders. A world free of nuclear weapons would be a global public good of the highest order, and will be the focus of my remarks today. I will speak mainly about nuclear weapons because of their unique dangers and the lack of any treaty outlawing them. But we must also work for a world free of all weapons of mass destruction.

Some of my interest in this subject stems from my own personal experience. As I come from the Republic of Korea, my country has suffered the ravages of conventional war and faced threats from nuclear weapons and other WMD. But of course, such threats are not unique to my country. Today, there is support throughout the world for the view that nuclear weapons should never again be used because of their indiscriminate effects, their impact on the environment and their profound implications for regional and global security. Some call this the nuclear "taboo".

Yet nuclear disarmament has remained only an aspiration, rather than a reality. This forces us to ask whether a taboo merely on the use of such weapons is sufficient.

States make the key decisions in this field. But the United Nations has important roles to play. We provide a central forum where states can agree on norms to serve their common interests. We analyse, educate and advocate in the pursuit of agreed goals.

Moreover, we have pursued general and complete disarmament for so long that it has become part of the Organization's very identity. Disarmament and the regulation of armaments are found in the Charter. The very first resolution adopted by the General Assembly, in London in 1946, called for eliminating "weapons adaptable to mass destruction". These goals have been supported by every Secretary-General. They have been the subject of hundreds of General Assembly resolutions and have been endorsed repeatedly by all our Member States.

And for good reason. Nuclear weapons produce horrific, indiscriminate effects. Even when not used, they pose great risks. Accidents could happen any time. The manufacture of nuclear weapons can harm public health and the environment. And of course, terrorists could acquire nuclear weapons or nuclear material.

Most states have chosen to forgo the nuclear option, and have complied with their commitments under the Nuclear Non-Proliferation Treaty. Yet some states view possession of such weapons as a status symbol. And some states view nuclear weapons as offering the ultimate deterrent of nuclear attack, which largely accounts for the estimated 26,000 that still exist.

Unfortunately, the doctrine of nuclear deterrence has proven to be contagious. This has made non-proliferation more difficult, which in turn raises new risks that nuclear weapons will be used.

Questions

Use words from the box given below to fill in the blanks.

1. Weapons that cause mass destruction pose a very .... problem.

2. The effort to build .... by the Institute was appreciated by the Secretary General.

3. The world-wide .... of nuclear weapons are indeed very serious.

4. Despite the implications of nuclear weapons, doing away with them has eluded us and it remains just a ....

5. Some states believe in the .... that having nuclear weapons would discourage use of such weapons against them.

weighty	acceptance	ramification	doctrine	theory	Credo
serious	yearning	harmony	grim	agreement	ambition
	purport	insinuation		inspiration	

6. **Another type of question will ask for a diagram to be labeled based upon a description given in a text. It could be the diagram of a device, an animal or insect, or any other.**

GRASSHOPPERS

Like all insects, the grasshoppers have three main body parts – the head, the thorax and the abdomen. They have six jointed legs, meaning a pair each of fore-legs, mid-legs and hind legs, two pairs of wings and two antennae jutting out from near their eyes. Their body is covered with a hard exoskeleton. Grasshoppers breathe through a series of holes called 'spiracles' which are located along the sides of the body. Most grasshoppers are green, brown, or olive-green.

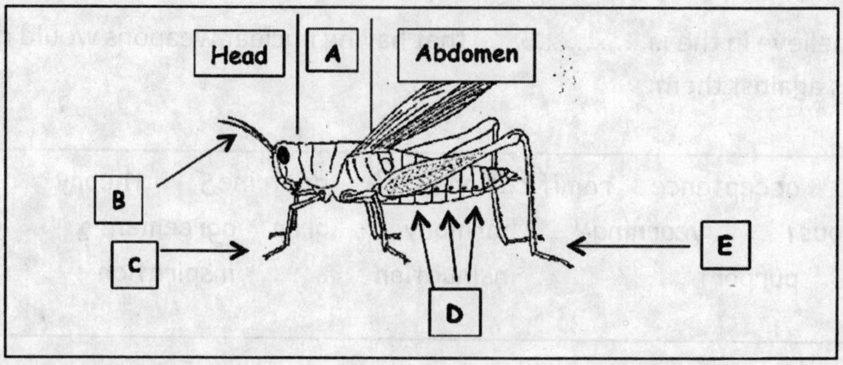

Name the body parts of the grass-hopper:

A ..Thorax..

B ..Antennae..

C ..fore legs..

D ..Spiracles..

E ..Hind legs..

(5)

7. **Apart from such diagram labeling question, there could be a labeling exercise based upon some other matter; for example, a street scene could be described and the question could be to label the landmarks on the street.**

Look at the sketch of the street scene below and answer the questions at the end:

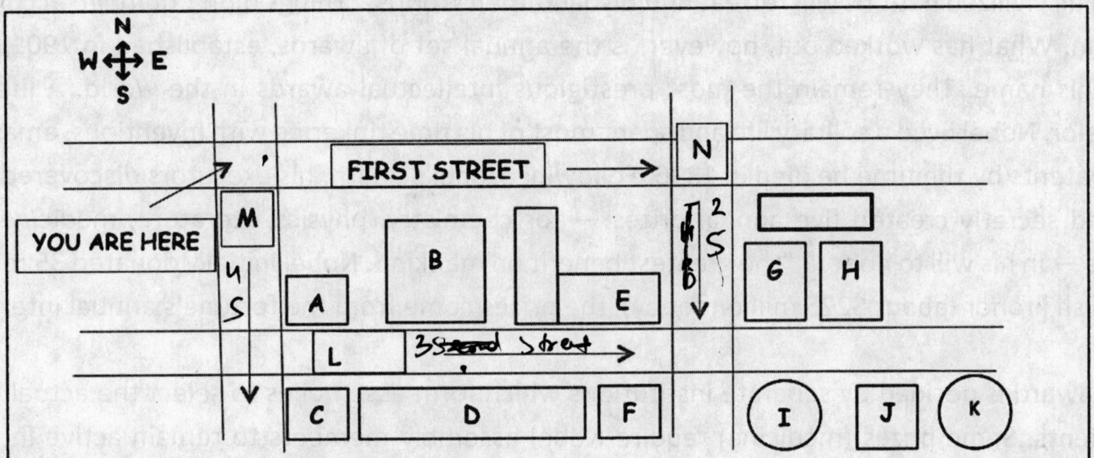

The First Street is parallel to the Third Street; going East from where you are, it intersects with the Second Street. The fourth street in this sketch is the Fourth Street. Of the two identical buildings side by side, the one on the left, if you face them, has a McDonald's outlet and the other has the Buddy's Gym. The building with the longest frontage in the diagram, houses a parking lot on the ground floor. The L-shaped building has a movie hall and the adjacent one has a drug store. The gas station is the eastern-most building in the sketch.

Questions

Where are the following located?

1. Drug store: ....
2. Parking Lot: ....
3. Buddy's Gym: ....
4. Gas Station: ....
5. Movie Hall: ....
6. Fourth Street: ....
7. McDonalds: ....

8. **In yet another type of question, a précis of the passage with blanks is given at the end; these blanks have to be filled up with a defined number of words taken from the text.**

THE NOBEL PRIZE

Alfred Nobel, the inventor of dynamite, was sure his creation would help bring about the end of war. "When two armies of equal strength can annihilate each other in an instant," he once wrote, "then all civilized nations will retreat and disband their troops." Things didn't quite go according to plan. What has worked out, however, is the annual set of awards, established in 1901, that bear his name. They remain the most prestigious intellectual awards in the world. A lifelong bachelor, Nobel lived a solitary life and spent most of his time tinkering with inventions, amassing 355 patents by the time he died in 1896. Following Nobel's death, his executors discovered that he had secretly created five annual prizes — for chemistry, physics, literature, medicine and peace — in his will to honour "the greatest benefit on mankind. Nobel initially donated 35 million Swedish kronor (about $225 million today); the prizes come from the fortune's annual interest.

Each award is decided by separate institutions which form assemblies to select the actual prize recipients. Some prizes (medicine) require Nobel assembly members to remain active in their fields, while others (literature) appoint members for life. The Peace Prize is actually decided by five members of the Norwegian parliament. Nobel Prize winners must be living; there are no posthumous awards. Each year, the Nobel committees distribute nomination forms to an undisclosed number of recipients — past winners, prominent institutions, respected members of the field — who are allowed to choose as many nominees as they want. Self-nomination is not permitted. The winner is decided by a simple majority vote.

The literature and peace prizes regularly inspire controversy. Jean-Paul Sartre rejected his 1964 prize in literature, though his family tried to claim the award money after his death. Pablo Neruda wanted a Nobel Prize so much that he reportedly wined and dined Swedish writers and academics at his seaside villa; he finally won one in 1971. In 2004, the literature prize went to Austrian feminist Elfriede Jelinek, a move so controversial that one assembly member resigned in protest. Henry Kissinger and Le Duc Tho shared a 1973 Peace Prize for negotiating the end of the Vietnam War. Tho rejected his award, saying there was no peace in his country. Kissinger's acceptance caused uproar: apparently the former National Security Adviser's role in a secret war against Cambodia and the overthrow of the Chilean government didn't sit well with some people.

Some Nobel Prizes have gone to discoveries that turned out to be wrong. The 1926 Nobel Prize in Medicine went to Johannes Fibiger for the discovery that roundworms cause cancer (they don't). A year later, psychiatrist Julius Wagner-Jauregg won for injecting patients with malaria to treat syphilitic dementia (not a good idea). Past laureates have espoused eugenics, opposed public school, joined the Nazi party and claimed that the Sept. 11 attacks were an inside job. But the majority of prizes have reflected sound discoveries (X-rays, quantum physics, penicillin) and respected leaders (Martin Luther King, Albert Einstein, Nelson Mandela). Much has been made of Obama's seemingly premature win and the committee's vague reasoning for awarding him the honor (they said he promoted "international diplomacy and cooperation between peoples"). Unfortunately, those seeking answers are out of luck: Nobel documents are sealed for 50 years.

Questions

Fill in the blanks in the sentences below using **NOT MORE THAN 2 WORDS AND/OR FIGURES** from the text.

Alfred Nobel, who had invented dynamite, felt that his invention would ensure countries did not go to war against each other, for if they did, the opposing armies would 1) Annihilate each other. While his conjecture has fallen through, he did establish the Nobel Prize, the first of which was given out in 2) ...1901..... Given for work in five areas, the award is funded from the interest earned on his donation of 3) $225 Million Each award has a set process by which the winner is determined, and they are not awarded posthumously. Forms inviting nominations are given out annually; the one who gets the most votes is the 4) winner. Some prizes have created controversies, while others were given to 5) Discoveries...... that later proved incorrect. The documents which could throw light on each award are not readily available, as they are not made public for 6) ....50 years.

3

9. **Another type of question would be a long passage divided into paragraphs, and one has to choose the correct paragraph heading from a given set of such paragraph headings. There may also be some questions at the end of the passage.**

The text has 8 SECTIONS, marked A to H. Choose the correct heading for each paragraph from the list of headings below.

i. The preferred customer interface
ii. Video is not just you tube
iii. Old is not gold
iv. It may not be natural but it is power-packed
v. Get personal
vi. Get ready for the new world ahead
vii. Why type when you can speak
viii. Use effective persuaders
ix. Siri and Alexa to the fore!

1. Paragraph A ....
2. Paragraph B ....
3. Paragraph C ....
4. Paragraph D ....
5. Paragraph E ....
6. Paragraph F ....
7. Paragraph G ....
8. Paragraph H ....

DIGITAL MARKETING

A. As 2019 approaches, the digital marketing landscape is witnessing a dramatic shift. There may have been a time when you could've dismissed artificial intelligence or visual search as gimmicks from the latest blockbuster science fiction film, but that time is long gone.
There are many new digital marketing trends and strategies that are evolving in the current high-tech, internet-connected era and businesses now need to use them to succeed in their efforts because what worked for you last year may not work this year.

B. Artificial intelligence will take over the world! AI can analyse consumer behaviour and search patterns, utilizing data from social media platforms and blog posts to help businesses understand how users and customers find their products and services. For example, Facebook messenger bots (which we'll talk more about later) can help you automate and optimize your customer service.

Artificial intelligence also offers information and tips to users by getting into conversations. According to Gartner, 25% of customer service will use chatbot technology by 2020, up from less than 2% in 2017.

C. Chatbots will continue to be an important part of digital marketing in 2019.
This AI-based technology uses instant messaging to chat in real-time, day or night, with your customers or site visitors. With 1.4 billion people interacting with chatbots, 80% of savvy businesses are already using or plan to use chatbots by 2020. And by 2022, chatbots will help businesses save over $8 billion per annum, especially in the banking and healthcare industries. Many customers prefer interacting with chatbots as they are responsive, give answers promptly, accurately recall your entire buying history, and never lose patience. These virtual assistants offer outstanding customer service, meeting customers' expectations and automating repetitive tasks – which mean you can focus on more important work.

D. If you want to stand out in 2019, you need to personalize your marketing – and that means personalized content, products, emails, and more. With the availability of data like purchase history, consumer behaviour and links clicked, custom content has never been easier. Businesses like Netflix and Amazon are already leveraging the power of personalization. Logging on to your Netflix account, for example, immediately shows you the evidence of this: the banner, carousels, order, artwork, text and search are all personalized for you.

E. These numbers show the importance of incorporating video into your digital marketing strategy in 2019:
70% of consumers say that they have shared a brand's video.
72% of businesses say video has improved their conversion rate.
52% of consumers say that watching product videos makes them more confident in online purchase decisions.
65% of executives visit the marketer's website and 39% call a vendor after viewing a video.
And don't just think YouTube. To witness higher engagement with your video marketing, you can make a video post or start a live broadcast on Facebook, Instagram or LinkedIn.
Live video is gaining popularity, with a large number of businesses using it for interviews, product demos and "behind the scenes" glimpses of events, life in the office, how products are made, etc.

F. Influencer marketing is a type of word-of-mouth marketing that focuses on using key leaders to drive your brand's message to the larger market.... Rather than marketing directly to a large group of consumers, you instead pay influencers to get out the word for you. Using influencers is a very effective marketing tool that works to attract customers. Influencers can be anyone from celebrities and Instagram or YouTube stars to well-known bloggers and journalists who help spread the word about your business or product through their social channels.

Because people generally trust consumer opinions over corporate statements, frozen food retailer Iceland ditched celebrities in favour of real people, tapping into a dedicated community of micro-influencers, increasing its approval rating by 72%.

G. Hey Siri, what time is Mission Impossible playing tonight?

Alexa, find me a recipe for apple butter.

The increasing use of voice search has made it important for companies to rethink their digital marketing strategies in 2019.

Voice search plays an important role in providing all the relevant information that people are searching for through audio content. Artificial Intelligence is getting smarter and the number of errors made by voice assistants like Alexa, Siri and Google has reduced.

Many brands have included voice search in their digital marketing strategies to deliver value-based content effectively to their customers. Domino's Pizza uses voice search technology as a way to increase its sales, thus allowing customers to order pizzas through Alexa. Smart speakers like Alexa and Google Home are also on the rise: 39 million Americans use smart speakers and 65% of them say they wouldn't want to go back to life without their voice-controlled assistant.

H. 2019 will be about better customer experience with personalization, automation and AI-powered technology, so to stay ahead of the curve and increase conversions in the coming year, you'll need to get better at producing custom, conversational content – particularly audio and video content – to share with your better-targeted audience.

Other questions on the passage may be of types already discussed earlier, i.e., Fill in the blanks, or TRUE/FALSE/NOT GIVEN type.

Being familiar with the various types of questions enables you to attempt your paper with greater confidence. The material for the practice tests that follow have been sourced extensively from the web and designed to expose the student to a variety of subjects and writing styles.

While practicing, be conscious of the time; the test is demanding in terms of time available; and remember to write only what is required. If the answer to be written is TRUE/FALSE/NOT GIVEN, write just one of those three options.

Once you are familiar with these test examples, go ahead and attempt the practice tests!

GT READING TEST 1

SECTION 1

Questions 1 – 14

Read the text below and answer Questions 1 – 8

HIMALAYAN TREKS

A. Beginning in Manali, this trek to Hampta Pass is exciting as it leads to enthralling meadows and green valleys. This trek across the river Rani, further leads to Chika, Balu ka Ghera, and Shea Gahru, through a stretch of tall forests of oak and alpine offering a totally spectacular view of the valley.

B. The Nag Tibba Trek is a relatively easy trek near Mussoorie with a maximum altitude of 9910 ft. It is considered as a weekend getaway trek as it is short and best suited for people with limited time. The trek takes you through thick Deodar forests with the chirping of birds in the background and the amazing view of the Bandarpoonch peak, the Gangotri group of peaks, and Kedarnath peak to name a few.

C. The Kedarkantha trek is a winter trek through forests covered with pine, maple, and Rhododendron trees in the state of Uttarakhand. It starts at Sankri a remote village around 200 kms from Dehradun. It is a popular winter trek because of the landscape and majorly for snow which makes it a delight for trekkers.

D. The Bhrigu Lake trek is a popular trek in the heart of Kulu Valley. The maximum altitude during this trek is 4267 meters/14000 feet. This trek is through the high-altitude alpine meadows and woody trails tucked away in the mountains of Kulu Valley. The views here are charming with the lake changing colors all through the day. The Bhrigu Lake has a mythical significance attached to it.

E. Dayara Bugyal trek is one of the most beautiful treks in Uttarakhand with beautiful valleys with streams of water running across high altitude meadows and vivid flora and fauna and is a perfect choice for beginners as the trek route is easy to traverse. The trek starts from Barsu a small village which is also the base camp for the trek.

F. When it feels like your life has lost all its charm due to the hectic schedule, just set out for the Chopta Chandrashila trek, via the sparkling Deoriatal Lake and rejuvenate yourself in the lush rhododendron forest and enthralling scenic views. The entire trail encompasses spectacular views from the great Chandrashila summit, plenty of forests, and uncountable varieties of plants and birds. It is the perfect escape for both nature and bird lovers.

Questions 1 – 8

Look at the six descriptions of treks. For which treks are the following statements true? Write A – F against questions 1-8 in your answer sheet. You may use any letter more than once.

1. This trek starts at a distant village: C
2. The trek takes you through dense Deodar forests: B
3. This is not a summer trek: C
4. This trek is to a lake with a fictional/imaginary significance attached to it: D
5. This trek is the ideal choice for those who haven't gone on treks before: E
6. This trek is for bird lovers: F
7. This trek offers remarkable views of the valley: A
8. This is best suited for people who have time constraints: B

8

Read the text below and answer Questions 9 – 14

ALL ABOUT GOLD'S GYMS

THE GOLD'S GYM FITNESS EXPERIENCE: Members enjoy access to the best coaches, personal trainers, and group exercise instructors in the business. That means access to motivating and knowledgeable experts dedicated to your success. Whatever your goal or experience level, our wide range of fitness classes and offerings can help you reach your goals. And you'll join a supportive community of members who share your aspirations. All of that adds up to an experience you won't find anywhere else. To see group exercise classes, personal training offerings, BOOTCAMP locations, GOLD'S STUDIO® programs & more, find a gym near you.

GOLD'S GYM CHALLENGE: The Gold's Gym Challenge is a 12-week body transformation challenge exclusively available to Gold's Gym members. By committing to 12 weeks you have the opportunity to experience the best of our coaching, our community and – most of all – you'll experience change.

In January, participants begin their new year Challenge journey with initial measurements and photographs. Then, 12 weeks later, final measurements and photographs will be taken to document results. Each participating Gold's Gym will choose their local winners who will then be eligible for the national prize pool featuring 30 cash prizes totaling $100,000.

GOLD'S GYM PERSONAL TRAINING: There's nothing better than having your very own coach, mentor and cheerleader. Need an extra push? That's why we're here. Our personal trainers are certified experts in exercise physiology, anatomy, training program development, exercise application and fitness assessments. And they excel at applying that knowledge to your own goals, no matter your age or fitness level.

GOLD'S GYM GROUP EXERCISE CLASSES: Achieve physical, emotional and spiritual well-being while strengthening your body in a Yoga class. Or challenge yourself with a Zumba class where Latin rhythms join cardiovascular exercise to create an aerobic routine. We offer classes that appeal to all interests and fitness levels.

GOLD'S GYM BOOTCAMP: It's time to change up your routine and your scenery with both in-gym and outdoor BOOTCAMP classes. BOOTCAMP offers a full-body, large group training workout led by a Certified Gold's Gym Coach and geared for all fitness levels. Not a Gold's Gym Member? Take advantage of a Free Pass at participating BOOTCAMP locations to see where your workout can take you.

Questions 9-14

Do the following statements agree with the information given in the text?

In boxes on your answer sheet, write

TRUE	if the statement agrees with the information
FALSE	if the statement contradicts the information
NOT GIVEN	if there is no information on this.

9. The New Year Challenge will begin in January:
10. Bootcamp is geared for beginners only:
11. Personal trainers are certified in assessing fitness:
12. Bootcamp offers a full body workout:
13. Zumba classes are held on alternate days:
14. The first prize in Gold Gym challenge is $100,000:

SECTION 2

Questions 15-27

Read the text below and answer Questions 15 – 21

TOP TIPS FOR EFFECTIVE PRESENTATIONS

1. Show your Passion and Connect with your Audience

It's hard to be relaxed and be yourself when you're nervous. But time and again, the great presenters say that the most important thing is to connect with your audience, and the best way to do that is to let your passion for the subject shine through. Be honest with the audience about what is important to you and why it matters. Be enthusiastic and honest, and the audience will respond.

2. Focus on your Audience's Needs

Your presentation needs to be built around what your audience is going to get out of the presentation. As you prepare the presentation, you always need to bear in mind what the audience needs and wants to know, not what you can tell them. While you're giving the presentation, you also need to remain focused on your audience's response, and react to that. You need to make it easy for your audience to understand and respond.

3. Keep it Simple: Concentrate on your Core Message

When planning your presentation, you should always keep in mind the question: What is the key message (or three key points) for my audience to take away? You should be able to communicate that key message very briefly. Some experts recommend a 30-second 'elevator summary', others that you can write it on the back of a business card, or say it in no more than 15 words. Whichever rule you choose, the important thing is to keep your core message focused and brief. And if what you are planning to say doesn't contribute to that core message, don't say it.

4. Smile and Make Eye Contact with your Audience

This sounds very easy, but a surprisingly large number of presenters fail to do it. If you smile and make eye contact, you are building rapport, which helps the audience to connect with you and your subject. It also helps you to feel less nervous, because you are talking to individuals, not to a great mass of unknown people. To help you with this, make sure that you don't turn down all the lights so that only the slide screen is visible. Your audience needs to see you as well as your slides.

5. Relax, Breathe and Enjoy

If you find presenting difficult, it can be hard to be calm and relaxed about doing it. One option is to start by concentrating on your breathing. Slow it down, and make sure that you're breathing fully. Make sure that you continue to pause for breath occasionally during your presentation too. If you can bring yourself to relax, you will almost certainly present better. If you can actually start to enjoy yourself, your audience will respond to that, and engage better. Your presentations will improve exponentially, and so will your confidence. It's well worth a try.

Questions 15-21

Complete the sentences below. Choose no more than two words from the text above for each answer.

15. The audience will .... if you are enthusiastic and honest.
16. You need to remain focused on your audience's response and .... to that.
17. At the planning stage, keep in mind the............ that you want your audience to take away.
18. Whatever you say must contribute to the............ message of your presentation.
19. Not only your slides, but .... also must be visible to your audience.
20. To be calm and relaxed during your presentation, concentrate on your ....
21. You can present better if you can bring yourself to............

Read the text below and answer Questions 22 – 27

WORK / LIFE BALANCE:
9 WORK HABITS TO GET YOU HOME ON TIME

1. Commit to a Departure Time Every Day: There's something very powerful about defined time frames. If you know you've got a drop-dead deadline to get out of your office at 5pm, you'll work smarter and harder all day to make that happen. Parents of young children in pricey daycares know the drill—many of them charge $5 for every minute past they're late past closing! Priorities come into sharp relief when you're racing against the clock and you'll skip that leisurely coffee, idle chit chat or social media check-up if it means shutting down on time.

2. Don't Insist on the Last (Email) Word: Ever had that email conversation that just wouldn't end? The thread in which the last three emails were comprised of responses like, "Thanks," "Okay," and "Will do"? Forget the niceties and, at the end of the day, let the conversation go. If you simply can't resist getting through a few emails before bed to lighten your load for the next day, queue them up and hit send in the morning.

3. Stop "Working" an Hour Before You Stop Working: Forget about taking a deep dive into a complicated project or booking a meeting an hour before you're set to leave. Instead, commit to making the last hour of your workday all about setting yourself up for success the next day. That might mean closing documents on your computer, answering those final emails for the day, tidying your desk and listing your priorities for the next day, so you're ready to swing back into action the minute you get in the next morning.

4. Protect Your Time & Preserve Your Work / Life Balance: Don't let your overcrowded calendar fool you into thinking you're uber-productive. If your days are packed from start to finish, the opposite is probably happening. And for good reason! If you're an ambitious entrepreneur, you want to be saying yes more than no and jamming your days full of ways to move the business forward. But you may be neglecting your basic human needs.

5. Leave Errands and Personal "Work" for After Hours: One of the greatest perks of being your own boss is having the flexibility to manage your own time. A quick errand or appointment outside the office will always take longer than you intend for it to and personal phone calls and social media take on a life of their own. If you want to leave on time every day—and avoid working all evening and on weekends—keep the workday items focused on work.

6. Plan Ahead: A highly-effective habit of proven leaders is to build a roadmap of priorities every week—and regularly keep an eye on it to ensure they're on task. Set aside some time every Friday

afternoon to assess what you need to accomplish the following week, prioritizing time-sensitive tasks as you go. You might assign certain tasks to certain days, including scheduled meetings. When you start the work week with a vision of what your week looks like and what you want to achieve, it's much easier to make that happen. Most importantly, be realistic. You're not going to start and finish an updated business plan in a day. For big projects, break it down into smaller, easily attainable pieces so you're always moving things forward, bits at a time.

Questions 22-27

Complete the sentences below using **ONE WORD ONLY** from the text for each answer.

22. You will ensure you leave your office on time if you have a.............. that cannot be avoided.
23. While exchanging emails at the end of the day one should forget ....
24. You should close the documents on your computer in the .... hour of your workday.
25. You may think that you are very productive if your .... is over-crowded.
26. You have .... to manage your time when you do not have a boss.
27. One should plan ahead for the following week on.............. afternoon.

SECTION 3

QUESTIONS 28 - 40

Read the text below and answer Questions 28 – 35

The text has 8 SECTIONS, marked A to H. Choose the correct heading for each paragraph from the list of headings below.

i. Effects of greenhouse gases
ii. Our lifestyle is responsible
iii. Low lying countries at risk
iv. The definition of global warming
v. Message for the future
vi. Reduced photosynthesis
vii. Food sources impacted
viii. Doing these could help
ix. Exploitation of fossil fuels

28. Paragraph A ....
29. Paragraph B ....
30. Paragraph C ....
31. Paragraph D ....
32. Paragraph E ....
33. Paragraph F ....
34. Paragraph G ....
35. Paragraph H ....

GLOBAL WARMING

A. What exactly is global warming and why is it worthy of consideration? Global warming is the scientific phenomenon linking an increase of the average earth temperature because of a trapping of radiation within the earth like a greenhouse. This has been a natural phenomenon throughout the natural history of the world but it has only become a problem in the last few hundred years because of an anthropogenic increase in greenhouse gasses.

B. Global warming is caused by an acute heating of the earth's atmosphere as a result of energy being trapped. Greenhouse gasses such as carbon dioxide and methane can cause the atmosphere to build up, leading to solar radiation becoming trapped within the earth like within a greenhouse, hence the name. Over time, the trapping of this radiation leads to the earth's atmosphere rising in temperature and the earth becomes warmer as a result. Once these greenhouse gasses become released, they can contribute to the buildup of the atmosphere and work to trap more solar radiation within the earth.

C. The reason as to why global warming is such an issue today is because of the problem that humans are creating with anthropogenic contributions to greenhouse gasses. Many of the practices that humans employ create enormous amounts of greenhouse gasses to be released and this has been well documented to be significantly harming the earth. Modernity, modern technology and new lifestyles have resulted in human activities that produce a lot of greenhouse gasses such as deforestation, the combustion of fossil fuels, industrial action and farming animals. The growing rise of industry around the world and the rise of consumerism have resulted in the production of many goods, all using fossil fuels either directly or indirectly. Consider the example of something trivial a mobile phone – creating something like this will lead to a large amount of components that need to be made using fossil fuels. Even if we want goods that have been grown on trees in our homes, they will need to be transported somewhere by transport that uses fossil fuels. There's no real escape from it – fossil fuels are in the fabric of modern life.

D. Deforestation is one of the biggest causes of global warming. Not only are trees cut down to make goods that need to be transported using fossil fuels, the removal of trees leads to a net loss of photosynthesis which is carried out by plants to make food. In this process, carbon dioxide can be absorbed and turned into oxygen, making food for the plants and cleaning the atmosphere as a result. The wide scale removal of trees and bio-diverse life results in a large amount of carbon dioxide that can't be converted to oxygen and so a huge problem for global warming.

E. The melting of polar ice caps poses one of the biggest problems for human society. As the earth's temperature increases, these large masses of ice and snow will melt and create the sea level to rise all over the world. In the same way, glaciers will also melt and create problems on land. According to scientific research, if all the snow and ice were to melt today, this would result in a raised sea level of over 200 feet worldwide and would be instantly detrimental to many low lying areas such as the Netherlands and other low lying islands around the world. It is the tragic case that most of the countries and areas that will be affected directly are often the ones that contribute the least to global warming.

F. As global warming occurs, biodiversity all over the world will suffer. Species will die off as they won't be able to adapt to their changing environments and the migratory patterns of many species will be ruined, e.g. birds will get lost migrating to get food. Food sources will be compromised, e.g. most primates are at significant risk as global warming results in less nutritious plant content to eat and a reduction in animal niches.

G. There are small choices that we can change about ourselves, for instance driving hybrid cars that reduce gasoline consumption. If a person needs to drive to work and pump their car many times a day, why do this when you can take public transport instead. Both of these solutions are actually cost effective for consumers but the problem is that people like to have the goods they want (e.g. cars) and there is little incentive for them to change their ways. It is also hoped that technology will lead to a reduction in global warming, with hardcore geo-engineering coming in to save the day, e.g. large mirrors to reflect radiation or pumping Sulphur into the atmosphere to influence global cooling. Efforts to create such technology would be worthwhile as the problems of incentives would not factor in.

H. There are many causes and effects of global warming. Unfortunately it is highly likely that the problems of global warming will persist unless immediate action is to be taken. Problems will exist unless hard geo-engineering is developed or if people are given sufficient incentives to change their actions for the better.

Questions 36 – 40

Choose ONE WORD ONLY from the text to complete the following:

36. Increased consumerism has resulted in the Production of many goods, using fossil fuels directly or indirectly.
37. There are many reasons of global warming, but Deforestation is the biggest one.
38. We can take public transport or drive...hybrid cars so that we use less gasoline.
39. Releasing...Sulphur... into the atmosphere may help to cool it down.
40. It is Unfortunate. but highly likely that problems of global warming will not go away.

(5)

37/40 8 bands

GT READING TEST 2

SECTION 1

Questions 1 – 14

Read the text below and answer Questions 1 – 8

LEMUR SPECIES

While many species of Lemurs have become extinct, it is believed that there are at least 99 of them that still survive, including subspecies.

A. Ring Tailed Lemur: It is a well-known Lemur, with a body very different from other primates. It is considered to be one of the most intelligent of them as well.

B. Red Ruffed Lemur: The Red Ruffed Lemur is a medium sized species. They don't associate with any other types of Lemurs. They seem to turn their noses up at them and won't even nest or feed in the same locations.

C. Indri Lemur: The Indri Lemur is also called the Babakoto in many regions. This is one of the largest Lemurs found in the world. They seem to have many behaviors that are humanistic. They have characteristics that are different from many other species of Lemurs.

D. Gray Mouse Lemur: It may be hard to believe that the Gray Mouse Lemur is a primate! In fact, many people would likely wager money that it is a rodent by the name and the appearance of it. Yet DNA doesn't lie and so it is correctly classified as a primate.

E. Golden Crown Sifaka: One of the medium sized primates is the Golden-Crowned Sifaka Lemur. They are very limited in number and location. There is hardly anything known about them and they were only identified as a unique species in 1974.

F. Coquerel's Sifaka: The Coquerel's Sifaka Lemur is a medium sized one and it belongs to the primate family. It features some very interesting behaviors as well as a look that is different from other Lemurs.

G. Collared Brown Lemur: The Collared Brown Lemur is a primate that is medium in size. There are 12 species of Brown Lemurs in the world. They are the most well-known of these Brown Lemurs.

H. Aye-Aye: Of all the Lemurs in the world, the Aye-Aye Lemur is the largest primate that is nocturnal. One may argue that point though, if they didn't realize that this was really a primate.

Questions 1 – 8

Look at the 8 descriptions of Lemur species. For which Lemurs are the following statements true? Write the correct letter A-H in your answer sheet.

1. Not much is known about these Lemurs.
2. These Lemurs are not active in the day time.
3. These Lemurs are not very sociable.
4. These are best known brown Lemurs.
5. Because of its looks, it is difficult to believe that this is a Lemur.
6. This is the most intelligent Lemur.
7. You will hardly find a Lemur larger than this one.
8. This Lemur does not look like other Lemurs.

Read the text below and answer Questions 9 – 14

WHITE WATER RAFTING RULES

1. **Wear Your Personal Flotation Device**
   While most of your raft trip will be spent on the raft, there may be times when you jump into the river to cool off or take an accidental plunge while riding some rapids. Wearing a personal flotation device (PFD) will help make sure you stay safe while cruising down the river.

2. **Stay on Board**
   Unless your raft guide gives you permission, don't jump out of the boat! On calmer sections of the river, your guide may let you jump in the water to cool off and cruise alongside the boat. Listen to your guide, and only take the plunge when he or she tells you it's safe.

3. **Keep Your Head Up**
   When your team paddles towards whitewater, ball game rules apply: keep your eyes ahead and on the objective. If you're thrown overboard, lie flat on your back—lean back into the PFD, which will help you float—with your head pointed upstream, and feet pointed downstream

4. **Wear Sun Protection**
   When you head out on the water, don sunglasses—but not your most expensive pair, in case they get tossed in the water or get smashed—and secure them around your neck with protective straps. Apply water-resistant sunscreen to your face, ears, neck and any other sections of exposed skin.

5. **Wear Closed-Toed Shoes**
   Don't wear flip flops—you'll most likely lose them overboard! Plus, your footing won't be stable for exiting the raft or wedging your feet into the raft's sides while riding the rapids. Instead, wear shoes that can be secured to your feet, like an old pair of tennis shoes.

6. **Bring a Bathing Suit**
   Don't be the lady or lad who forgets their bathing suit when they walk out the door for a water adventure. For the record: There are usually lost-and-found bins at most raft headquarters, which you can fish through to find a suit to borrow.

7. **Laugh—A Lot**
   It might be impossible to not laugh at the surprises and feats that are faced while rafting. But, more importantly, laugh at your river guide's jokes. They might be dry, but hey, these water lovers aren't professional standup comedians! They need encouragement, too.

Questions 9 – 14

Do the following statements agree with the information given in the text?

In boxes on your answer sheet, write

TRUE if the statement agrees with the information

FALSE if the statement contradicts the information

NOT GIVEN if there is no information on this.

9. You can jump into the water whenever you feel like.
10. If thrown overboard, you should lie down flat such that your feet pointing in the direction opposite to the current of the river.
11. You should wear your best pair of sunglasses for proper protection from the sun.
12. You should wear shoes that can be secured to your feet.
13. You can find a fish in lost and found bins at most raft offices.
14. Your guide will tell you a lot of jokes.

SECTION 2

Questions 15 – 27

Read the text below and answer Questions 15 – 21

YOGA

Yoga is a form of exercise that originated in ancient India and is practiced widely across the world today. Yoga not only enhances your physical strength but also contributes largely towards your mental health and spiritual growth.

Yoga not only keeps you fit but also has a lot of long-term benefits when you make it an integral part of your lifestyle. Some benefits of yoga include:

1. Better posture
   Yoga helps in keeping the spine erect, enabling you to sit straight and not slouch. It also helps alleviate the stress on your spine, exerted through incorrect posture. Consistent practice of Yoga helps in keeping the spine strong and prevents fatigue.
2. Improved bone health
   Many postures in yoga require you to lift your own weight which helps in making the bones stronger and helps ward off osteoporosis.
3. Increased blood flow
   The inverted and twisting nature of Yoga poses wring out the venous blood from the internal organs and allow oxygenated blood to flow. This also boosts the haemoglobin and red blood cells count.
4. Improved heart health
   When you practice Yoga regularly, you get your heart into the aerobic range. This not only lowers the risk of heart attack but also relieves depression.
5. Lowered blood pressure
   The sarvasana (corpse pose) helps people with hypertension. This pose is said to be have resulted in great improvement in people with these kinds of problems.
6. Improved balance
   Yoga involves focusing on holding postures for extended periods of time. This helps in improving your body balance and developing muscle tone.
7. Relaxation and sleeping aid
   Yoga can help you to relieve the stress of modern life and helps you sleep deeper. Yoga encourages you to relax and slow your breath and to focus on the present. Restorative asanas and meditation also encourage a turning inward of the senses, which relaxes the nervous system.
8. Improved lung health

Yoga draws attention to your breathing pattern and makes you aware of breathing correctly which filters the air, warms it and humidifies it removing the pollen and the dirt, and supplying fresh oxygen into the lungs.

9. <u>Reduced digestive problems</u>

Yoga like any other physical exercise can ease constipation and lower the risk of colon cancer. The movements of Yoga improve the transport of food and remove waste through the bowels. This helps in getting rid of the waste from the system more effectively.

10. <u>Eases your pain</u>

Yoga can ease your pain and help people who suffer from arthritis, back pain and other chronic conditions. When you relieve pain, you're in a much better mood and are inclined to be more active.

Questions 15-21

Choose one word from the text above for each answer.

15. The various Yoga poses helps to take out the .... blood from our internal organs.
16. You can sit upright because Yoga exercises helps to keep your backbone..................
17. Movement of food through the bowels is improved by the ....of Yoga.
18. Because your aches are better, your .... also improves with Yoga.
19. People with high blood pressure are helped by ....
20. By practicing Yoga, we can .... the tensions and pressures of day to day living.
21. The practice of Yoga was born in ....

Read the text below and answer Questions 22 – 27

HOW TO INCREASE EMPLOYEE MOTIVATION

Here are three immediate actionable tips to increase employee motivation.

1. **Improve communication**

   The easiest way to increase employee motivation is by having positive communication at the workplace. Not relying only on emails but by making sure that managers talk to their employees in person and even on a personal level, if possible.

   Try setting aside some time each day to talk with employees or you can join them during coffee breaks instead of sitting at your desk. By doing so, you actually make employees feel as though you are part of the team; a leader instead of just the boss.

   Employees also want to see the company that they are working for succeed. Many have excellent ideas, ranging from money saving to operational improvements. Management must make an effort to take some time to ask for and listen to suggestions. Nothing is more worthwhile than feeling valued.

2. **Value individual contributions**

   Management should ensure their employees know how their individual efforts and contribution plays an important part in the achievement of the company's overall goals and direction. Employees will take pride and be engaged in their work if they are aware how their efforts create an impact the organisation; regardless of how big or small their contributions are.

   Management does not have to reward their employees with gifts every time they did a good job. At times, a simple "Thank You" or "Great job" will suffice. These meaningful words acknowledge effort, build loyalty and encourage people to work even harder.

3. **Positive workplace environment**

   Sometimes, employees lack motivation because their workplace does not have a positive work environment. To fix this, management could send out surveys to get feedback and solve the issues that they may face.

   Management could also post a positive quote or picture by the copier, coffee machine or somewhere else that is visible and that receives high foot traffic so that others can see it. Flora and fauna also helps create a serene workplace environment for your employees, so why not add a couple of plants around the office.

In Summary

A positive workplace is the basic element that will get your company to the top. We understand that it may be time consuming and difficult to encourage employee motivation at the workplace. However, in order to achieve a high level of employee productivity, management needs to encourage a positive workplace environment.

Questions 22-27

Complete the sentences with ONE WORD ONLY from the passage for each answer.

22. One should try to schedule some time every day to .... to employees.
23. The most worthwhile thing for an employee is to feel ....
24. For the company to meet its objectives, each person's .... is important.
25. Whenever someone does a good job, he does not have to receive a ....
26. In order to find out the employees' point of view, one should conduct ....
27. .... posters should be put up at places which are more frequented by employees.

SECTION 3

Questions 28 -40

Read the text below and answer Questions 28 – 35

The text has 8 SECTIONS, marked A to H. Choose the correct heading for each paragraph from the list of headings below.

i. How the problem exacerbated

ii. Likely scenario by the mid of 21st century

iii. Water borne plastic

iv. Single use disposable plastic the major culprit

v. Inadequate recycling adds to the problem

vi. What can be done

vii. Economic growth = more plastic waste

viii. Impact on animals and human health

28. Paragraph A ....
29. Paragraph B ....
30. Paragraph C ....
31. Paragraph D ....
32. Paragraph E ....
33. Paragraph F ....
34. Paragraph G ....
35. Paragraph H ....

PLASTIC POLLUTION

A. Our planet is drowning in plastic pollution. This World Environment Day, it's time for a change. While plastic has many valuable uses, we have become addicted to single-use or disposable plastic — with severe environmental consequences. Around the world, one million plastic drinking bottles are purchased every minute, while up to 5 trillion single-use plastic bags are used worldwide every year. In total, half of all plastic produced is designed to be used only once — and then thrown away. Plastic waste is now so ubiquitous in the natural environment that scientists have even suggested it could serve as a geological indicator of the Anthropocene era. So how did we get here?

B. From the 1950s to the 1970, only a small amount of plastic was produced, so plastic waste was relatively manageable. By the 1990s, plastic waste generation had more than tripled in two decades, following a similar rise in plastic production. In the early 2000s, our output of plastic waste rose more in a single decade than it had in the previous 40 years. Today we produce more than 300 million tons of plastic waste every year. That is nearly equivalent to the weight of the entire human population.

Researchers estimate that more than 8.3 billion tons of plastic has been produced since the early 1950s. About 60% of that plastic has ended up in either a landfill or the natural environment.

C. We're seeing some other worrying trends. Since the 1950s, the rate of plastic production has grown faster than that of any other material. We've also seen a shift away from the production of durable plastic, and towards plastics that are meant to be thrown away after a single use. More than 99% of plastics are produced from chemicals derived from oil, natural gas and coal — all of which are dirty, non-renewable resources. If current trends continue, by 2050 the plastic industry could account for 20% of the world's total oil consumption.

D. We need to slow the flow of plastic at its source, but we also need to improve the way we manage our plastic waste, because right now, a lot of it ends up in the environment. Only 9% of all plastic waste ever produced has been recycled. About 12% has been incinerated, while the rest — 79% — has accumulated in landfills, dumps or the natural environment. Cigarette butts — whose filters contain tiny plastic fibres — were the most common type of plastic waste found in the environment in a recent global survey. Drink bottles, bottle caps, food wrappers, grocery bags, drink lids, straws and stirrers were the next most common items. Many of us use these products every day, without even thinking about where they might end up.

E. Rivers carry plastic waste from deep inland to the sea, making them major contributors to ocean pollution. A staggering 8 million tons of plastic end up in the world's oceans every year. How does it get there? A lot of it comes from the world's rivers, which serve as direct conduits of trash from the world's cities to the marine environment.

These 10 rivers alone carry more than 90% of the plastic waste that ends up in the oceans

Chang Jiang (Yangtze River) 1,469,481 tons

Indus 164,332 tons

Huang He (Yellow River) 124,249 tons

Hai He 91,858 tons

Nile 84,792 tons

Meghna, Brahmaputra, Ganges 72,845 tons

Zhujiang (Pearl River) 52,958 tons

Amur 38,267 tons

Niger 35,196 tons

Mekong 33,431 tons

F. Plastic waste — whether in a river, an ocean, or on land — can persist in the environment for centuries.

The same properties that make plastics so useful — their durability and resistance to degradation — also make them nearly impossible for nature to completely break down. Most plastic items never fully disappear; they just get smaller and smaller. Many of these tiny plastic particles are swallowed by farm animals or fish who mistake them for food, and thus can find their way onto our dinner plates. They've also been found in a majority of the world's tap water. By clogging sewers and providing breeding grounds for mosquitoes and pests, plastic waste — especially plastic bags — can increase the transmission of vector-borne diseases like malaria.

G. If current trends continue, our oceans could contain more plastic than fish by 2050. While the United States, Japan and many European countries generate significant amounts of plastic waste, they're also relatively good at managing it. About half of all of the plastic waste that ends up in the oceans comes from just five countries: China, Indonesia, the Philippines, Thailand and Viet Nam. These countries are experiencing rapid economic growth, which is reducing poverty rates and improving the quality of life for hundreds of millions of people. But as these economies grow, consumption booms — and so does the use of plastic goods.

H. The global volume of plastic waste continues to grow, and some of the biggest producers don't manage their waste effectively. But the world is waking up to the problem, and governments are starting to act.

There are a number of things that governments can do — from running public awareness campaigns, to offering incentives for recycling, to introducing levies or even banning certain products outright. In the last decade, dozens of national and local governments around the world have adopted policies to reduce the use of disposable plastic. And the number continues to grow. Africa stands out as the continent where the most countries have adopted a total ban on the production and use of plastic bags. Of the 25 African countries that have banned the bags, more than half have done so in the last four years alone.

An impressive — and growing — number of national and local governments have taken action against plastic pollution. We have seen a lot of positive action, but the truth is that we all need to do more.

Questions 36 - 40

Choose ONE WORD ONLY from the text to complete the following:

36. The weight of plastic produced is almost equal to the weight of all the .... in the world put together.
37. If nothing changes, by the middle of the century the plastic industry could account for one fifth of the world's................ consumption.
38. The .... is the fifth largest polluting river in the world.
39. 50% of the plastic waste in the oceans is generated by .... countries.
40. ....growth leads to generation of more plastic.

8:42

GT READING TEST 3

SECTION 1

Questions 1 – 14

Read the text below and answer Questions 1 – 7

THE TAJ MAHAL

The Taj Mahal is a significant Mughal Empire architectural marvel, still standing in all its beauty and finesse in Agra in India. It is a white marble mausoleum built by the Mughal emperor Shah Jahan in memory of his third wife, Mumtaz Mahal. As if to show-case the expanse of the Mughal Empire, it combines architectures from all the corners of the Empire including Islamic, Persian, Ottoman Turkish and Indian architectural styles.

1. The Taj Mahal was built by a whopping 22,000 laborers, painters, stone-cutters and embroidery artists, and took 17 years to be built.

2. Legend has it that Emperor Shah Jahan intended to build another Taj Mahal in black marble across the river but a war with his sons interrupted these plans.

3. The changing moods of the Emperor's wife are well captured by the changing hues of the Mausoleum at different times of the day. It takes a pinkish hue in the morning, milky white in the evening and a golden glow at night when illuminated by moonlight.

4. The most recognizable feature is the white dome at the peak of the mausoleum. Often called the 'onion dome', it rises to about 35 meters, and is surrounded by four other domes.

5. Taj Mahal is a famous Indian landmark and tourist magnet, attracting more than a million tourists every year.

6. The materials that were used to build Taj Mahal were transported to the construction site by a whopping 1,000 elephants.

The Taj Mahal is indeed a beautiful place. When you visit, make sure you take a picture of yourself and your spouse with the mausoleum as the background...who knows, the love that the emperor had for his wife to dedicate these kind of resources for her remembrance after death might rub off on you.

Questions 1 – 7

Do the following statements agree with the information given in the text.

Write:

TRUE	**if the statement agrees with the information**
FALSE	**if the statement contradicts the information**
NOT GIVEN	**if there is no information on this.**

1. **The Taj Mahal is the most famous of all Mughal architectural marvels.**
2. **The hues of the mausoleum reflect the moods of Mumtaz Mahal.**
3. **Islamic, Turkish, Persian and Indian laborers built the Taj Mahal.**
4. **The Taj Mahal has 5 domes in all.**
5. **Shah Jahan had three wives.**
6. **Shah Jahan also built a black Taj Mahal.**
7. **The Taj Mahal combines architectural styles from all across the world.**

Read the text below and answer Questions 8 – 14

SWIMMING POOL RULES AND REGULATIONS

1. All rules and requests made by lifesaving personnel must be followed.
2. All patrons entering the facility during Recreational/Lap Swim times are required to pay the facility admission fee. Parents wishing to watch their children that are 7 years and older during recreation swim are not required to pay the adult admission fee, but must remain in the designated spectator area.
3. Children under 7 years old or less than four feet tall must be accompanied by a parent or responsible person in a swim suit at all times including in the water, on the deck and in the restroom. While in the water, the parent/responsible person must remain within arm's reach at all times.
4. Persons in the water must wear acceptable swim suits. T-shirts are not allowed. A tight fitting rash guard is acceptable.
5. Animals are not allowed in the building or pool area, with the exception of guide/service dogs. Guide/service dogs are allowed on deck, but not in the water.
6. Candy, food or beverages are not allowed. There are designated areas provided for eating or drinking. No glass items, chewing gum or smoking is permitted in the facility.
7. All patrons must shower before entering the pool. Persons with open cuts, sores, bandages, colds, coughs or infected eyes are not permitted in the pool.
8. Everyone must pass a swim test before entering deep water. Weak or non-swimmers must remain in shallow water no deeper than their armpits.
9. Dangerous practices are prohibited. Patrons must not run on decks; climb, sit or jump from fences; dive in shallow water (less than 9 feet deep); dunk, push, pull or splash swimmers. Jumps are permitted feet first. Back jumps, twisting and flips are not permitted at any time.
10. Diving in water less than nine (9) feet deep, back dives, somersaults and cannon balls from the side of the pool or any other unsafe activities are not permitted.
11. Emergency procedures must be observed. Swimmers must leave the pool area immediately upon the signal or request of the Pool Manager.
12. Walk at all times!!! DO NOT RUN!!!

Questions 8 – 14

Do the following statements agree with the information given in the text?

In boxes on your answer sheet, write

TRUE	if the statement agrees with the information
FALSE	if the statement contradicts the information
NOT GIVEN	if there is no information on this.

8. Parents wishing to watch their ten year old children during recreational swim are not required to pay the adult admission fee.
9. No food is allowed to be taken to the swimming pool.
10. Persons with open cuts and sores must shower before entering the pool.
11. A child who is 4 ft. tall has to be accompanied by a parent or responsible person:
12. It is preferred that women wear a two piece swim suit.
13. When you jump into the water, your feet must touch the water first.
14. Diving in 10 ft. deep water is permitted.

SECTION 2
Questions 15 – 27
Read the text below and answer Questions 15 – 20

JOB BRIEF: RECEPTIONIST

We are looking for a Receptionist to manage our front desk on a daily basis and to perform a variety of administrative and clerical tasks.

What does a Receptionist do?

As a Receptionist, you will be the first point of contact for our company. Our Receptionist's duties include offering administrative support across the organization. You will welcome guests and greet people who visit the business. You will also coordinate front-desk activities, including distributing correspondence and redirecting phone calls.

To be successful, you should have a pleasant personality, as this is also a customer service role. You should also be able to deal with emergencies in a timely and effective manner, while streamlining office operations. Multitasking and stress management skills are essential for this position. This role may require working in shifts, so flexibility is a plus.

Ultimately, your duties and responsibilities are to ensure the front desk welcomes guests positively, and executes all administrative tasks to the highest quality standards.

Responsibilities

- Greet and welcome guests as soon as they arrive at the office
- Direct visitors to the appropriate person and office
- Answer, screen and forward incoming phone calls
- Provide basic and accurate information in-person and via phone/email
- Receive, sort and distribute daily mail/deliveries
- Maintain office security by following safety procedures and controlling access via the reception desk (monitor logbook, issue visitor badges)
- Order front office supplies and keep inventory of stock
- Arrange travel and accommodations, and prepare vouchers
- Keep updated records of office expenses and costs
- Perform other clerical receptionist duties such as filing, photocopying, transcribing and faxing

Requirements

- Proven work experience as a Receptionist, Front Office Representative or similar role
- Proficiency in Microsoft Office Suite
- Hands-on experience with office equipment (e.g. fax machines and printers)
- Professional attitude and appearance
- Solid written and verbal communication skills
- Excellent organizational skills
- Multitasking and time-management skills, with the ability to prioritize tasks
- Customer service attitude
- High school degree; additional certification in Office Management is a plus

Questions 15-20

Choose no more than two words from the text above for each answer.

15. Whenever a visitor comes into the office, you will be the........... person to meet him or her.
16. The position of a Receptionist is also a .... role.
17. Since the role requires .... you should be able to work in shifts.
18. One of the responsibilities is to keep track of the..................... in the office.
19. The tasks required to be performed are not only administrative in nature, but also..................
20. The computer SW that you should be well versed in is ....

Read the text below and answer Questions 21 – 27

SOME POPULAR TYPES OF LIFE INSURANCE POLICIES IN INDIA

1. **Term Life Insurance:** Term insurance is the simplest form of life insurance plan, easy to understand and affordable to buy. This plan provides death risk cover for a specified period. In case of death during the policy period, the life insurance company pays the benefit to the nominee. It is a pure risk cover plan that offers high coverage at low premiums. The death benefit is payable as lump sum, monthly payouts, or a combination of both.
   There's no payout if the life assured outlives the policy term.
   Benefit of Term Plan: In case of an untimely death of the breadwinner, the family is supported with an enormous amount of money- the sum assured, which helps them to replace the loss of income caused due to the breadwinner's death.

2. **Unit Linked Plans (ULIPs):** A unit linked plan is a combination of insurance and investment. The premium paid is partly used as a risk cover (insurance) and partly invested in funds. One can invest in different funds offered by the insurance company depending on one's risk appetite.
   Benefit of ULIP: Invest money as per your risk appetite in equity, debt or in hybrid funds with complete transparency.

3. **Whole Life Insurance:** A whole life insurance policy covers the life assured for whole life, or in some cases, up to the age of 100 years, unlike term plans, which are for a specified term.
   The sum assured or the coverage is decided at the time of policy purchase and is paid to the nominee at the time of the death claim of the life assured.
   However, if the life assured outlives the age of 100 years, the insurance company pays the matured endowment coverage to the life insured.
   Benefit of Whole Life Plan: Lifelong protection to the insured and an opportunity to leave behind a legacy for heirs.

4. **Child Plan:** Child plan helps to build corpus for a child's future, and helps to build funds for a child's education and marriage. Most Child Plans provide annual installments or one time payout after the age of 18 years.
   Benefit of Child Plan: Helps in fulfilling your child's dream.

5. **Retirement Plan:** This plan helps to build a corpus for your retirement.
   If the person passes away during the policy term - immediate payment is payable to the nominee by the insurance company.
   Benefit of Retirement Plan: Helps in building corpus for retirement.

Questions 21 – 27

Complete the sentences below. Choose no more than two words from the text for each answer.

21. Whole Life Policy is one of the .... types of life insurance policy.
22. The Term Life Insurance is.....................
23. The amount for which I am insured will be decided when I take the policy if I am buying a .... insurance policy.
24. One can receive either a lump-sum or money every year under the .... policy.
25. If you wish to have access to a pile of money once your working life is over, you should opt for a.........................
26. A...................... insurance policy is unlike policies that have a specific term.
27. If I take a .... policy, some of my funds can be invested in various funds.

SECTION 3

Read the text below and answer Questions 28 – 40.

Questions 28 -35

The text has 8 SECTIONS, marked A to H. Choose the correct heading for each paragraph from the list of headings below.

i. Demands other than meat
ii. Countries involved
iii. Whaling for sustenance
iv. The origins
v. Growth of the industry
vi. Looking ahead
vii. The moratorium
viii. Initial regulatory attempts
ix. Establishment of IWC

28. Paragraph A ....
29. Paragraph B ....
30. Paragraph C ....
31. Paragraph D ....
32. Paragraph E ....
33. Paragraph F ....
34. Paragraph G ....
35. Paragraph H ....

WHALING

A There are two kinds of whaling, ASW or Aboriginal Subsistence Whaling, and Commercial Whaling. In some parts of the world, whale products play an important role in the nutritional and cultural life of native peoples. Four International Whaling Commission (IWC) member countries conduct aboriginal subsistence hunts today: Denmark (Greenland), Russia (Chukotka), St Vincent and the Grenadines (Bequia) and the United States (Alaska) and also potentially a resumption of hunts previously undertaken by the Makah Tribe of Washington State).

From the outset, the IWC recognized that indigenous or aboriginal subsistence whaling is not the same as commercial whaling. Aboriginal whaling does not seek to maximize catches. It is categorized differently and is not subject to the moratorium. The IWC recognizes that its regulations have the potential to impact significantly on traditional cultures, and great care must be taken in discharging this responsibility.

B. Commercial whaling began in the 11th century with the Basque inhabitants of the French and Spanish coastlines of the Bay of Biscay. In the ensuing centuries, as they depleted local populations of whales starting with right whales, Basque efforts expanded north. This influenced other nations in northern Europe and eventually North America to begin their own whaling operations. Great Britain started hunting bowhead whales around the North American colonies in 1611 and American colonists began whaling (a practice known as Yankee whaling) out of Nantucket, Massachusetts, in 1712.

C. Through the 18th and 19th centuries, whaling was driven by demand not for meat, but for whale oil, which literally lit the lamps and greased the wheels of the industrial revolution. Other whale products also held value, including ambergris (a stomach excretion of sperm whales used as a perfume fixative) and baleen (most famously used to stiffen women's' corsets).

D. As whaling ships became faster (with the advent of steam vessels) and larger, whaling became both more efficient and more competitive, with whaling nations establishing remote land stations and deploying factory ships that could spend months at sea processing whale oil on board. By the 20th century, industrial-scale commercial whaling had begun to target whales on their feeding grounds in the Antarctic, decimating whale populations. Scientists estimate that 2.9 million whales were killed between 1900 and 1999 and many species suffered catastrophic declines. Some populations, including the North Atlantic gray whale, were lost forever. Others, such as the North Atlantic right whale, number in the low hundreds even after decades of protection.

E. The major industrial whaling nations of the early 20th century included Great Britain, the United States, Norway, the Netherlands, Japan, Germany, and the Soviet Union, but whalers from Australia and Brazil also had a significant presence in the southern hemisphere. As whale populations began to dramatically decline, governments started to recognize the importance of "managing" whaling and conserving whale stocks, not just for future human generations but also for their own sake.

F. Early attempts at regulating whaling fell short as Japan and other leading whaling nations refused to participate. In 1946, however, shortly after the close of the Second World War, governments of the main whaling nations came together to negotiate the International Convention for the Regulation of Whaling (ICRW), recognizing the "interest of the nations of the world in safeguarding for future generations the great natural resources represented by the whale stocks." The ICRW established the International Whaling Commission (IWC) whose (then) 15 member nations (known as contracting governments) were authorized to adopt, by three-quarters majority vote, binding regulations on catch limits, whaling methods, protected areas, when whaling was permitted, and what species (including minimum sizes) could be killed.

While this system brought some measure of control to ongoing commercial whaling operations and offered respite for some of the most threatened species, commercial whaling largely continued unchecked under the auspices of the IWC. The IWC was unable to detect violations by its member nations or enforce its regulations, and the Soviet Union killed 180,000 more whales than it reported to the IWC over a 25-year period. Underreporting of catch data is also known to have occurred in Japan's coastal whaling.

G. The IWC was also unable to prevent whaling from occurring as a result of two provisions included in the ICRW—a provision allowing governments to take objections to, and exempt themselves from, regulations they did not support and a clause authorizing governments to issue "special permits" for scientific research whaling on whales. With declining demand for whale products, a growing awareness of the intelligence and sentience of whales and their role in the ecosystem, and increased understanding of whale suffering at the hands of whalers, the IWC, at its meeting in 1982, agreed to a moratorium on all commercial whaling. At that meeting, the IWC set all commercial whale quotas to zero with an effective date of 1986 for coastal and 1985/86 for pelagic (open sea) whaling seasons.

The commercial whaling moratorium was a landmark event and remains one of the most effective decisions ever made by an international body for the protection of wildlife. Before it went into effect, tens of thousands of whales were being killed annually by whaling nations, reaching a peak of as many as 72,000 whales a year in the 1960s. By 1986, when the moratorium went into effect, four of the remaining whaling nations had stopped whaling, and the Soviet Union stopping commercial whaling at the end of the 1986/1987 Antarctic whaling season. However, Norway, Iceland and Japan have persisted, continuing to hunt hundreds of whales a year for commercial gain in defiance of the moratorium and despite the widely held belief that commercial whaling is no longer necessary or acceptable.

H. It is difficult not to be slightly concerned for the fate of whales in a future ocean. There is a range of factors that seem stacked against them: over-fishing, resumption of commercial whaling, pollution, entanglements, ship strikes and ultimately climate change. Yet at the same time, many populations of great whales are demonstrating their resilience by returning from the massive over-exploitation of earlier centuries. We are learning more about the extraordinary ecology of whales every year and are coming to understand their critical role in the ecosystem. Hopefully with the realization that whales are not merely of value as blubber, meat and bone, we will come to treasure these giants of the ocean because they add value to the marine ecosystems—and to the lives of those privileged enough to observe them.

Questions 36 – 40

Choose one word only from the text to complete the following:

36. The Makah tribe of Washington State engages in whaling for..................
37. In order to increase efficiency, countries started to establish whaling stations in .... areas.
38. In the beginning, the main product for which whaling was done was whale..................
39. The decision to stop whaling was a .... event.
40. In spite of extensive whaling over the years, these gentle creatures are resurging back, showing their..................

GT READING TEST 4

SECTION 1

Questions 1 – 14

Read the text below and answer Questions 1 – 7

SOME OFF-BEAT DESTINATIONS NEAR DELHI

A. Pangot

A charming little hill town near Nainital, Pangot is a paradise for nature lovers and bird watchers. With around 580 bird species recorded in this area, you are bound to encounter a few fluttering colourful feathers. The resorts here are gorgeous and will make your holiday worthwhile.

B. Fagu

Fagu is an enchanting little hill town in the Kufri region of Shimla. You can have a glimpse of the majestic Himalayan summits from here. Dotted by little stone walled houses and lush green plantations, it's definitely one of the most charming offbeat weekend getaways near Delhi.

C. Darang

Another Himachali beauty, Darang is located near Mcleodganj on the road to Palampur. Walk through lush tea gardens and get mesmerized by the sounds of toads and chirping of birds. From here you can view the majestic Dhauladhars standing tall over delightful hamlets.

D. Pithoragarh

Pithoragarh district is located in the Kumaon region of Uttarakhand. The beauty of this place is beyond explanation. Surrounded by towering snow clad peaks, alpine forests, green valley and perennial rivers; it is one of the most gorgeous offbeat places near Delhi that is still un-spoilt by commercialism.

E. Kausani

Another undiscovered Kumaoni beauty, Kausani is the best place to view the majestic massifs of Nanda Devi, Trishul and Panchachuli. There are a few 12th century temples in Baijnath that you can visit and the view points from where you can witness the mountains. It is one of the offbeat weekend getaways near Delhi that has managed to retain its natural form.

F. Naukuchiatal

Naukuchiatal, flanked by Bhimtal and Nainital on either side, is a picturesque hill town best known for its placid and beautiful lake, the deepest in the region, which is said to be fed by an underground river. Another amazing feature of this place is its must-visit temples.

Questions 1 – 7

Look at the 6 descriptions of off-beat destinations near Delhi.
For which destinations are the following statements true?
Write the correct letter A-F in your answer sheet.

1. This destination has rivers which flow all through the year. D
2. You can see small villages here. C
3. You can visit very old temples at this off-beat destination. E
4. Those into ornithology would love to visit this place. A
5. Though an off-beat destination, the places to stay here are really very good. A
6. In this off-beat destination you can still find an old-world charm. B
7. The lake here is very deep. F

Read the text below and answer questions 8 – 14.

NAPKIN ETIQUETTE

Napkin Etiquette is essential in practicing proper table etiquette and having good manners.

An elegantly set table will display table linens and fine china. Delicate details such as the choice of napkins never go unnoticed. Guests love the feel and look of a beautifully set table. A formal dinner is not only a feast for the palate but a feast for the eye.

We should make an effort to use cloth napkins with most of our meals. Paper napkins should not be used for home dinners, except for very casual meals or outdoors BBQ, picnic or fast food restaurants.

Napkins vary in colors, patterns, fabrics and sizes. The formal dinner napkin will always match the table cloth color and fabric and is bigger in size than her lunch and breakfast counterparts. White and cream are the colors you will find for very formal functions. Colors and patterns are to be expected in theme or less formal events.

In a formal setting you should find your napkin to the left of the fork. In a less formal setting you can find the napkin in a water or wine glass, under the fork, or on the table near the plate. Within a few minutes of sitting you can unfold your napkin gently and place it on your lap. A dinner napkin does not need to be opened completely you can place it on your lap folded in half. For lunch, brunch, breakfast or tea party, the napkin is usually smaller in size and can be placed on your lap completely open. Your napkin should not leave your lap throughout dinner, if you really must get up, place the napkin left of your plate or fork gently unfolded.

Do not use your napkin to clean utensils, or to dip in water to clean a stain, or to blow you nose, or to wipe your face.

Never tuck your napkin in your shirt collar, like a bib.
Never spit food into your napkin.
When dinner is over, place your used napkin unfolded on the left of you plate, never on your plate.

Questions 8 – 14

Do the following statements agree with the information given in the text?

In boxes on your answer sheet, write

TRUE	if the statement agrees with the information
FALSE	if the statement contradicts the information
NOT GIVEN	if there is no information on this.

8. Whenever we are having a meal, we must use cloth napkins.
9. Napkins should not be tucked into your trousers.
10. Paper napkins can be used for informal meals.
11. You should have your napkin as long as you are sitting on the dining table.
12. The color of the tablecloth and the napkin should be the same.
13. The size of the dinner napkin is larger than the napkins used for other meals.
14. Fold your napkin neatly once dinner is over.

SECTION 2

Read the text below and answer Questions 15 – 27

Questions 15 - 21

IMPORTANCE OF DISCIPLINE AND PUNCTUALITY AT WORKPLACE

Discipline and punctuality are the two most essential traits required in a professional to be successful. Discipline ensures individuals behave in an acceptable way at the workplace and also adhere to the rules and regulations of the organization. Individuals who are disciplined are not only successful professionally but also in their personal lives. Disciplined employees are liked and appreciated by not only their superiors but also other fellow workers.

Misbehaving at the workplace spoils the entire work culture eventually leading to zero or very less productivity. You need to understand that there is a difference between office and home and you just can't behave in the same way at work as you behave at home.

Would you be able to concentrate on your work if the colleague sitting next to you is constantly over the phone and chatting with his girlfriend? Obviously, NO. In fact no one can. Discipline ensures individuals maintain silence at their workplace and work as a single unit with their team members to achieve organizational goals and objectives. Discipline is in fact the lifeline of an organization.

Punctuality ensures employees attend office daily and also complete their working hours. Managers need to ensure that their team members reach office on time and do not unnecessarily sit till late. It is always better to leave on time and come back fresh and completely recharged the next day. Believe me, individuals who are not punctual are often not reliable.

How would you feel if you want to meet someone on an urgent basis and if the other person never comes on time and always comes up with a new excuse? Would you ever believe or want to meet this person again? Being late to meetings is indeed a crime in today's business scenario where your client has access to unlimited alternatives just at the click of a button.

Discipline and punctuality make you a confident professional. Employees who concentrate on their work rather than interfering in their colleague's, finish their work on time and do not have to sit beyond the working hours. Trust me, being disciplined and punctual allow you to enjoy your work and the office never becomes a boring place. Disciplined employees seldom find their names dragged into controversies or nasty politics. Trust me, no one would respect you if you are not disciplined and punctual.

Questions 15 – 21

Choose NO MORE THAN TWO WORDS from the text above for each answer.

15. There are ....very important requirements for a working person to be successful.
16. An employee must not conduct himself the way he does at .... when he comes to the work.
17. If somebody in your workplace is engaging in casual conversation, you cannot .... on your work.
18. The .... of an organization is discipline.
19. You would not .... someone who always has a reason to be late.
20. If you have the qualities of being a disciplined worker and are punctual, it will make you a .... professional.
21. Employees who are focused on their work, and do not meddle in other people's assignments, do not have to stay at the office post .... hours.

Read the text below and answer the Questions 22 – 27

HOW TO MAKE A DAY TRIP TO THE TAJ MAHAL FROM DELHI

The first option I'm going to talk about is to just add Agra into your itinerary and go there by public transportation from Delhi and then move on to the next place from Agra. The problem with this is that going onward from Agra sometimes means coming back to Delhi as it's a big hub to catch long trains and buses. Because of this, passing through Agra isn't always a great option but you should see if it works for you.

Public transportation is easy and there are many buses that go from Delhi to Agra throughout the day. If you want to get there for sunrise you need to leave by 3.30 in the morning. Women traveling solo might not be okay with that, so in that case, I recommend not taking a local bus but instead a "tourist bus". Here's some information about booking buses in India. Keep in mind during some times of the year, there is too much fog to drive on the highway that early in the morning and tours will not run.

If you're more interested in taking a "tourist bus" this would mean booking it either online at makemytrip.com or redbus.in if you can get your international card to work. You can also just pop into any tourist agency (you'll see them everywhere) or ask your hotel to book this for you. Prices for a local bus could be as cheap as 50 rupees while a tourist bus might cost you 400 rupees. Moving on to more options, you might prefer a private A/C car ride there. These can be arranged through your hotel or an agency once you reach there. They will charge you commissions on this which could be quite high. If you would rather book this ahead of time with a reputable company then I recommend either of these two options:

1. Get Your Guide $80. This tour started at $17 and has gone up in price as it's become so popular, which is a little sad but at least you know it's good. 321 people have given this "tour" a 4.8/5-star rating. They will pick you up from your hotel in Delhi and get you to the Taj Mahal by sunrise, then take you back to Delhi. The tour pass allows you to skip the line at the Taj Mahal and you also get taken to Agra Fort and Mumtaz Mahal. The price does not include entrance tickets but there is a guide who will go with you through the attractions. This translates to about 1000 rupees which is literally a better deal than you can find anywhere else. This price will fluctuate as the peak tourist season rises and falls.

2. Viator $80. This is actually a better deal. 96 people have given it a 5-star review. With this option, the entrances to the Agra Fort and Taj Mahal are both included as well as breakfast. I think the entrance to both would cost around $20 so it saves you that money. Lunch isn't included and

they take you to a 5-star hotel buffet – so that's a little bit up to you if you want to pay for a lunch like that or if it's just you and your friends on the tour you can say no thank you to stopping at the hotel. Prices also go up if you are just one person.

3. Viator Shopping Tour $25. This is a kind of weird one but might work for some people. You go to Agra from Delhi and see the Taj Mahal from the outside for sunrise, don't go in, and then do a unique shopping tour. Like the others, it's a return trip back to Delhi but you could just stay in Agra and then the next day go to the Taj Mahal and go inside. The price is so cheap that it's kind of like paying for a ride there and getting a free shopping tour before you explore Agra on your own. Someone will go to the Taj with you so they can take your picture in front of it and help keep people from swarming you for selfies. It's so affordable and booking it ahead would just take off all your stress.

Questions 22-27

Complete the sentences with **NO MORE THAN TWO WORDS AND/OR A NUMBER** for each answer.

22. Based upon the time of the year, the buses may not be plying to Agra because of too much of ....
23. If you want to book a bus on-line, your .... has to work.
24. One of the options to book a tour to Agra is to ask a ...., which are available in plenty.
25. The price of Get Your Guide tour has increased manifold because it is extremely ....
26. If you want to have your breakfast as part of the tour, you should book the .... tour.
27. The tour that costs $25 is the only one where you also get to go on a .... in Agra.

SECTION 3
Read the text below. And answer Questions 28 – 40.
Questions 28 -35

The text has 8 SECTIONS, marked A to H. Choose the correct heading for each paragraph from the list of headings below.

i. The need for a contingency plan
ii. Symbol of the spirit of the games
iii. The German connection
iv. The Greek connection
v. The engineering behind the flame
vi. Harnessing the laws of physics
vii. Not just one torch
viii. Mistakes do happen

28. Paragraph A ....
29. Paragraph B ....
30. Paragraph C ....
31. Paragraph D ....
32. Paragraph E ....
33. Paragraph F ....
34. Paragraph G ....
35. Paragraph H ....

THE HISTORY OF THE OLYMPIC TORCH

A. Oddly, it all began with Hitler. For the 1936 Olympic Games in Berlin, Adolf Hitler wanted to draw on the ancient Greeks to bring a certain authoritative, classical air to modern Germany. The head of the Reich sports office had just the plan to do it: hold an elaborate relay to bring a symbolic Olympic flame from Greece to the games.

The original design by the German engineering giant, Krupp Company, was simple, with one primary function: to keep the flame burning. That's still the goal today. Since 1936, the torch has taken on a different form for every Olympic relay and undergone various transformative redesigns to make it more resilient and less likely to burn out. It's a strangely singular goal for an engineering project, but it allows for almost limitless creativity: The torch design can vary in almost every aspect, it just can't go out.

B. Engineers all over the world have, through the years, set about designing a flame that resists extinction, to varying degrees of success. But Olympic organizers know better; each year they arrange complex contingency plans in an effort to ensure that the final torch did, somehow, come from that original fire lit in Greece. The reason for these elaborate backup plans is a good one: carrying a flame for thousands of miles and across varying landscapes is, unsurprisingly, an incredibly difficult feat. There are so many steps along the way that can wreak havoc — that starts with the initial lighting.

C. The original Olympics looked almost nothing like the modern ones, but we like to draw on the ancient origins and so we still hold a ceremony at their birthplace: Olympia, Greece. Like children igniting ants with a magnifying glass, the actresses playing the part of Greek priestesses light the initial Olympic torch with a mirror. Specifically, they use a parabolic mirror, which is curved and looks a bit like a small satellite dish. The curvature focuses light in one spot, where the beams all meet at a single, intense spot. The one used in the ceremony at the Temple of Hera in Olympia has a focal point just above the mirror's surface. A "priestess" simply has to hold the torch in that spot and wait for the light to heat the fuel enough for it to ignite.

D. The ceremonial lighting is always held in Greece, and the flame is then symbolically transferred from person to person in an elaborate relay to whichever city is hosting the games. Greece is a fairly sunny place, so lack of available focalizing light is rarely a problem. But just in case, Olympic organizers hold a dress rehearsal on a bright day leading up to the real ceremony and light a flame, thus creating a backup source should the mirror fail to work during the ceremony.

E. And thus begins a little-known Olympic tradition: keeping a backup flame. Yes, that flame that's never supposed to extinguish sometimes probably does — we just never hear about it. To ensure that no one has to lie and say that the flame used to light the torch at the opening ceremony of the games isn't actually derived from that initial light, they light multiple miners lamps from the original flame and keep those backups lit, just in case.

As the relay moves along its course, each torch-bearer only carries a lit flame for a short while — about 20 minutes according to one report. That's because the fuel in a torch of that size simply can't last very long. The fuel should, in theory, last for longer than that to ensure that if something goes wrong on a leg of the relay, the team has some wiggle room. Still, rain and wind have put out the torch before, and organizers have had to relight the flame from the backup lanterns every time.

F. The 1972 Munich games were the first to use liquid fuel, which today is usually some combination of butane, propane, and propylene. Mixing each in varying amounts helps to control the brightness and color of the flame. Each chemical gives off a certain characteristic color of light and burns at a slightly different temperatures; a higher temperature results in a brighter color.

Most importantly, having a pressurized tank of fuel allows for a pilot light hidden inside the top of the torch. This little flame can reignite the whole thing if the main flame goes out, which is crucial given that torch-bearers have to sometimes run in the rain and up mountains where the air gets thin. In an interview, Sam Shelton, who created the torch for the 1996 Atlanta games, said that he tested the torch's endurance by having members of his team carry it to the top of Pikes Peak in Colorado, a 15,000 foot summit.

G. At the opening ceremony, engineers need to ensure everyone there is able to see the famed flame. Sometimes they design the fuel to smoke a bit, making the light more visible. Other times they just need to make the flame brighter by igniting more gas at once or choosing a fuel that burns at a higher temperature.

This went disastrously wrong in 1956, when the Olympics where held in Melbourne. The engineers had put a combination of magnesium and aluminum inside the torch so the flame would sparkle and burn brightly, which it did. But it also spewed bits of hot metal and sparks that burned the arm of the poor torch-bearer. Now, designers mostly use liquid fuels that have a more brilliant or larger flame to increase the visibility.

H. No matter what, though, the flame you see igniting the cauldron at the opening ceremony did somehow come from a fire lit in Olympia. It just takes an intricate system of backups and contingency plans to do it. And even if all of those plans failed, rest assured that you will never know the difference. The next time you see the Olympic flame being carried in a relay through your country, you can feel smug in the knowledge of the bearer may never know how many times the flame has been re-lit, or even if this is the torch the runner was supposed to be carrying, or a back-up one! But the audience most likely does not know or even care; the torch is a symbol, signifying the essential spirit of the games, and that is all that really matters.

Questions 36 – 40

Choose **ONE WORD OR A NUMBER** from the text to complete the following:

36. There were no Olympic torches before ....
37. The Greek priestesses who light the flame are actually ....
38. The flame burns brighter if the fuel used burns at a .... temperature.
39. The accident at the Melbourne Olympics was a result of an effort to make the torch burn ....
40. Organizers have to have elaborate .... plans to ensure that the flame stays lit through its journey from Greece to the venue of the Olympics.

GT READING TEST 5

SECTION 1

Questions 1 – 14

Read the text below and answer Questions 1 – 8

BEST DIVE SPOTS IN THE PHILIPPINES

A. **Apo Island:** This Island is named one of the 100 best dive sites in the world, thanks to the administrators who have taken all efforts in ensuring that the island lives up to world class standards. Locals supported initiatives of scientists from Silliman University to make the island one of the most well-documented and best protected marine sanctuaries in the country.

B. **Monad Shoal:** Divers from all over the world flock to Malapascua Island to see the elegant, oddly-shaped thresher sharks that breach the waters off the island, moving their way into the depths of Monad Shoal, where divers patiently wait for a sighting. A second dive through the blue waters of Malapascua in the afternoon will show you manta rays taking over the shoal.

C. **Anilao:** Most Manila-based divers will point to Anilao when asked about their favorite dive site. There are dozens of dive sites in Anilao as weekend warriors troop to the place for a good weekend dive. Anilao has good diving conditions all year round and it has an incredibly rich marine life and fantastic underwater landscapes you need not go far to enjoy.

D. **WWII Wrecks:** in Coron Bay, Palawan. The sunken remains of the WWII Japanese warships have been an interesting diving attraction in this dive site in Coron Bay where some of the most diverse and richest marine life thrives.

E. **Barracuda Lake:** in Coron Island, Palawan. Apart from wreck diving, Coron Island has Barracuda Lake, an underrated dive site in the Philippines. This lake is full of sharp thermoclines and alien underwater landscapes. Add to that the legend of the centuries-old monster-sized barracuda said to be the size of five large oil barrels.

F. **Ticao Pass:** This is known as "the Manta Bowl". The rough waters off Ticao provide a perfect spot for the majestic manta rays. Divers can enjoy truly breathtaking sightings of these gentle giants gliding overhead. There are also whale sharks that use the pass on their way to Donsol – a favorite snorkeling spot.

G. **Honda Bay:** This is an affordable luxury dive site. Teeming with rich marine life, Honda Bay has the advantage of being dotted with spectacular islands with sparkling white-sand beaches.

H. **Blue Hole in Romblon Island, Romblon.** This site may not be as popular as the others since Romblon is a largely unvisited province. Blue Hole is a product of the efforts of the three German-Filipino Eschweiler brothers – Peter, Philipp, and Patrick. And it is an underwater sinkhole where divers can stare into a bottomless abyss.

Questions 1 – 8

For which dive spots are the following statements true?

Write the correct letter, A-H, in boxes 1- 8 in your answer sheet.

You may use any letter more than once.

1. A lot of divers come here on Saturday and Sunday.
2. Bright white beaches are found here.
3. This dive site received the support of the local population.
4. The sight of large sea life here will take your breath away.
5. A very wide variety of marine life can be found here.
6. This site receives visitors from different parts of the world.
7. This dive site is much better than the rating people give it.
8. Three siblings helped develop this dive site.

Read the text below an answer Questions 9 – 14.

THROWING EVENTS IN TRACK AND FIELD ATHLETICS

Discus Throw: In this event, the athlete will attempt to throw a heavy disc as far as he/she can. The discus is usually made of plastic, wood, fiberglass, and carbon fiber. Then the athlete will spin counter clockwise around one and a half times through the circle, after which the athlete can release his/her throw.

The six key movement of discus throw are: wind up, move in rhythm, balance, right leg engine, orbit, and delivery.

Shot Put: Shot put is a track and field event in which the athlete will throw a shot - a heavy metal ball, the farthest that he can without leaving a circle that is 7 feet wide.
This sport was known to have started by the Ancient Greeks, but the first event of it on record was in Scottish Highlands during the first century. In 1896, shot put for men became an official event for Olympics; women were included in 1948.

During the throw or put as it is called, there are different styles can be used to get the maximum distance. The glide style involves rotating 180 degrees towards the putting direction and there's the spin style in which the thrower faces the rear, then spins to the throwing direction but giving the upper body a hard twist to get the highest possible throwing momentum.

Javelin Throwing: The javelin throw is part of the track and field event. A javelin or a spear about 8 feet long is to be thrown. The participant first runs within a predetermined area and then throws the javelin. The participants must hold the javelin at its grip and throw over hands, over the participant's upper arm or shoulder.

Javelin is a part of the men's decathlon and the women's heptathlon.

Hammer Throw: Hammer throw is one of the oldest events in track and field competitions. A heavy object on the end of a thin wire is hurled for maximum distance. The game dates back to the 15th century.

It was used to be thought of as a strength event, but now it's based more on speed.
The action of throwing involves two swings, then around three or four body rotations in circular motion using a heel-toe movement of the foot. This is then moved in a circular path. It gradually increases its velocity, and then the participant throws the ball from the circle.

Questions 9 – 14

Do the following statements agree with the information given in the text.

Write:

TRUE	If the statement agrees with the information
FALSE	If the statement contradicts the information
NOT GIVEN	If there is no information on this.

9. Discus throw is not part of the women's heptathlon event.
10. Hammer Throw is one of the earliest events introduced in the Olympics.
11. Shot put for women was introduced into the Olympics more than half a century after it was introduced for men.
12. The last key movement in a discus throw is delivery.
13. Strength is the key in doing well in the Hammer Throw.
14. The Javelin cannot be more than 8 ft. in length.

SECTION 2

Read the text below and answer Questions 15 – 27

Questions 15 – 20

FIRE SAFETY

Fire safety is a fundamental consideration in building design and management, but unfortunately, one that is often overlooked. Assess fire safety measures in your built environment with the help of this checklist:

1. Provide adequate means of escape: The first rule of fire management requires sufficient escape routes out of the building, in accordance with its scale and occupancy. The number, size and location of exits are specified in the National Building Code (NBC) 2005, a detailed set of guidelines for constructing, maintaining and operating buildings of all types. Office occupiers must additionally ensure that staircases, stairwells and corridors are well-maintained, ventilated and free of obstacles in order to be effective in an emergency.

2. Install smoke detection systems: The first few minutes of a fire are crucial in containing it. Automatic fire alarm systems such as smoke and heat detectors are mandatory elements in international building codes, and particularly useful in spotting fires during times when occupancy in the building is low.

3. Maintain smoke suppression systems: Fire extinguishers are only useful if they work, so check them regularly. High-rise buildings, which are harder to access and evacuate, should consider installing automatic sprinkler systems. It is estimated that automatic suppression systems lower the cost of damage by 60%.

4. Conduct regular fire drills: Regular fire drills familiarize people with emergency evacuation methods at little cost, and also prevent panic. Nominate a fire safety officer in every building to ensure that this becomes standard operating procedure.

5. Use flame-retardant materials: Materials used in the interiors can save or endanger lives. The combination of wood, paper and textiles makes workstations highly combustible. An increasing number of companies, especially multinationals, request fire-resistant fabrics despite their price premium. Doors are also assigned a fire-resistance rating, measuring how long they can remain resistant to excessive temperatures and flames without collapsing.

6. Ask the local fire brigade to assess safety: Fire departments, for a nominal fee, will independently assess your building's level of fire safety. Storage of hazardous or inflammable materials, old and

unstable structures, inadequate escape routes or electricity overloads are potential death traps that are best assessed by professionals.

7. Comply with National Building Code: “Green buildings" are in vogue but safe structures are sadly not. Both the Mumbai Fire Brigade and BMC commissioner concede that 80% of buildings likely violate accepted codes of building safety, with ignorance and personal whims leading to illegal modifications after gaining requisite occupancy permission.

Questions 15 – 20

Choose no more than one word from the text above to complete each sentence.

15. When a building is constructed, it is essential to consider what should be done in case of a fire however, this aspect is often......................
16. It is compulsory to have smoke .... as per the international building codes.
17. If regular fire drills are conducted, it ensures that if there is a fire, people do not..................
18. Although their costs are at a ...., many organizations are using fire-resistant materials in their buildings.
19. Nowadays people make eco-friendly buildings, but they are not necessarily ....
20. The very first thing one has to ensure is that there are .... ways to get away from a building in case of fire.

Read the text below and answer Questions 21 – 27

7 TIPS FOR THE PERFECT RUNWAY WALK

Whether you are in a haute couture assemble or vogue-ing in a living room, here are a few tips to get you on the road to your inner diva. Physical balance, inner confidence and a sparkling personality are all necessary to make a charming performance. The catwalk is easy to learn, but can take a lifetime to master. However, what makes runway technique so interesting is how it requires both outward and internal calibration. Physical balance, inner confidence and a sparkling personality are all necessary to make a charming performance.

1. Posture: Think tall. While walking, stand up straight leaning slightly back so your legs can go first. Keep your toes pointed forward, so they aren't turned out. Then walk with one foot in front of the other as if walking on a tightrope.

2. Hips: Most people think you need to do a lot of hip swaying. Your hips will move naturally so exaggeration isn't necessary.

3. Arms: Let your arms swing naturally. However, take care they are not too stiff or have big movement. The clothing you have on will help you decide what to do with your hands, you may need to hold something or stick one in a pocket.

4. Attitude: Be commanding and flirty. This will make you fun for the audience.

5. Rhythm: Get into a rhythm and let the loud music be your uplifting motivation. When a natural bounce to the beat happens add to it by thinking about holding your head high and keeping your shoulders back.

6. Eyes: You should never look down. Always look straight ahead at the cameras or pick a spot on the wall ahead of you so you won't get distracted by anything else around you.

7. Posing: When you reach the end of the runway pause, and then lean on one hip with lots of attitude.

By following these simple tips you'll be on your way to a natural, confident and fun runway presence to make the entire designers clothes look amazing or your living room look like a major fashion event.

Questions 21-27

Do the following statements agree with the information given in the text?
In boxes on your answer sheet, write

TRUE	if the statement agrees with the information
FALSE	if the statement contradicts the information
NOT GIVEN	if there is no information on this.

21. Always keep one hand in your pocket while walking.
22. It is not difficult to learn how to walk on the ramp.
23. Practice walking on a tight-rope to improve your walking style.
24. Stop for a while at the end of the walk-way.
25. Sway your hips from side to side for maximum effect.
26. You should carefully listen to the loud music to motivate you.
27. Look down once in a while to ensure you don't trip over and fall.

SECTION 3

Read the text below and answer questions 28 – 40

Questions 28 -35

The text has 8 SECTIONS, marked A to H. Choose the correct heading for each paragraph from the list of headings below.

i. Drilling for oil and gas
ii. Consequences of burning fossil fuels
iii. Impacts of coal mining
iv. Lower negative impact of renewable energy
v. Risks during transportation
vi. Impact on water
vii. Our civilization is at risk
viii. Hidden cost of fossil fuels

28. Paragraph A ....
29. Paragraph B ....
30. Paragraph C ....
31. Paragraph D ....
32. Paragraph E ....
33. Paragraph F ....
34. Paragraph G ....
35. Paragraph H ....

FOSSIL FUELS

A. We've all paid a utility bill or purchased gasoline. Those represent the direct costs of fossil fuels; but those expenses don't reflect the total cost of fossil fuels to each of us individually or to society as a whole. Known as externalities, the hidden costs of fossil fuels aren't represented in their market price.

Externalities are sometimes easy to see, such as pollution and land degradation, and sometimes less obvious, such as the costs of asthma and cancer, or the impacts of sea level rise. Many consequences are far removed from our daily lives and may only affect a minority or marginalized subset of the population.

Costs accrue at every point of the fossil fuel supply chain. Extraction processes generate air and water pollution; transporting fuels from the mine or well causes air pollution. When e fuels are burned, they emit toxins and global warming emissions. Even the waste products are hazardous to public health and the environment.

Understanding these impacts is critical for evaluating the true cost of fossil fuels.

B. The most obvious and severe cost of underground coal mining is the threat it poses to the health and safety of coal miners. Many coal miners are injured, sometimes fatally, on the job each year. Adverse impacts to the environment are another significant cost of underground coal mining. Mines can collapse or gradually subside, affecting surface and subsurface water flows. If active and abandoned coal mines are not properly managed, water can sometimes flow through the mine and become highly acidic and rich in heavy metals.
Surface mining involves removing the overlaying soil to access the coal below. Huge volumes of excess rock and soil are typically dumped into adjacent valleys and streams, altering their ecosystems and diverting the natural flow of streams. In the long term, coal removal sites are left with poor soil that typically only supports exotic grasses.

C. The environmental and health costs of onshore and offshore oil and gas drilling are also significant, and often unseen.
When oil and gas are extracted, water that had been trapped in the geologic formation is brought to the surface. This "produced water" can carry with it naturally-occurring dissolved solids, heavy metals, hydrocarbons, and radioactive materials in concentrations that make it unsuitable for human consumption and difficult to dispose of safely.
A large amount of land is disturbed by the drilling wells, access roads, processing facilities, and pipelines associated with oil and gas drilling operations. In particular, noise and habitat fragmentation can harm wildlife populations.
Natural gas's climate emissions are not only generated when it's burned as a fuel at power plants or in our homes. The full global warming impact of natural gas also includes methane emissions from drilling wells and pipeline transportation.
Oil drilling can also produce methane. Although it can be captured and used as an energy source, the gas is often either vented (released) or flared (burned). Vented methane contributes greatly to global warming, and poses a serious safety hazard.

D. In most cases, coal is transported from mines to power plants. In 2014, approximately 68 percent of the coal used for electric power in the US was transported by rail: 13 percent was transported on river barge and another 11 percent by truck. Train cars, barges, and trucks all run on diesel fuel, a major source of nitrogen dioxide and soot, which carry substantial human health risks.
Natural gas is transported over long distances by transmission pipelines, while distribution pipelines deliver gas locally to homes and businesses. But natural gas is also highly flammable, making the process of transporting it from wellhead to homes and businesses dangerous.
Oil is transported across the ocean in supertankers, and it is moved over land by pipeline, rail, and truck. In every case, the risk of oil spills poses a serious environmental threat.

E. Some of the most significant hidden costs of fossil fuels are from the air emissions that occur when they are burned. Unlike the extraction and transport stages, in which coal, oil, and natural gas can have very different types of impacts, all fossil fuels emit carbon dioxide and other harmful air pollutants when burned. These emissions lead to a wide variety of public health and environmental costs that are borne at the local, regional, national, and global levels.
Of the many environmental and public health risks associated with burning fossil fuels, the most serious in terms of its universal and potentially irreversible consequences is global warming. Non-fossil fuel energy generation technologies, like wind, solar, and geothermal, contributed less than 1 percent of the total energy related global warming emissions.
Coal-fired power plants are the largest source of mercury emissions to the air. As airborne mercury settles onto the ground, it washes into bodies of water where it accumulates in fish, and subsequently passes through the food chain to birds and other animals.

F. Across the United States, the demand for electricity is colliding with the need for healthy and abundant freshwater. Nationwide, fossil fuel and nuclear power plants have been found to withdraw as much water as all farms and more than four times as much as all residences. More than 80 percent of this power plant cooling water originates in lakes and rivers, directly impacting local ecosystems and often competing with other uses, such as agriculture and recreation.
Power plants that return water to nearby rivers, lakes, or the ocean can harm wildlife through what is known as "thermal pollution." Thermal pollution occurs due to the degradation of water quality resulting from changes in water temperature.

G. Burning coal, oil, and natural gas has serious and long-standing negative impacts on public health, local communities and ecosystems, and the global climate. Yet the majority of fossil fuel impacts are far removed from the fuels and electricity we purchase, hidden within public and private health expenditures, military budgets, emergency relief funds, and the degradation of sensitive ecosystems.
Renewable energy—such as wind and solar power—carries far fewer negative impacts at increasingly competitive prices. The Union of Concerned Scientists has worked for decades on transforming the electricity and transportation sectors, and is committed to policies and practices that encourage clean energy.

H. There is no doubt that fossil fuels and their usage has been a prime factor in the engine for the growth of our civilization. Fossil fuels power our homes, our transportation systems on land, sea and air, factories and so on. The impact of fossil fuels on the environment and therefore the health, well-being and even survival of all living species has only been fully understood in recent years. Research and development of alternate sources of energy is taking place across the world at a fairly rapid pace. We need fuel in various forms to sustain life. Our future is dependent upon developing alternate fuel sources successfully and economically and making it available at a reasonable cost to everyone as soon as possible. There are no winners or losers in this race, our civilization will sink or swim together.

Questions 36 - 40

Choose **ONE WORD ONLY** from the text to complete the following:

36. The price we pay for using fossil fuels includes the cost at which we buy them plus ....
37. .... released in the air is a safety hazard
38. Coal is mostly moved from where they are extracted to plants that generate................
39. Since it can catch fire very easily, the process delivering gas to the ultimate end user is highly.....................
40. The negative impact on the quality of water due to changes in its temperature is known as .... pollution.

GT READING TEST 6

SECTION 1

Questions 1-14

Read the text below and answer questions 1-8

THE BEST BEACHES OF GOA

A. **Arambol Beach:** Let the sea and the sun kiss your soul as you spend pensive hours on Arambol Beach. A handful of shacks offer unforgettable sea food and a mix of cuisines to delight you. Quite close to the Dabolim Airport, this beach sees ardent beach lovers in winters. Perfect for a sunny day out, Arambol is where you can engage in a game of volleyball at the beach.

B. **Morjim Beach:** The calm ambience of Morjim Beach is going to sooth all your travel fatigue. Take a stroll for unsurpassed beauty and calm that only a few beaches in Goa offer even in the peak of winters. Attracting a wide species of birds and, not to forget, its popularity as one of the hatching sites for the Olive Ridley turtles, Morjim is a must-visit for the love of all things wild!

C. **Vagator Beach:** A huge hit with backpackers, Vagator Beach in Goa is lined with numerous shacks, quaint cafes, a slew of budget shacks and hotels as well. A typical evening at this beach in Goa sees swimmers, volleyball lovers and even scooters wading through knee deep water at the banks!

D. **Baga Beach:** One of the most recognizable and famous beaches in Goa, Baga is a must-visit for everyone! Especially for the shopaholics, who are keen for bargain deals and more. Also popular as a party hub, this beach sees beach lovers flocking late into the night.

E. **Anjuna Beach:** The fun begins in Goa when you hit the popular Anjuna Beach along with your friends! A number of popular beach clubs and shacks in its vicinity make it a favourite. An equal and apt competitor to Baga, this popular Goa beach is much loved by hippies, sun lovers and anyone into water sports. A host of cheap yet surprisingly good eateries by the beach are an added attraction.

F. **Calangute Beach:** Just 15 km from the Goan capital, Panaji, Calangute is the largest beach in Goa. Mid-way between Candolim and Baga, it is lined with a host of backpacker and luxury accommodations to make the dream of a beach side stay in Goa quite feasible.

G. **Candolim Beach:** The waters of Candolim Beach take different hues as the day passes by! A must-visit for photographers, this is one place you cannot skip from your itinerary.

Questions 1 – 8

Look at the 7 descriptions of the beaches of Goa.

For which beaches are the following statements true? Write the letter A-G on your answer sheet

1. **You can buy stuff here at cheap prices.**
2. **This beach is located between two other popular beaches of Goa.**
3. **If you fly into Goa, you will find this beach quite close by.**
4. **If you have a camera with you, you should go to this beach.**
5. **Those fond of ornithology will find this beach interesting.**
6. **You will be surprised by the good quality of food at this beach.**
7. **Meet fellow back-packers at this beach.**
8. **This beach is a worthy competitor to the most recognizable beach of Goa.**

Read the text below and answer Questions 9 – 14.

PLACES TO VISIT IN MANALI

Here is the best mix of tourist attractions in Manali and its vicinity.

A. **Hadimba Temple:** This beautiful temple, dedicated to Hadimba, the wife Bhima, is one of the best places to visit in Manali. The most striking feature of this temple is that it is located in the Dhungri Forest and is surrounded by pine trees. The pagoda-shaped temple is unique in its architecture. It is one of the most popular religious attractions in Manali.

B. **Museum of Himachal Culture and Folk Art:** A stone's throw from the Hadimba Temple, the Museum of Himachal Culture & Folk Art allows a walk through time. It houses a unique collection of unknown antiques including religious relics, household objects, weapons, instruments, and scale models.

C. **Tibetan Monasteries:** Manali also boasts of a Tibetan settlement. The famous Tibetan monasteries draw a large number of tourists, and are among the most visited and certainly the best places to visit in Manali. One can meditate here and shop for unique Tibetan art and craft objects.

D. **Manu Temple:** Nearly 3 km away from the famous Mall Road of Manali, the famous Manu Temple is among the frequently visited tourist places in Manali. Dedicated to Lord Manu, the temple's premises offer a sense of peace and serenity to the devotees walking in. It is frequented by religious tourists and foreigners and is among the most popular attractions in Manali.

E. **Vashisht Hot Water Spring:** Almost 3 km away from Manali, the Vashisht Temple is famous for its natural hot water springs. The premises enclose a pyramid-shaped stone temple dedicated to Sage Vashisht; the hot water spring, where tourists take a bath, is said to have medicinal properties to relieve aches and pains.

F. **Jogini Falls:** The breath-taking Jogini Falls, located beyond Vashisht Hot Springs towards the Vashisht Village, is another major tourist attraction near Manali. Melodious sounds of nature, stunning views, and some sumptuous authentic Himachali delicacies – Jogini Falls has it all for the backpackers and nature lovers.

G. **Solang Valley:** The Solang Valley is among the most popular places to visit near Manali. It lies about 14 km from Manali and is the venue for winter skiing festival that is held here every year.

People of all age groups love to visit this place during winters to enjoy skiing and other adventure sports.

Questions 9 – 14

Do the following statements agree with the information given in the text? In boxes on your answer sheet, write

TRUE	if the statement agrees with the information
FALSE	if the statement contradicts the information
NOT GIVEN	if there is no information on this.

9. Jogini Falls is further from Manali than Vashisht Temple.
10. If you are tired, a bath in the Vashisht Hot Water Springs will rejuvenate you.
11. The Museum of Himachal Culture and Folk Art is quite far from Hadimba Temple.
12. There are Tibetans living in Manali.
13. The Hadimba Temple is the only religious place of tourist interest in and around Manali.
14. The winter skiing festival held at the Solang Valley is extremely popular with people of all age groups.

SECTION 2

Questions 15 – 27

Read the text below and answer the Questions 15 – 20.

BANQUET MANAGER: DUTIES AND RESPONSIBILITIES

- Maintain complete knowledge of and comply with all departmental policies/service procedures/standards.
- Maintain complete knowledge and strictly abide by state liquor regulations, particularly those prohibiting service to minors and intoxicated persons.
- Be familiar with all hotel services/features and local attractions/activities to respond to guest inquiries accurately.
- Inspect all aspects of the outlet environment ensuring compliance with standards of cleanliness and order and ensure immediate rectification of deficiencies.
- Anticipate guest's needs, respond promptly and acknowledge all guests, however busy and whatever time of day.
- Resolve guest complaints, ensuring guest satisfaction.
- Ensure that each liquor bottle ordered is backed up by an exchange of an empty bottle of the same liquor.
- Monitor Happy Hour set-up and service, ensuring agreement to Hotel standards.
- Responsibility for the creation of cocktail menus and Update menu changes on the Point of sale (POS) terminal.
- Monitor and maintain cleanliness, sanitation and organisation of work areas.
- Coordinate music tapes and entertainment, ensuring correct volume and appropriateness to clientele.
- Establish par levels for supplies, liquor, beer, wine and equipment. Complete requisitions to replenish shortages or additional items needed.
- Responsibility for all beverage purchases, inventories and stock levels.
- Regularly check storage areas for proper supplies, organisation and cleanliness.
- Review sales and beverage costs for previous day; resolve discrepancies with Accounting. Track actual against budget.
- Conduct pre-shift meeting with staff and review all information pertinent to the day's business.
- Inspect grooming and attire of staff; rectify any deficiencies.
- Inspect, plan and ensure that all materials and equipment are in complete readiness for service; rectify deficiencies with respective personnel.
- Prepare weekly work schedules in accordance with staffing guidelines and labour forecasts. Adjust schedules throughout the week to meet the business demands.
- Ensure that staff report to work as scheduled. Document any deviations.

Prerequisites:

Must be able to communicate in English (writing and speaking); knowledge of any other languages would be advantageous. Broad understanding of tight stock management procedures; a target orientated individual with the ability to work to set deadlines.

Education:

Graduates bachelor degree and/or diploma in hotel or other related field; experience and proficiency in MS office, Point of Sales, Inventory and store programs.

Experience:

Previous experience in similar Job role or three to five years management experience in large up-scale hotel / restaurant preferred.

Questions 15 – 20

Choose **ONE WORD ONLY** from the text to fill in the blanks in the passage below:

The Banquet Manager has a number of duties and responsibilities. Before starting his day at work, he should (15).............. all that is known about what to expect during the day's work. with his staff. There are certain rules and regulations pertaining to alcohol and he should (16)........... by them. As and if and when any guest has reason to find fault, he should be able to take care of the guest's concern to the (17)............. of the guest. Since the volume of work may vary from day to day, he should (18) .... the duties of staff appropriately. If any of his staff members do not come to work, he should take note and (19).................. the same. If he is able to speak Punjabi, it will be (20)....................

Read the text below and answer Questions 21 – 27.

INSTRUCTIONS FOR COMPLETING MANUAL TIME SHEETS

All part-time employees must use web time entry when recording and submitting hours worked. If an employee is unable to access web time entry and has been unsuccessful in resolving the issue with the payroll department, or has missed the web time entry deadline, he or she may use the manual (paper) time sheet titled "BO-029 Payroll Part-Time Hourly Time Sheet" and follow the instructions below.

1. Access a manual (paper) timesheet online at http://www.fsw.edu/payroll/forms
2. Complete the following information:

   a. Enter your Banner ID Number (available on your Connect Card)

   b. Enter your legal name (First Name, Last Name)

   c. Choose the "Pay Beginning Date" by clicking to the right to show the drop down feature. Scroll down and click on the correct date. This will automatically generate the days and dates for the pay period

   d. Check to make sure the pay period begins on the correct day/date and ends on the correct day/date.
3. Hours Worked

   Enter the total number of hours physically worked each day rounded to the nearest quarter hour. Do not include any lunch breaks, holidays or any other time away from work. Peak Partners are required to complete In/Out times, the electronic time sheet will calculate and enter your hours each day. The electronic time sheets will also sum the "Grand Totals for this Pay Period". If you do not have access to a computer a paper copy can be used. You will need to enter in the correct information for each day worked and total the time sheet.
4. Additional Hours to be Paid - Holiday Pay: All regular part-time employees are eligible for holiday pay. Temporary employees are not eligible for holiday pay. Examples of temporary employees are student assistants, work study and peak partners. Holiday pay for eligible employees will only be paid if the employee was normally scheduled to work on that day and for only the hours scheduled to work. For example, John Smith is scheduled to work five (5) hours on Christmas Day. Christmas Day is designated as a college holiday in 2008. John Smith will receive five (5) hours of holiday pay.
5. Required Signatures: Both the employee and the supervisor must sign/approve the time sheet. It is the supervisor's responsibility to verify the hours and calculations prior to signing the time sheet.
6. Payroll Schedule: Time sheets must be turned into the payroll office by the posted deadlines. Any time sheets received after the deadline could result in non-payment for that pay period. If this

occurs, the employee will receive payment on the next scheduled pay cycle. To access the current payroll schedule, go to http://www.fsw.edu/payroll/forms, and then click on Payroll Calendar.

7. Corrections to Time Sheets: Any corrections or changes to time sheets must be recorded on a new time sheet and marked "AMENDED" with the original pay beginning date. The corrected time sheet must again be signed and approved by the employee and supervisor.

Questions 21 – 27

Do the following statements agree with the information given in the text?

In boxes on your answer sheet, write

TRUE	if the statement agrees with the information
FALSE	if the statement contradicts the information
NOT GIVEN	if there is no information on this.

21. All part – time employees are required to fill in manual time sheets.
22. Nick names should not be entered on time sheets.
23. Total hours spent at the office, including hours physically at work, and meal and bio breaks should be aggregated and entered.
24. A student assistant will be paid for the hours worked on a holiday.
25. Time sheets must be submitted on time, otherwise payment for that time period will lapse.
26. If an employee is unsuccessful in resolving any issue with the payroll department, he should contact his supervisor.
27. All time sheets are required to be validated and signed by the supervisor.

SECTION 3

Read the text below and answer questions 28 – 40

Questions 28 -35

The text has 8 SECTIONS, marked A to H. Choose the correct heading for each paragraph from the list of headings below.

i. How big is the problem?
ii. Of population growth and poverty
iii. Solutions: improving life in rural areas
iv. Characteristics of an urban slum
v. Causes and effects of urban poverty
vi. Govt. accountability
vii. Urban slums in India
viii. Slum rehabilitation in urban areas

28. Paragraph A ....
29. Paragraph B ....
30. Paragraph C ....
31. Paragraph D ....
32. Paragraph E ....
33. Paragraph F ....
34. Paragraph G ....
35. Paragraph H ....

URBAN SLUMS

A. Urban slums are settlements, neighborhoods, or city regions that cannot provide the basic living conditions necessary for its inhabitants, or slum dwellers, to live in a safe and healthy environment. The United Nations Human Settlements Program (UN-HABITAT) defines a slum settlement as a household that cannot provide one of the following basic living characteristics:

a. Durable housing of a permanent nature that protects against extreme climate conditions.
b. Sufficient living space, which means not more than three people sharing the same room.
c. Easy access to safe water in sufficient amounts at an affordable price.
d. Access to adequate sanitation in the form of a private or public toilet shared by a reasonable number of people.
e. Security of tenure that prevents forced evictions.

B. In India, the causes of urban poverty can be linked to the lack of infrastructure in rural areas, forcing inhabitants of these regions to seek out work in India's mega-cities. However, as more and more people make this migration, the space left to accommodate them becomes less and less. Urban development can't keep up with the growing numbers of informal settlers and no one wants to be held accountable for the slums or their residents. As a result, nearly one in four urban resident lives in a slum.

Urban poverty in India is unique, particularly in the way that it follows certain patterns of growth. Though the proportion of urban poor has reportedly declined over the past decades, the numbers keep adding up, fuelling the persistent nature of slums.

C. In 2001, according to the National Report about 23.5% of urban households were slum dwellers. This percentage had decreased to 17% by 2011 even though the total number of households living in slums had gone up from 10.5 million in 2001 to 13.75 million in 2011.

India's present urban system includes about 7933 cities and towns of varying population sizes, and many of these cities and towns are included in the massive expansion of urban growth that was registered over the 2001- 2011 decade. Given the present lack of affordable housing, these numbers are anything but reassuring. If the causes of urban poverty and the lives of millions of slum-dwellers are to be improved, many changes must be made

D. As agriculture is barely a lucrative option, the only job option for villagers who have migrated to the cities is to seek out work in the cities' informal economies. Millions migrate to the cities every day to take up informal jobs such as domestic help, drivers, construction site work, etc. However, this creates overcrowding in the already packed urban infrastructure.

Lack of affordable housing leaves these people address-less on paper. They settle wherever they can, but as more people join, a whole community of undocumented settlers emerges. This further complicates the procedure of accessing basic services like electricity, water and sanitation, etc. as the authorities and public utilities can only serve those registered on paper – this is how poverty begins. Overcrowding is another major factor in informal settlements. There is often just one bathroom for 50 to 100 people in each illegal building, and lack of awareness of personal hygiene practices pushes families further into the waiting arms of diseases and infections.

The low income of these communities means that standard medical help is often a far-fetched dream, not to mention unaffordable. Therefore, on occasions when it rains or the neighbourhood is flooded, these settlements become breeding grounds for various parasites and infections and the cycle repeats itself.

E. Tackling the causes of urban poverty in India – is also a key way to curb India's fertility rate. The demographic transition refers to the process through which all countries in the world are going through (or have completed) whereby their population goes from:

High birth rate and high death rate (mostly for children under 5) to

High birth rate and lower death rate (for those same children) to

Low birth rate and low death rate (most families have only 2 children who survive)

The middle stage causes the world population to grow, but we can see very clearly that the majority of developing countries tend to have 4-5 children per family and the number keeps going down as the world economy improves.

Recent studies and statistics worldwide have shown that people living in poverty are more likely to have more children. So in a way, it's safe to say that, in this day and age, poverty is one of the causes behind overpopulation. It wasn't the case before because basic medicine wasn't available. And the reason for this is simple, families living in poverty lack access to education and contraception but mostly they often have no pension system (they expect their children to take care of them in their old age) and they expect that many of their children die before the age of five.

F. Traditionally, institutional corruption has played a major role in the slow rate of provision of affordable urban housing. Over the past decades, officials at different levels of operation have been known to harass slum dwellers by asking them to pay up for documents they lacked. They also ignored bureaucratic procedures by "justifying" delays in housing provision, forcing them to permanently settle in these unsustainable settlements. Although public service delivery has improved over the past decade, there is a general desperate feeling that nothing will ever change. Given the current scale of the problem, hopelessness would not be an irrelevant emotion given the poor record of management and rate of addressing the issue so far.

G. In order to control large-scale migrations from rural to urban areas, the current state of rural infrastructure must be addressed. What's also important is giving slum-dwellers access to some form of credit and resources, if not the causes of urban poverty will continually wear down on generations to come.

India is taking the right step in promoting small and medium scale industries in rural areas, as well as promoting other income-generating opportunities. However, more investment into satisfying the demand for more jobs, equal pay, more career and movement opportunities in the tertiary or agriculture sector, could ease the increasing pressure on urban infrastructure services.

H. As India ambitiously progresses in line with other rapidly developing cities, informal settlers are increasingly left behind. Although considered a persisting problem, slums weren't just born overnight. They are a product of decades, even centuries of neglect and lack of development planning.

Life in the slums will only improve when its residents' living situations are upgraded or bettered on a basic level. That's why one of our key programmes in India consists in rehabilitating and upgrading: building safe and decent homes for the millions of socially excluded families in India's big cities. Through rehabilitation, we ensure that these families have access to clean water, electricity, better jobs (via skills training), and the right to live in their homes.

Questions 36 – 40

Choose not more than two words from the text to complete the following sentences:

36. In our country, there is a connection between poverty and the state of .... in the villages.
37. Since there is a shortage of........................ accommodation, migrants to urban areas settle down wherever possible.
38. The number of children per family is inversely proportional to the state of the ....
39. Given the manner in which the issue has been managed and addressed so far, one may tend to feel ....
40. Urban slums are a major problem, but these did not materialise ....

GT READING TEST 7

SECTION 1

Questions 1 – 14

Read the text below and answer Questions 1 – 8

LONDON UNDERGROUND

The London Underground rail network or "the Tube" is a great way to travel to and from central London and will be an integral part of most people's stay in the UK capital.

Greater London is served by 11 Tube lines, along with the Dockyards Light Railway (DLR) and an interconnected local train network. Underground trains generally run between 5am and midnight, Monday to Saturday, with reduced operating hours on Sunday.

For more detailed traveler information on which stations to use and suggestions for the best route to reach your destination, use Transport for London's Journey Planner.

What are the London Underground zones?

London's public transport network, locally called the London Tube, is divided into nine travel zones. Zone 1 is in central London and zones 6 to 9 are on the outskirts of the city.

What are the London Tube prices?

Buy a Visitor Oyster card, Oyster Card, Travelcard or use a contactless payment card to get the best value as cash is the most expensive way to pay. Check out our guide to cheap travel for more money-saving tips when travelling in London.

An adult cash fare on the London metro for a single journey in zone 1 is £4.90. The same Tube fare with Visitor Oyster card, Oyster card or contactless payment card is £2.40. For more details about London Tube prices, see the Transport for London website.

For contactless payment cards issued outside the UK, please check for transaction fees or bank changes.

There are various discounts available for children, students, and elderly travellers on the London subway.

If you plan on travelling around London to do some sight-seeing and visit some of London's best attractions, why not get a London Pass and save even more money.

Questions 1 – 8

Do the following statements agree with the information given in the text above? Write:

TRUE	If the statement agrees with the information
FALSE	If the statement contradicts the information
NOT GIVEN	If there is no information on this

1. There are 11 Tube Lines in all, including the DLR.
2. Zones 2 to 5 of the London Tube are located between Zone 1 and Zones 6 to 9.
3. An adult cash fare on the London metro for a single journey is £4.90.
4. It is more economical to pay for travel using a card than paying cash.
5. If you are studying in school, you can get a discount on the London subway.
6. If you are buying a contactless payment card outside the UK, you may have to pay charges more than the cost of the card.
7. The cheapest option to travel around London, including sight-seeing, is using a London Pass.
8. There are fewer trains on Sundays as compared to weekdays.

Read the text below and answer Questions 9 – 14

THE SEVEN MOST PRESTIGIOUS MARATHONS IN THE WORLD

If you want to take your love of running to the extreme, hop on a plane and compete in one of these prestigious marathons around the world.

A. Boston Marathon: Although it has grown to elicit a new meaning after the terrorist attacks in 2013, it has always been a well-known event. The first Boston Marathon was held in 1897, making it the oldest marathon in the United States today. Qualifying standards are so rigorous that runners earn bragging rights just for qualifying. Racers gather on Patriots' Day outside of Boston in Hopkinton and run through several New England towns before finishing in the center of Boston.

B. Great Wall Marathon: Not only does this marathon, held each May, put you at the scene of history, but it's also known as one of the hardest marathons to run. Throughout the race, you'll have to climb 5,164 steps of The Great Wall of China, and because of that, it will probably take you about 50% longer than normal to complete. However, the views of China's countryside are fantastic and you'll race through beautiful Chinese villages and past rice fields before finishing in Yin and Yang Square.

C. New York City Marathon: Started in 1970 with just 55 finishers, it has now grown to be the largest marathon in the world – with over 50,000 people finishing the race in 2014. Despite the large number of racers, this is actually a tough marathon to get into. Should you qualify, you'll race through all five New York City boroughs, so it's the perfect run if you love the urban setting.

D. Athens Marathon: The Athens Marathon is one of Greece's biggest sporting events. Go back to where it all started, and run the route from Marathon to Athens as Pheidippides did in 490 B.C., where the term "marathon" got its name. Although the course is mostly uphill, the marathon has a rich history that makes joining the 13,000 other runners worthwhile.

E. London Marathon: The London Marathon is an in-demand race that takes you past London's greatest landmarks like The Tower of London and the London Eye before finishing in front of Buckingham Palace. It's also one of the largest races worldwide. In 2014, despite nearly 170,000 runners applying to the race, around 35,800 finished. Most years average between 34,000 and 37,000 finishers.

F. <u>Tokyo Marathon:</u> Also one of the largest marathons in the world, this marathon features around 35,000 runners and 1.6 million spectators. The race takes you through a flat, urban setting past many of Tokyo's landmarks, such as the Imperial Palace, Tokyo Tower, and Tokyo Station.

G. <u>Berlin Marathon:</u> Taking place in September, the Berlin Marathon has grown from 286 runners in 1974 to over 40,000 racers in 2015. In all categories, including inline skating, wheelchair, and Breakfast Run divisions, the 2015 race saw 58,776 participants from 127 nations. This race takes you through areas of German history, but it's also a quick race. In 2014, Dennis Kimetto won with an impressive time of 2:02:57

Although these races are some of the most well-known, they're just the tip of the iceberg. Wherever you want to travel, there's sure to be a marathon scheduled nearby. Simply slip on your shoes and socks and get started with your training!

Questions 9 – 14

Which marathons do the following statements refer to? Write the letter A - G referring to the Marathon in your answer sheet.

9. This run takes you through towns and cities and the route does not have ups and downs.
10. This route follows the same route as was run more than 2500 years ago.
11. Of all the marathons mentioned here, this one will take the longest to complete.
12. You can participate in this marathon even if you are handicapped.
13. Qualifying for this marathon is a matter to boast about.
14. This marathon attracts the maximum number of participants.

SECTION 2
Read the text below and answer Questions 15 – 27
Questions 15 – 20

DEFINING DRESS CODES – WHAT TO WEAR FOR EVERY OCCASION

A. SMART CASUAL

Women: Wear a pencil skirt or dress pants, paired with a silk or button-down top and high heels.
Men: Opt for dressy trousers, paired with a collared shirt and loafers.
When to wear it: office parties, happy hours, business luncheons.

B. DRESSY CASUAL

Women: Avoid wearing denim, tennis shoes, and cotton tees. Instead, opt for silk pants, dress pants, or a skirt. Pair with a patent leather flat, or one with nice embellishments such as a bow, buckle, or a print.
Men: Wear trousers and a dress shirt with oxfords. Pair with a blazer or sport coat. Avoid showing up with wrinkles or clothes one size too big, too small, or in a non-coordinating color. A tie is optional.
When to wear it: church, dinner, or an invite received via phone or e-mail.

C. COUNTRY CLUB CASUAL

Women: Choose an open-necked or polo shirt. You can also opt for dresses and skirts with minimal accessories.
Men: Wear an open-necked or polo shirt, paired with khakis. Accessorize with leather shoes and a belt.
When to wear it: cruise lines, the country club, friend's home for dinner, nice restaurant.

D. BUSINESS CASUAL

Women: Put on a skirt, khakis, or dress pants paired with long sleeve or three-quarter sleeve tops. A casual dress and flats are options as well.
Men: Wear a button-down or a polo shirt, paired with khakis, or dress pants. If you so desire, layer with a v-neck sweater, a blazer, or a sports coat. A tie is optional.
When to wear it: company party, daily work attire, business lunch meetings.

E. COCKTAIL ATTIRE

Women: Wear a shorter dress with some frill. The classic little black dress makes for great cocktail attire, and is the easiest to show your personality by accessorizing to suit your mood.
Men: Wear a dark suit, coat, and tie. Opting for dark jeans paired with a jacket and tie is also acceptable at some cocktail events, depending on how casual the atmosphere is.
When to wear it: adult birthday parties, evening social events.

F. LOUNGE

Women: Wear a dress that would be appropriate for brunch or afternoon tea. It should fall to, or slightly above, the knee, and not be too sparkly or low-cut. Incorporate a jacket or shawl to cover the arms.

Men: Opt for a dark suit, paired with a French-cuffed, crisp white shirt. You can go with or without a tie. Opting for a vest instead of a tie adds to the informality of the look.

When to wear it: daytime engagement parties, business breakfasts, afternoon tea.

G. WHITE TIE

Women: A floor-length ball gown is a must. Accessorize with opera length gloves, glamorous jewels, and up-do hairstyles.

Men: Wear a short or waist length black tailcoat (tails should reach the back of your knees,) white bow tie, starched white shirt, and a cummerbund (optional). Sport high-quality black pants.

When to wear it: charity fundraisers, government ceremonies, weddings, and the opera.

H. BLACK TIE

Women: Gussy up in a floor-length ball gown. A very dressy cocktail dress may be acceptable depending on the venue of the event.

Men: Wear a dark suit or a tuxedo without tails. Pair with a white shirt and a tie, or a bow tie with or without a vest and a cummerbund.

When to wear it: charity fundraisers, political dinner parties, weddings.

I. BLACK TIE OPTIONAL

Women: Look glamorous in a long gown, cocktail dress, or luxurious separates. Accessorize with items such as long gloves, clutches, and jewelry to top off the whole look.

Men: If you own a tuxedo, put it on, else, wear a suit in a dark color such as charcoal or black, paired with a white dress shirt, and a solid colored tie. Make sure patterns are kept to a minimum. Accessorize your look with a pocket square and cuff links.

When to wear it: elegant events such as galas, silent auctions, weddings, formal dinners.

Questions 15-20

In which paragraph will you find the answer to the following questions?

15. The occasion when men can wear lace-less shoes.

16. When should women not wear too many items of jewellery?

17. For women, the dress you choose to wear will depend upon the location of the occasion.

18. What you wear if you are at a party where the host is blowing out two score candles on his birthday cake.

19. Events where ladies accessorize their shoes.

20. The dress to wear when you are meeting a client over breakfast.

Read the text below and answer Questions 21 – 27

COMPANY POLICY ON PROVIDING CABS TO EMPLOYEES

- All vehicles shall display standard size sticker of 6" x 9" name and logo of our company. If the vehicle does not have a sticker, we request you not to board the vehicle.
- All vehicles will be provided with a first aid kit, umbrella and fire extinguisher.
- Smoking and or food consumption in vehicles is prohibited.
- Pickup and drop will be strictly from point to point (home to office to home)
- The permitted speed limit is 40 kms per hour in residential areas and 60 kms per hour on normal roads and highways.
- Employees are requested not to give their land phone/mobile numbers to any of the drivers.
- Drivers will not wait for more than five minutes at each pick up point. You are expected to board the car within this time failing which you may have to make own arrangements for commuting.
- In case of any vehicle break down while in commute, replacement of vehicle shall be provided immediately; however if there is a delay in providing the replacement vehicle, the expenses incurred by the employee for commuting from the breakdown point to their office/residence shall be reimbursed. However, between 8pm to 7am employees are requested to wait for company transport.
- All women employees will be picked up from the front of their residence and will be dropped back in front of their residence.
- Employees are requested not to board the car in case there are any unknown persons in the cab along with the driver (other than our security personnel).
- Employees should request for a cab at least 15 minutes before their log out time. This will give us time to organize for a cab for your drop back to home.
- Any female employee being asked to work beyond 8pm will be entitled to use the cab facility for their drop back to home. However, the request for a cab needs to be sent by the line manager to the local travel desk at least four (4) hours in advance.
- Female employees working between 8pm to 7am will be provided with an escort guard, if they are the first pickup and last drop.
- Employees should ensure they fill in the trip sheets and sign the same after every pickup and drop.
- Routing and clubbing will be done by the transportation team and the same will be shared with all users. Employees are requested to follow the routing accordingly.
- Cab facility will not be provided for those employees leaving office before their working hours.
- At the time of drop, if there is any other employee who stays on the same route and expected to logout within 15 minutes time, the employee may be requested to wait for a maximum of 15 minutes for the other employee and clubbing would be done accordingly.

- Employees are requested to keep the local travel desk informed at least a day in advance, if they do not require a pickup / drop. Last moment cancellation is not encouraged.
- During the commute, if there is a conflict between the driver and other commuter for whatsoever reason, employees are requested not to get down from the cab and if you feel necessary, please inform us on 1234567890.

Questions 21 – 27

Do the following statements agree with the information given in the text?
In boxes on your answer sheet, write

TRUE	if the statement agrees with the information
FALSE	if the statement contradicts the information
NOT GIVEN	if there is no information on this.

21. If the vehicle does not have a first aid kit, umbrella and fire extinguisher, you should report the matter to the Transport Department.
22. You may smoke in the cab as long as you are holding the cigarette outside the window of the c r.
23. The cab can travel at 50kmph on highways.
24. If the Security Guard in the cab is unknown, do not board the cab.
25. If your shift is up to 5 pm, and you leave at 4.30 pm, you will be provided with a cab.
26. If a female employee gets off work at 9 pm, she will be given a cab as long as she requests for it four hours before 8 pm, that is, by 4 pm.
27. Male employees will not be picked up from in front of their residences.

SECTION 3

Read the text below and answer questions 28 – 40

Questions 28 -35

The text has 8 SECTIONS, marked A to H. Choose the correct heading for each paragraph from the list of headings below.

i. The urban landscape
ii. As you sow so shall you reap
iii. Matters of fashion
iv. A legacy to be proud of
v. Money matters
vi. Not just a roof above the head
vii. The geographical span
viii. All beginnings have an end

28. Paragraph A ....
29. Paragraph B ....
30. Paragraph C ....
31. Paragraph D ....
32. Paragraph E ....
33. Paragraph F ....
34. Paragraph G ....
35. Paragraph H ....

THE INDUS VALLEY CIVILISATION

A. The Indus Valley Civilization (IVC) was a Bronze Age civilization extending from what today is northeast Afghanistan to Pakistan and northwest India. Along with Ancient Egypt and Mesopotamia it was one of three early civilizations of the Old World, and of the three the most widespread. It flourished in the basins of the Indus River, and the Ghaggar-Hakra River, which once coursed through northwest India and eastern Pakistan.

At its peak, the IVC may have had a population of over five million. Inhabitants of the ancient Indus river valley developed new techniques in handicraft (carnelian products, seal carving) and metallurgy (copper, bronze, lead, and tin). The Indus cities are noted for their urban planning, baked brick houses, elaborate drainage systems, water supply systems, and clusters of large non-residential buildings

Until 1999, over 1,056 cities and settlements had been found, of which 96 have been excavated.

B. The IVC encompassed most of Pakistan and parts of northwestern India, Afghanistan and Iran, extending from Baluchistan in the west to Uttar Pradesh in the east, northeastern Afghanistan to the north and Maharashtra to the south.

The IVC was in a highly similar situation to those in Egypt and Peru, with rich agricultural lands being surrounded by highlands, desert, and ocean. Recently, Indus sites have been discovered in Pakistan's northwestern Frontier Province as well.

Other IVC colonies can be found in Afghanistan while smaller isolated colonies can be found as far away as Turkmenistan and in Gujarat. An Indus Valley site has been found on the Beas River near Jammu, India, and at Alamgirpur on the Hindon River, only 28 km from Delhi.

C. A sophisticated and technologically advanced urban culture is evident in the Indus Valley civilization. The quality of municipal town planning suggests knowledge of urban planning and efficient municipal governments which placed a high priority on hygiene. The streets of major cities were laid out in a perfect grid pattern. The houses were protected from noise, odors, and thieves.

This urban plan included the world's first urban sanitation systems. Within the city, individual homes or groups of homes obtained water from wells. From a room that appears to have been set aside for bathing, waste water was directed to covered drains, which lined the major streets. Most city dwellers appear to have lived with others pursuing the same occupation in well-defined neighborhoods. Although some houses were larger than others, Indus civilization cities were remarkable for their apparent egalitarianism. For example, all houses had access to water and drainage facilities.

D. The Indus civilization's economy appears to have depended significantly on trade, which was facilitated by major advances in transport technology. The IVC may have been the first civilization to use wheeled transport. These advances may have included bullock carts that are identical to those seen throughout South Asia today, as well as boats. Most of these boats were probably small, flat-bottomed craft, perhaps driven by sail, similar to those one can see on the Indus River today.

Judging from the dispersal of Indus civilization artifacts, the trade networks integrated a huge area, including portions of Afghanistan, the coastal regions of Persia, northern and western India, and Mesopotamia. Such long-distance sea trade became feasible with the innovative development of plank-built watercraft, equipped with a single central mast supporting a sail of woven rushes or cloth.

E. The nature of the Indus civilization's agricultural system is still largely a matter of conjecture due to the limited amount of information surviving through the ages. Some speculation is possible, however.

Earlier studies (prior to 1980) often assumed that food production was imported to the Indus Valley by a single linguistic group ("Aryans") and/or from a single area. But recent studies indicate that food production was largely indigenous to the Indus Valley.

Agriculture must have been highly productive; after all, it was capable of generating surpluses sufficient to support tens of thousands of urban residents who were not primarily engaged in agriculture. It relied on the considerable technological achievements of the pre-Harappan culture, including the plough. Still, very little is known about the farmers who supported the cities or their agricultural methods.

F. Houses were one or two stories high made of baked brick, with flat roofs, and were just about identical. Each was built around a courtyard, with windows overlooking the courtyard. The outside walls had no windows. Each home had its own private drinking well and its own private bathroom. Clay pipes led from the bathrooms to sewers located under the streets. These sewers drained into nearly rivers and streams.

Their towns were laid out in grids everywhere. These people were incredible builders. Scientists have found what they think are giant reservoirs for fresh water. They have also found that even the smallest house at the edge of each town was linked to that town's central drainage system. It is possible that they not only drained waste water out, but also had a system to pump fresh water into their homes, similar to modern plumbing.

G. Men and women dressed in colorful robes. Women wore jewelry of gold and precious stones, and even wore lipstick! Among the treasures found was a statue of a woman wearing a bracelet. Bracelets with similar designs are worn today in India.

Clothing was for the most part, similar for both men and women. The basic costume of ancient society was a length of cloth wrapped around the lower part of the body, and a loose fitting garment for the upper body, which was usually another length of fabric. A headdress was also worn, mainly by the men.

Women in Vedic society wore a variety of garments, the first being a skirt type garment (dhoti), with a blouse (choli) and scarf. The second was a sari, which is a length of fabric and wound around the body with the loose end (pallu) thrown over the shoulder. Sometimes a choli would be worn with this. Men also had a choice in their clothing though not as varied as the women.

H. Around 1900 BCE, signs of a gradual decline begin to emerge. People started to leave the cities. Those who remained were poorly nourished. By around 1800 BC, most of the cities were abandoned.

Many scholars believe that the collapse of the Indus Civilization was caused by drought and a decline in trade with Egypt and Mesopotamia. It has also been suggested that immigration by new peoples, deforestation, floods, or changes in the course of the river may have contributed to the collapse of the IVC.

A possible natural reason for the IVC's decline is connected with climate change that is also signaled for the neighboring areas of the Middle East: The Indus valley climate grew significantly cooler and drier from about 1800 BCE, linked to a general weakening of the monsoon at that time.

According to a theory, the slow eastward migration of the monsoons across Asia initially allowed the civilization to develop. The monsoon-supported farming led to large agricultural surpluses, which in turn supported the development of cities. As the monsoons kept shifting eastward, the water supply for the agricultural activities dried up. The residents then migrated towards the

Ganges basin in the east, where they established smaller villages and isolated farms. The small surplus produced in these small communities did not allow development of trade, and the cities died out.

Questions 36 – 40

Choose not more than two words from the text to fill in the blanks:

36. In a group of houses, you would hardly find someone engaged in a dissimilar..................

37. What we know about the .... during that period is a mainly based on presumptions.

38. The houses were very well planned and built to a similar pattern; the IVC people had .... abilities when it came to build houses.

39. The dresses worn by the IVC people were very..................

40. Some believe that a lack of rainfall and declining commerce led to the .... of the IVC.

GT READING TEST 8

SECTION 1

Questions 1 – 14

Read the text below and answer Questions 1 – 8

MELAS OF INDIA

A. Kumbh Mela is celebrated every twelve years at four holy places: Prayagraj (Allahabad), Haridwar, Ujjain and Nashik. The grand event is held by rotation, on the banks of the sacred rivers: Godavri, Kshipra, Yamuna and the Ganges, where pilgrims gather for a holy bath. The major attractions of this biggest religious fair are the procession of Naga Sadhus.

B. Sonepur Mela is cattle fair held on a full moon day in Bihar, on the confluence of rivers Ganges and Gandak. This fair is also known as the Harihar Chhetra Mela, and is the only one of its kind in the world. Haathi Bazaar is one of the major attractions of the fair, where elephants are lined up for sale. Apart from this, all breeds of buffaloes, donkeys, ponies and birds are also available for sale. The largest animal fair in India attracts people from all around Asia.

C. Pushkar Fair is one of the world's largest camel fairs, held in the oldest city of Rajasthan, Pushkar. The fair, held on the banks of the Pushkar Lake, attracts a large number of visitors from all around the world, especially from Israel. It is an important tourist attraction.

D. The Hemis Gompa Fair is a religious fair and one of the most auspicious occasions for the Buddhist community in India. The grand fair is held in the months of January/February at the world famous Hemis Gompa, the biggest Buddhist monastery in Ladakh. The most esoteric of festivities are the mystic mask dances, referred collectively as Chams Performance, which is essentially a part of Tantric tradition, performed only in those gompas which follow the Tantric Vajrayana teachings.

E. Chandrabhaga Mela, also known as Magha Saptam Mela, is held in February at Khandagiri near Bhubaneswar Orissa. This important fair is celebrated every year during the full moon phase. During the seven day fair thousands of pilgrims gather to bathe in the holy Chandrabhaga river.

F. Gangasagar Mela is the second largest congregation of mankind after the holy Kumbh mela. This big religious fair is held annually where the holy river Ganges meets the Bay of Bengal in West Bengal. During the time of the fair, thousands of people congregate here for a holy bath.

G. Ambubasi Fair: The Ambubasi Fair is one of the numerous religious fairs and festivals celebrated across India. This three-day traditional fair is organized every year during the monsoons in the

Kamakhya temple at Guwahati, Assam. Tens of thousands of devotees from different parts of the country throng the Kamakhya Temple for the three-day fair.

H. Baneshwar Fair: The Baneshwar fair is the most popular tribal fair held in Dungarpur district in Rajasthan during the month of February. This is a religious fair with simple and traditional rituals to worship Lord Shiva. This fair attracts a large number of tribals from the neighboring state of Madhya Pradesh.

Questions 1 – 8

Look at the 8 descriptions of popular Melas of India. For which Melas are the following statements true? Write the letter A-H in columns 1-8 of your answer sheet. You may repeat any letter more than once.

1. From start to finish, this mela lasts seven days.
2. The banks of a lake are witness to this mela.
3. This mela witnesses the largest congregation of mankind.
4. This mela is held during the rainy season.
5. This mela is held at a junction of two rivers.
6. A lot of people from different tribes come to this mela.
7. Only the Kumbh mela witnesses a larger gathering of visitors than this mela.
8. You cannot see the faces of the people dancing at this fair.

Read the text below and answer Questions 9 – 14

THE ORIGINS OF THE OSCAR: HOW THE PRIZED STATUE GOT ITS NAME

Since 1929, Hollywood has revolved around the golden Oscar statue. The prized award has gone through facelifts since first debuting as a knight figure. Here are five fun facts about the history of Hollywood's little golden man.

<u>The first Oscar statue sketch was not how it looks today:</u> MGM art director Cedric Gibbons sketched the first figure of a knight holding a sword and standing on a reel of film with spokes representing the five branches of the Academy (actors, directors, producers, technicians and writers). The sword represented the protection for the welfare and advancement of the industry. Later, Los Angeles sculptor George Stanley redesigned the statue with an improved knight figure, but removed the reel of film.

<u>One popular story suggests the "Oscar" was named after someone's uncle:</u> It's been said that Academy librarian and eventual executive director Margaret Herrick thought the statue resembled her Uncle Oscar. In 1934, Sidney Skolsky used the name in his Hollywood column to describe Katharine Hepburn's first best actress win. The name caught on and the Academy made the name official in 1939.
The Oscar was first officially named the Academy Award of Merit. It stands 13.5 inches tall and weighs 8.5 pounds.

<u>Over 3,000 statuettes have been presented:</u> R.S. Owens & Company produces new statuettes each January in Chicago, but this year Polich Tallix Fine Art Foundry will take on the job and hand-cast the trophies in bronze before they receive their 24-karat gold finish. R.S. Owens & Company, who has been casting the Oscar mold since 1982, will continue to service existing Oscars and create other awards for the Academy.

<u>The Oscar was first gold-plated solid bronze and later gold-plated metal:</u> Due to a metal shortage during World War II, Oscars were made of painted plaster for three years. Following the war, the Academy invited recipients to redeem the plaster figures for gold-plated metal ones.

<u>The Academy keeps a second set of additional Oscar statues on hand just in case:</u> Weeks before the Oscars in 2000, the annual shipment of Oscars were stolen. The Academy now stays prepared and locks extra trophies from the ceremony in a vault to be used the next year.

Questions 9 – 14

Do the following statements agree with the information given in the text?

In boxes on your answer sheet, write

TRUE	if the statement agrees with the information
FALSE	if the statement contradicts the information
NOT GIVEN	if there is no information on this.

9. The Oscar derives its name from director Margaret Herrick's Uncle Oscar.
10. During World War 2, the Oscars were not made of metals due to a shortage of money.
11. The first Oscar was given in 1929.
12. The design and material of the statuette has changed five times since it was first introduced.
13. The Oscars to be awarded in the year 2000 were stolen one week before the event.
14. The Oscar had a different name earlier.

SECTION 2

Read the text below and answer Questions 15 – 27

Questions 15 – 21

VARIABLE PAY - THEN AND NOW

The practice of linking pay to performance has been around for a while. However, what's new is that the percentage of pay that is linked to performance and the way in which the same is structured around different components of performance.

In recent times, the concept of linking pay to performance has taken on an entirely new dimension with the introduction of variable pay. This article discusses some aspects of the variable pay and performance linked incentives in place in the contemporary organizations.

How it Works:

One of the key components of this variable pay or incentive plan is the strategy of linking pay to performance. This is a strategy that has been followed by many Multinational companies across the world and consists of the overall pay structure being broken down into components. These components would include the basic pay, benefits and the variable pay. The variable pay would be paid out as a percentage of the whole subject to the performance of the employee. For instance, if the employee gets a grade of 2 on a scale of 1 to 4, the variable pay would be 70-80% of the eligible amount and if the employee gets a grade of 3, the variable pay would be 100-120% of the eligible amount. Accordingly, the performance of the employee determines the variable component of the salary. The international practice is to increase the component of the variable pay higher according to the hierarchy. This would mean that at senior levels of the employee hierarchy, the variable component can be as high as 50-60% of the overall pay.

Categories of Variable Pay:

Further, there can be different categories of variable pay. The first component of the variable pay can be linked to individual performance, the second component can be linked to group performance and the third component can be linked to company performance. The idea behind variable pay is that it provides an incentive for employees to feel a sense of ownership and take responsibility for their jobs and relate to the overall group and company. By introducing variable pay, the management would ensure that employees are motivated to contribute individually and as a group and finally as part of the whole company.

Conclusion:

In conclusion, variable pay and performance linked incentives is a necessary evolution to a system where merit is recognized more than it is being done now. Given the fact that many organizations in India follow this approach, it is time for the employees and prospective employees to attune themselves to this concept and work accordingly.

Questions 15-21

In the passage below, fill in the blanks using NOT MORE THAN ONE WORD for each blank from the text above.

The overall pay-out to employees has included an amount linked to performance. However, in recent times, the (15) .... of this amount has changed. The overall pay structure being broken down into various components is a (16) .... adopted by many organizations working in multiple countries. The amount of variable pay that a person can earn is entirely dependent upon his or her (17) .... The (18) .... one is in the company hierarchy, higher the percentage of the incentive as against the overall compensation. The variable pay component of an individual can have different (19)...................., and is structured so that everyone is (20) .... to work not only towards his or her personal goals, but also for the objectives of the organization. The variable pay plan has to ensure that (21) .... is rewarded much more than what was happening earlier.

Read the text below and answer Questions 22 – 27

SOME EQUIPMENT USED IN GYMNASIUMS

A. **BENCH PRESS:** This is used for upper body strength training exercises, where you are pushing weight upwards as you're lying on your back. You want the perfect chest? This is one of the tools you use to train for that chest.
MUSCLES USED: Biceps, Triceps, Lats, Shoulders, Chest, and Upper Back.

B. **INCLINE BENCH PRESS:** Essentially an elevated bench press, but the elevation affects the muscle being targeted.
MUSCLES USED: The upper chest is targeted by the incline, as well as shoulders and triceps. It is not uncommon to use dumbbells in conjunction with or instead of a barbell on an incline bench.

C. **HAMMER STRENGTH MACHINE:** A favorite among athletes, this mechanic focuses on explosiveness.
MUSCLES USED: Different types target different muscle groups; primarily chest, then shoulders and triceps, to traps, and others.

D. **CABLES AND PULLEYS:** Very diverse workout machine in the amount and types of exercises that can be performed by attaching grips to the end of the cables.
MUSCLES USED: The inherent design and versatility of this machine allows for it to essentially touch upon every muscle in the body.

E. **DUMBBELLS:** Pretty much the go-to gym equipment most people first think of when they think of bodybuilding. Varying in weight, but having the same concept, a handle bar with weights on opposite ends is similar as regards muscles targeted is concerned. A must have free weight for any fitness regimen. There are even adjustable dumbbells with differing weights all in one piece.
MUSCLES USED: You can target a good amount of muscles with dumbbells. These exercises work the biceps, shoulders and triceps. Some of the muscles you can work with dumbbells are: chest, shoulders, triceps, traps, biceps, lats, glutes, quads, hamstrings, and calves.

F. **PULLUP BAR:** The best tool for upper body exercise and strengthening. You can pull yourself up with any grip, though palms facing forward are the most popular one seen in demonstrations. Different grips and hand positions can affect different muscles. You pull yourself up, until your chin is over the bar.

MUSCLES USED: Trunk, arms, shoulders, abs, pelvic floor muscles, hands and forearms. Different types of pull-ups effect different muscles. Some of the more common types of pull-up exercises are: behind the neck, underhand grip, pull-up to waist, wide/butterfly grip.

G. **LAT PULLDOWN MACHINE:** Used for strengthening your latissimus dorsi muscle, or lats as they are known. Pull downwards toward you, keeping your elbows and back straight. Google a picture of Bruce Lee and you'll see the lats you're capable of attaining with this machine.
MUSCLES USED: Upper and lower back; biceps, and lats in particular (as is evident by the name of this exercise machine).

Questions 22-27

Which of the above equipment best matches the description given below?
Write the letter A-G in columns 22-27 of your answer sheet.
You may repeat any letter more than once.

22. Use this to exercise every practically every muscle in the body:

23. This equipment is used quite often along with another one, both mentioned here:

24. The name of the machine tells you the muscles exercised:

25. You can hold this equipment in different ways to exercise different muscles:

26. The most commonly found equipment in gyms:

27. Athletes love to use this machine:

SECTION 3

Read the text below and answer questions 28 – 40

Questions 28 -35

The text has 8 SECTIONS, marked A to H. Choose the correct heading for each paragraph from the list of headings below.

i. Pap objectives
ii. How will the pap get done
iii. Why have a pap
iv. Who will get it done
v. Who is supposed to do what
vi. What happens after the appraisal
vii. What lies ahead
viii. What is this about

28. Paragraph A ....
29. Paragraph B ....
30. Paragraph C ....
31. Paragraph D ....
32. Paragraph E ....
33. Paragraph F ....
34. Paragraph G ....
35. Paragraph H ....

PERFORMANCE APPRAISAL POLICY (PAP)

A. This policy provides a guide to employees on the purpose of performance appraisal and to ensure that the work performance and training needs of every employee is managed effectively and fairly. While this policy applies to all employees of The Best Company (TBC), there may be some cases where the process is amended so that it is appropriate to the role.

B. A performance appraisal gives individual employees and their managers an opportunity to review performance, work content, loads and volumes, to look back on what has been achieved during the past year and then agree on future objectives. It is also the time an employee can agree on personal objectives, and any learning and development requirements which may help.

<u>The appraisal system is designed to:</u>

- Be a positive process.

- Raise the quality of services provided by motivating.
- Increase job satisfaction.
- Identify appropriate training and development requirements.

C. TBC recognizes that employees perform most effectively when they have clear expectations of their job role and purpose, their own targets or objectives, and of the wider aims of TBC.

The policy aims to ensure that employees:

- Know what is expected of them i.e. the required standard of performance and how they should do their jobs.
- Receive feedback which aims to improve and develop performance and recognize their achievements.
- Identify areas where improvement is required and training and development needs.
- Have a mutually agreed plan to achieve both development goals and employee career development.

D. TBC is responsible for:

- Setting sustainable standards.
- Providing advice and guidance to managers on implementing the policy.
- Ensuring that appropriate training and development is available for managers and employees.
- Holding an appraisal meeting and an appraisal review each year.
- Appraising employees in a fair and objective manner against agreed objectives and action plans.
- Following up actions arising from appraisals.
- Ensuring that a written record of the appraisal meetings is completed.
- Informing employees how the appraisal scheme works and how it will affect them.

Managers are responsible for:

- Ensuring each member of staff in their team is clear about what is expected of them.
- Ensuring that new employees have work targets and objectives set as part of induction.
- Meeting employees on a regular basis to review progress.

Employees are responsible for:

- Taking an active role in reviewing their performance appraisal and target setting.

E. Employees must be informed of the appraisal at least 4 weeks before the appraisal one-to-one meeting. A copy of the appraisal self-assessment form should be given to the employee so the employee has an opportunity to contribute. A copy of the completed self-assessment form should be returned to the manager 1 week before the appraisal one-to-one meeting.

The manager will use the appraisal performance checklist to prepare for an appraisal meeting by considering what criteria to use to measure employee performance; this will set the measure for performance over the next year.

The appraisal one-to-one meeting will be carried out in private so as to provide for confidentiality. Sufficient time will be allocated so that the meeting is unhurried and any discussion is properly considered. However, it must be understood by the employee and the manager that information discussed in an appraisal may need to be disclosed to others.

The one-to-one form should be used to record an employee / manager meeting. The manager should complete this form at, or immediately following the meeting, ensuring that it is signed by both him and the employee. A copy will be given to the employee.

F. When an appraisal is completed, it should be recorded using the appraisal form. This form should be completed by the appraiser and countersigned by the employee and the appraiser's manager so the employee is aware of the competencies that are critical for effective performance of that role. A copy of the form should be given to the employee as soon as possible. Employees may use as a last resort TBC grievance procedure to resolve any problems as to the accuracy or the fairness of the appraisal.

All employees have a role to play in enforcing the policy and are required to deal with any observed or reported breaches. Should employees feel apprehensive about their own safety in regard to addressing any breach, they should seek senior management support. Failure to comply with this policy may lead to a lack of clarity over job role, learning needs or expected standards of performance, resulting in reduced effectiveness or efficiency, underperformance and putting service delivery at risk. Any member of staff refusing to observe the policy will be liable to disciplinary action in accordance with TBC 's Disciplinary Policy up to and including dismissal.

G. Overall responsibility for policy implementation and review rests with TBC senior management. However, all employees are required to adhere to and support the implementation of the policy. TBC will inform all existing employees about this policy and their role in the implementation of the policy. They will also give all new employees notice of the policy on induction to TBC.

This policy will be implemented through the development and maintenance of procedures for appraisals and one-to-one meetings, using template forms, and guidance given to both managers and employees on the process.

H. The policy will be monitored on an on-going basis; monitoring of the policy is essential to assess how effective TBC has been.

This policy will be reviewed and, if necessary, revised in the light of legislative or codes of practice and organizational changes. Improvements will be made to the management by learning from experience and the use of established reviews.

Should any amendments, revisions, or updates be made to this policy it is the responsibility of TBC senior management to see that all relevant employees receive notice. Written notice and/or training will be considered.

If you require any additional information or clarification regarding this policy, please contact your manager. In the unlikely event where you are unhappy with any decision made, you should use TBC's formal Grievance Procedure.

To the extent that the requirements of this policy reflect statutory provisions, they will alter automatically when and if those requirements are changed.

Questions 36 – 40

Choose ONE WORD ONLY from the text to complete the following:

36. Among other things, when a performance review is done, it enables both the one being appraised and his supervisor plan for the...............
37. The PAP is so designed that it enhances the .... one derives from ones work.
38. The company is responsible to ensure that employees are evaluated in an .... manner.
39. Because an employee appraisal is not disclosed to the general public, these meetings will be done in........................
40. If an employee feels his manager was not fair in conducting the appraisal, he may fall back on the company .... procedure.

GT READING TEST 9

SECTION 1

Questions 1 – 14

Read the text below and answer Questions 1 – 8

PENGUINS

Penguins are aquatic, flightless birds that are highly adapted to life in the water. Here is a list of some types of penguins:

A. **Emperor Penguins**

Standing just over 4 feet tall and weighing up to 100 pounds, the stately Emperor Penguin is the tallest and heaviest of all penguin types and among the largest birds on the planet. This species is at home along the entire coastline of Antarctica.

B. **King Penguins**

King Penguins are the second largest penguin species, inhabiting several island chains in the sub-antarctic. As serial monogamists, these penguins form massive colonies every breeding season, several of which are composed of well over 100,000 pairs, each working in tandem to hatch just a single egg.

C. **Chinstrap Penguin**

With a distinctive band of black feathers across their necks to either side of their heads, Chinstrap Penguins look somewhat like they're wearing a biker's helmet. The species, which congregates on icebergs and small, barren islands in the sub-Antarctic region, are said to be the boldest and most aggressive of all penguin species.

D. **Gentoo Penguin**

Gentoo Penguins are the third largest of all penguins, standing around 35 inches tall. The penguins can be found in colonies on the continent of Antarctica as well as islands throughout the sub-Antarctic. Gentoos are listed as "near threatened," with some populations having experienced declines of two-thirds in the last 25 years.

E. **Little Blue Penguin**

Growing just 13 inches tall, Little Blue Penguins certainly earn that name when compared to their larger counterparts. The species is found on the southern coasts of Australia and New Zealand, and like many flightless birds there, they are prone to attack by invasive predators.

F. **Magellanic Penguin**

Magellanic Penguins are native to South America. The species numbers in the millions, but are still considered under significant threat from climate change and oil spills along their migration routes, which is responsible for the deaths of tens of thousands of young penguins every year.

G. **Galapagos Penguins**

The only penguin species that lives entirely in the Northern Hemisphere, Galapagos Penguins take their name from the archipelago they inhabit. During the 1980s, the penguins' numbers declined by around 70 percent, reducing the population to just around 1,500 by 2004. Conservation efforts are helping Galapagos Penguins to recover, though they are still listed as an endangered species.

H. **Snare Penguins**

These take their name from the small group of islands they are found in, off the coast of New Zealand, The Snares. Snare Penguins are distinguished by black coloring on the base of their beaks. Though not directly under threat, because of their centralized population, they are particularly vulnerable to sudden environmental changes.

Questions 1 – 8

For which penguins are the following statements true? Write the correct letter, A-G, in boxes 1-8 in your answer sheet.

1. You will not find this penguin south of the Equator.
2. These penguins are just over one foot tall.
3. Not only are they the largest penguins, they are also among the largest birds on the planet.
4. In some colonies of these penguins, only one in three have survived in the last quarter of a century.
5. These penguins are very loyal to their mates and do not change partners.
6. These penguins are not afraid to pick up a fight if need be.
7. Although numbering more than a million, these penguins are still considered to be threatened.
8. They take their name from the small cluster of islands which they inhabit.

Read the text below and answer Questions 9 – 14

RULES RELATED TO THE FREE WEIGHT AREA AND EXERCISE ROOM OF THE RECREATIONAL AREA OF A PARTICULAR US STATE UNIVERSITY ARE GIVEN BELOW.

- Users are responsible for sanitizing equipment. Each user may bring his or her own towel, or use the dry paper towel dispensers located in the workout area to remove sweat. Gym Wipes for sanitizing are located throughout each area to disinfect machines after each use. You are encouraged to clean each machine before and after use.
- Personal belongings are to be secured in a locker or cubby.
- Please report broken equipment to the Exercise Room desk.
- Exercise Room staff will provide orientation for general and cardio equipment only. See the Fitness Center staff for fitness assessment, exercise prescriptions, and personal training.
- Only Recreational Services staff, during their university employment, may provide personal training, sport instruction, fitness instruction, or coaching in any of our facilities (e.g. cueing and form correction).
- Users must return all equipment to their proper storage location after use.
- Weight belts are not allowed on exercise equipment if the buckle contacts the upholstery.
- Users must allow others waiting for equipment to work into your rotation.
- Slamming weight stacks or dropping Olympic bars, weight plates, barbells or dumbbells is prohibited. Olympic bars, weight plates, barbells and dumbbells must be below the knee before placing down.
- Users are recommended to have a spotter when excessive weight is lifted.
- Spring collars should be used on all bars with plates added.
- Olympic lifting is prohibited (e.g. power clean, power clean and jerk, split jerk and power snatch).
- Cell phone use whether talking or texting is prohibited while exercising. Patrons talking on their cell phones while in the Exercise Room or Free Weight Area will be asked to move to the lobby or stairwell area until their conversation is over. Please respect your fellow patrons.
- Patrons must use the equipment for its intended purpose or function. Improper use of any plate-loaded machines, selectorized machines, or cardiovascular equipment will not be tolerated.
- Be sure to check the Clothing policy specific to this area.

Questions 9 – 14

Do the following statements agree with the information given in the text?

In boxes on your answer sheet, write

TRUE	if the statement agrees with the information
FALSE	if the statement contradicts the information
NOT GIVEN	if there is no information on this.

9. Before and after each use, users should disinfect the equipment using towels they may have brought from home or using towels from dry paper towel dispensers located in the workout area.
10. Personal belongings are to be securely kept in the locker in the lobby.
11. If you wish to sign up for Personal Training, please go the Exercise Room Desk.
12. It is the responsibility of the user to place back any equipment removed from its place for us.
13. To show respect to your fellow patrons, please keep your cell phones on the silent mode at all times.
14. You must be aware of the proper attire for the area you are in.

SECTION 2

Read the text below and answer Questions 15 – 27

Questions 15 – 21

HOT VEGETABLES THIS SUMMER

The following is list of vegetables that will be hot this summer season:

1. **Arugula**

Arugula is an excellent source of folate and vitamin C. Although arugula is typically mildly flavored, larger leaf varieties can have a more peppery, almost hot taste than the smaller, softer leaf variety, so choose your arugula accordingly! Arugula is typically best served in a salad with olives, hard-boiled eggs, onions and salty cheeses.

2. **Avocados**

Although available year round, avocados are at their peak in the summer months! Touted most frequently for their high quantity of good fat avocados are also an excellent source of potassium, folate and vitamins C and B6. To pick the perfect avocado, look for those that have a uniform and unblemished skin that gives gently when pressed.

3. **Cucumbers**

A member of the squash family, cucumber's high water content makes it a refreshing addition to summer menus. Cucumber is also a good source of vitamin C and silica, which is important for connective tissue health and also does wonders for the skin (both when ingested and applied topically to reduce swelling or redness). In addition, the skin of the cucumber is a great source of fiber, potassium and magnesium.

4. **Eggplant**

Although it is assumed that an eggplant would have a purple skin, eggplants can come in just about any shade from black to a near-translucent white. Although selecting an eggplant is easy enough – again, just look for those with smooth, taut skin and those that feel heavy for their size –cooking can be a little bit more complicated. If the eggplant is young, the skin is edible, but if it's a little bit older, the skin will taste bitter and is best removed.

5. **Kohlrabi**

Often referred to as cabbage turnip, this green vegetable looks almost like an oversized radish, complete with a ball-like bulb and bushy sprouting leaves. When selecting a kohlrabi, look for smallish, firm bulbs less than 3 inches in diameter. Kohlrabi is an excellent source of vitamin C as well as potassium. When raw, it can be added to salads and vegetable platters or served as relish. When cooked, it can be steamed for inclusion in casseroles or hollowed out, and stuffed with a meat or vegetable filling.

6. **Mushrooms**

Different types of mushrooms are available the year around. With low sodium and fat content and high levels of fiber and riboflavin, niacin, potassium and riboflavin, mushrooms are an excellent way to add bulk to a meal without dramatically changing the nutrition content of foods.

When shopping for mushrooms, they should be dry and firm and, if open, should have gills that are intact and appear fresh.

7. **Shallots**

Of all the vegetables in the onion and leek family, shallots have one of the highest concentrations of antioxidants. In addition, they have also shown to have anti-bacterial, anti-inflammatory, and anti-allergic properties. Shallots are associated with a reduction in risk for several cancers, including those affecting the liver and colon as well as heart disease and diabetes.

Questions 15-21

Fill in the blanks, using not more than two words for the text above.

15. The Arugula you buy should be based upon what kind of a .... you prefer.
16. If the avocado feels slightly soft, then it is probably ....
17. Even if you eat it, cucumbers are very beneficial for the ....
18. It is okay to ingest the skin of eggplant if the eggplant is ....
19. The Kohlrabi looks like a .... that has grown much larger than its normal size.
20. Adding mushrooms is a great way to increase the .... of the meal, without compromising on its nutrition value.
21. In this family of vegetables, shallots have the most densely packed ....

Read the text below and answer Questions 22 – 27

SEVEN TIPS TO NAIL A SKYPE INTERVIEW

A. **Look the Part**

Do your research: Check out the company's website, Facebook page and Twitter feed to get a feel for how employees dress and behave, then take your cues from that when prepping for your interview.

Next, clean up. If your at-home appearance leans towards the casual, take some time to polish up. It's always better to err on the side of freshly-scrubbed—even if you're an aspiring trek leader, carefully dressed in her best khakis.

Assuming your bottom half will be hidden under a desk, you may be tempted to wear your favorite sweatpants, but it's best to dress from head to toe. What if you have to stand up to adjust your equipment?

B. **Prepare Your Surroundings**

Take your call in a quiet, businesslike setting, ideally in a room with a door. Look behind you, because that's what they'll see. A cluttered background may distract your audience, not to mention send the wrong idea of your organizational skills. Also, rid the area of personal items—no need to share too much information. A blank or neutral background is best, with a well-organized desktop.

Be sure to inform anyone else at home about the meeting; you don't want to be interrupted by a sudden blast of stereo music or someone bellowing your name.

C. **Practice It First**

Your first few video calls are bound to feel awkward as you figure out where to look, what to do with your hands, or how loudly to speak. But it's easy to work out those kinks ahead of time. Conducting a practice interview with a friend can be very helpful; record it so that you'll have an accurate idea of how you come across on video," advises Cheryl Palmer, career coach and owner of Call to Career, a career coaching service.

D. **Don't Forget to Smile!**

At an in-person interview, you'd naturally smile upon arrival, and try to keep a pleasant facial expression for the duration.

It's more difficult to do this with a remote interview. Lacking a 'live' person in front of you, and sidetracked by thoughts of equipment or cameras, you might be less likely to smile reflexively. If that's the case, you can seem like you're staring wide-eyed at the camera. Smiling is the best way to break the ice and develop rapport with your interviewer.

E. Stay Present

One may suggest interjecting listening sounds ("hm," or "yes") as your interviewers speak. In addition to making your conversation more pleasant, it also reassures the other party that the technology is functioning correctly and you are, indeed, still listening.

And even though they can't see you, never tinker with your computer during a call.

F. Go Ahead and Cheat

One advantage to a video interview is that you don't have to remember everything you want to mention. You can have notes in front of you—without your interviewer knowing. Place your resume in front of you, news about the company, questions you want to ask and potential talking points.

Of course, you don't want to be reading off the page verbatim, so make sure you're familiar with your material.

G. Address Tech Problems Immediately

When you're relying on video equipment, there's a good chance you'll experience a technical glitch: a weak connection, interference or garbled signals.

You may hesitate to draw attention to the problem, but you don't want to give an inaccurate answer because you didn't understand the question.

If you're getting too many blips, it's good to stop the call and redial.

Questions 22-27

Choose the right option for each of the questions below.

22. When dressing for the interview

a) Since the interview is from home, you may dress casually.

b) Check how the company employee dress at work and get an idea from there as to how to dress for the Interview.

c) Although you will be seated, it is good to wear formal, laced shoes.

23. For your surroundings during the interview, you should:

a) Lock the door to keep interruptions out.

b) Ensure the background is not cluttered, because it could be distracting for you and your audience.

c) Inform others at your home that you will be at an interview.

24. As you practice the call, you may find:

a) Your friend with whom you practice is very helpful.

b) All the kinks can be rectified before the actual interview.

c) Initially you will not know what to look at.

25. The point about smiling during an interview is:

a) It develops rapport with the interviewer.

b) It is not more difficult to smile during a remote interview.

c) Since you are side-tracked by thoughts of cameras and equipment, you are only able to smile reflexively.

26. One advantage of a video interview is:

a) You can cheat the interviewer.

b) Since you cannot read off the page verbatim, you should commit the points to memory.

c) You need not memorize all that you want to ask.

27. The thing about technical glitches during video interviews is that:

a) They should be fixed immediately before they get worse.

b) You should hesitate before drawing attention to the problem.

c) If there are too many blips, it is better to stop the call and re-dial.

SECTION 3

Read the text below and answer questions 28 – 40

Questions 28-35

The text has 8 SECTIONS, marked A to H. Choose the correct heading for each paragraph from the list of headings below.

i. Easing the guilt
ii. Working daughters most likely had working moms
iii. A mom's employment choices do not harm her children
iv. Very welcome findings from the initial research
v. Casting the research net wider
vi. Employed mum equals higher pay for daughters and vice-versa
vii. Male offspring are influenced differently
viii. Working woman? Likely she had a working mom

28. Paragraph A ....
29. Paragraph B ....
30. Paragraph C ....
31. Paragraph D ....
32. Paragraph E ....
33. Paragraph F ....
34. Paragraph G ....
35. Paragraph H ....

KIDS OF WORKING MOMS GROW INTO HAPPY ADULTS

A. In 2015, preliminary results of a groundbreaking study found that the daughters of employed mothers often perform better in their eventual careers than the daughters of stay-at-home moms. Now the full study has been released, and it brings even more good news for the children of working moms: They wind up just as happy in adulthood as the children of moms who stayed home.

Harvard Business School Professor Kathleen McGinn hopes the findings bring a big sigh of relief for guilt-ridden mothers who either have to hold down a job to make ends meet or simply choose to work outside the home while raising their children. "People still have this belief that when moms are employed, it's somehow detrimental to their children," says McGinn, the Cahners-Rabb Professor of Business Administration. "So our finding that maternal employment doesn't affect kids' happiness in adulthood is really important."

This isn't about raising happier kids, she continues. "When women choose to work, it's a financial and personal choice. Women should make that choice based on whether they want or need to work, not based on whether they are harming their children—because they are not."

B. Three years ago, McGinn and colleagues got some pushback when preliminary findings were included in a New York Times article. The research found that adult daughters whose moms worked outside the home are more likely to work themselves, hold more supervisory responsibilities, and earn higher wages than women whose mothers stayed home full time.

"Some asked if children of stay-at-home moms were happier," McGinn says. "Many decried the research as another installment of the 'mommy wars.' But the most common response was from mothers who suffered guilt, self-doubt, and disapproval from others. They found our preliminary results to be welcome news."

C. After the preliminary findings were publicized, McGinn, Mayra Ruiz Castro of Kingston University in the UK, and Elizabeth Long Lingo of Worcester Polytechnic Institute added a second international data set to their study. To make sure their findings could be replicated across both time and geographic distance, they compared two cross-national social surveys, the "Family and Changing Gender Roles" section of the International Social Survey Program from 2002 and 2012, as well as the "Generations and Gender Survey Core Questionnaire" in the Generations and Gender Program from 2002 through 2013.

All told, the two surveys of more than 100,000 men and women across 29 countries revealed how the employment of mothers affects their adult children, both in terms of their own employment as well as how much time they spend at home caring for children and doing housework.

D. Some critics questioned if the preliminary findings might have nothing to do with whether mothers work, but were tied to the moms' education level instead. After controlling for the mother's education, final results still showed that a mother's work experience is strongly linked to her daughter's future work performance, according to the recently published full study, 'Learning from Mum: Cross National Evidence Linking Maternal Employment and Adult Children's Outcomes', which was featured in Work, Employment and Society.

Compared to women whose mothers stayed home full time, women raised by an employed mother are 1.21 times more likely to be employed; 1.29 times more likely to supervise others at work; and they spend 44 extra minutes at their jobs each week.

They also earn more money. Among the women who responded to the survey in the United States in 2012, employed daughters of employed moms earned an average of $1,880 more per year than employed daughters of moms who stayed home full time.

E. Only adult daughters—not sons—see their careers influenced by whether their mothers work outside the home. It may not affect sons' employment choices simply because men tend to be employed, and also, as other research shows, sons' occupations and earnings map closely to their fathers' employment, McGinn explains.

In non-work ways, however, sons may be influenced by their working mothers, the study suggests. They spend an extra 50 minutes each week caring for family members.

Sons are influenced in other ways when their moms work. The sons of employed mothers hold significantly more egalitarian gender attitudes—even more so than the daughters of stay-at-home moms, a finding that surprised McGinn because it shows that the influence of maternal employment may even outweigh well-documented sex differences when it comes to shaping people's mindsets about appropriate roles for men and women.

"Sons of employed moms also tend to choose wives who are employed, and they have more egalitarian gender attitudes about women and men in the workplace as well," McGinn says. "So having an employed mom affects the choices these sons are making."

F. Employed moms strongly shape their daughters' gender attitudes and provide role models for them to imitate, McGinn says. So when these daughters grow up, they often follow in the footprints of their working mothers.

"Having an employed mom makes daughters think that employment is compatible with parenting," McGinn says. "If you're actually observing an employed mom manage a complex life and handle multiple demands—a job, a family, a household—you see that it can work. Everything we know about role models and social learning suggests that children are actively picking up life skills from the adults around them. It's all about what they're exposed to as children."

Also on the domestic front, daughters of employed mothers spend about an hour less on housework compared with the children of stay-at-home mothers.

Meanwhile, when both daughters and sons were asked about their overall life satisfaction, adult children of employed moms reported being just as happy as adult children of moms who didn't work outside the home.

G. The research uncovered other interesting findings:

Both sons and daughters of employed mothers have significantly more education than children of mothers who are not employed.

The employment rates of adult daughters are affected by their mothers' employment, regardless of whether the moms held high-skill or low-skill jobs. But only women whose mothers worked medium- or high-skill jobs are more likely to have supervisory positions than women whose mothers weren't employed.

The influence of mothers' employment on their daughters' careers is less important when girls see a lot of other women with jobs, because these women can act as alternative role models. For sons, however, their own mothers' employment is critical to how much they pitch in with their own children, even when they are raised around a lot of other employed women.

"For girls, seeing other employed moms can provide some of the same effects on attitudes and skillsets," McGinn says. "For boys, their own moms and other women in the community are complements; each reinforces the other."

H. While previous research has shown that young children and teenagers do just fine when their moms work, McGinn is hoping this longer-term view into adulthood provides reassurance for employed mothers who feel conflicted when they kiss their kids goodbye to head to the office. "Women are socialized to believe mothers should stay home with their children, so when you separate from your kids every day for work, it can be painful," she says. "As we gradually understand that our children aren't suffering, I hope the guilt will go away."

Working moms can also take comfort from their own kids. In a panel discussion with female executives and their grown children about maternal employment at Caterpillar Inc., McGinn asked the adult children, "What advice do you have for employed moms, given what you experienced as a child?"

Every one of these adults who grew up with a working mother delivered essentially the same message: Just chill. We're doing great.

Questions 36 – 40

Use NOT MORE THAN TWO WORDS from the text to fill in the blanks:

36. The findings of the study are a huge consolation for moms who were working raising their children; it helps them to feel less..............
37. The initial results of the study was very .... to mothers who had doubted themselves and felt others did not approve of their being at work while their children were growing up.
38. The study reveals that a working girl who had a working mother will be earning............ money as compared to one whose mother did not work.
39. Sons of working mothers are not............. in the same way as daughters.
40. Children of working mothers have remarkably more................ than children whose mothers do not work.

GT READING TEST 10

SECTION 1

Questions 1-14

Read the text below and answer Questions 1 – 7

SOME THINGS YOU MAY NOT KNOW ABOUT CACTI

Cacti are special in many ways. Many people think that cacti live in deserts. Nothing can live in a real desert, but 'desert' cacti are adapted in many ways to live in dry and sometimes hot places.

1. **Are they indestructible?**

No, if you've ever killed a cactus you are not alone. The easiest way is by over watering, poor drainage and using the wrong compost. Ordinary potting compost holds water well, which is a huge bonus for most plants but not for cacti, they need very good drainage.

2. **Do they flower?**

Cacti are all flowering plants, but some have more prominent blooms and there are a few, such as Mammillaria, Gymnocalycium and Parodia, that will flower quite easily with impressive, colourful displays.

3. **How do I get them to flower?**

Cacti flower on fresh growth, so if your plant just sits there, unchanging year after year, it's very unlikely to flower. What you should do is to get the plant to follow its natural growth cycle. It needs to go dormant in winter and then wake up in spring. So, put it somewhere dry and cold, but not dark, over winter, and stop watering all together. In spring give it as much sunshine as possible and start to water it.

4. **Which are the best varieties for beginners?**

Moon cacti have very colourful tops, usually red or yellow. These aren't flowers so the colour is there all year round. Bunny ears, also known as polka dot cacti, have spots of golden bristles against a green background so they look modern and geometric. Probably the most common variety is a tiny 'pin cushion' cactus, it's easy to grow and has lovely little pink flowers.

5. **Are all cacti prickly?**

What we usually think of as cacti are desert cacti, but there are also forest cacti without the bristles, however the range available as houseplants is quite small.

6. **How long do they live?**

In the wild cacti can live for hundreds of years. Indoors they may survive for 10 years or more. The trouble with old ones is that every single knock, scratch or blemish they get stays with them, so they tend to look less appealing as they get older.

Questions 1 – 7

Do the following statements agree with the information given in the text?

In boxes on your answer sheet, write

TRUE	if the statement agrees with the information
FALSE	if the statement contradicts the information
NOT GIVEN	if there is no information on this.

1. Cactus plants live in real deserts.
2. If you water a cactus too much you are likely to kill it.
3. Most cactus plants will flower.
4. If the cactus has not flowered for a few years it is hardly likely to flower.
5. Cacti grown as houseplants are very small in size.
6. Cacti can live for two hundred years in the wild.
7. All cacti have bristles which can prick.

Read the text below and answer Questions 8 – 14

TRY THIS FUN TEST OF SPEED AND ACCURACY, USING RIFLES, PISTOLS AND SHOTGUNS

One of the fastest growing shooting sports in the country right now is the action-packed multi-gun competition commonly known as "3-gun."

The reason for the name is somewhat obvious; competitors use three different firearms — a modern sporting rifle (MSR) that is a rifle built on an AR-platform; a pistol; and a shotgun. Matches generally involve courses where the shooter must move through different stages and engage targets in a variety of different positions. Each stage will generally require the use of different firearms and require the shooter to transition between them.

The targets might include clay pigeons, cardboard silhouettes, steel targets of varying sizes and anything else designated as a target. Distances of the targets might vary from 1 yard to 500 yards or anything in between. The shooter who hits the most targets — and avoids certain "no shoot" ones — in the least amount of time is the winner.

Although local ranges might opt to alter the rules somewhat, most abide closely by those set up by the International Multi-Gun Association (IMGA) or the United States Practical Shooting Association (USPSA), which regulates some matches. Each of these organizations has guidelines and rules, but the ability to adapt them for specific matches is what makes 3-gun competition dynamic and exciting.

Just as it is with the practical pistol matches, 3-gun simulates combat or self-defence situations. A stage provides a certain scenario for using one or more of the guns in a specific sequence. Each stage in each match will usually be different than any you've shot before.

Rifles: Most serious competitors choose MSR in .223 calibre with fairly short barrels in the 18- to 20-inch range and 30-round magazines. But any semi-automatic rifle that will handle larger magazines is normally permitted.

Shotguns: Any reliable auto-loading or pump-action shotgun will work. For serious competition, it should have an extended magazine tube, a good set of sights and interchangeable chokes. Both shot-shells and slugs are used in most 3-Gun matches.

Pistols: Most shooters use 9mm semi-autos, but the .38 Super and .40 S&W are also popular in some divisions.

Getting started in 3-gun competition is easy. Find a shooting range in your area that puts on 3-gun matches. Then spend some time to watch and to learn; also, don't be afraid to ask questions. Once you decide to take the plunge, go easy and don't spend a lot of money on anything too fancy. It's a learning process, and it's about having fun.

Questions 8 – 14

Use not more than **ONE WORD ONLY** to fill in the blanks below.

8. 3-gun is a sport where one shoots through different stages and competes in a ……………. competition.
9. Since the competition requires the use of a rifle, a pistol and a shot-gun, its name is more or less ………………
10. There are three stages and in each stage, the shooter has to use a ………………. fire-arm.
11. Each stage creates a ………………. in which the shooter has to shoot using one or two or three of his guns.
12. The 3-gun creates a situation as if you are in a …………………
13. A semi-automatic rifle with a magazine capacity of more than 30 rounds may be ……………………
14. Before you start engaging in this sport, you should go to a range as a spectator to ………………… about it.

SECTION 2

Read the text below and answer Questions 15 – 27

Questions 15 – 21

WRITING THE RIGHT RESUME

Hiring managers and recruiters alike say they've seen more poorly written resumes cross their desks recently than ever before. Attract offers for more interviews and ensure your resume doesn't eliminate you from consideration by following these six key tips:

1. <u>Format Your Resume Wisely</u>

No matter how well written, your resume won't get a thorough reading the first time through. Generally a resume gets scanned for 25 seconds. Scanning is more difficult if it is hard to read, poorly organized or exceeds two pages.

- Use a logical format and wide margins, clean type and clear headings
- Selectively apply bold and italic typefaces that helps to guide the reader's eye
- Use bullets to call attention to important points (i.e. accomplishments)

2. <u>Identify Accomplishments not Just Job Descriptions</u>

Hiring managers, especially in technical fields like engineering, seek candidates that can help them solve a problem or satisfy a need within their company. Consequently, you can't be a solution to their problems without stating how you solved similar problems in other companies and situations.

- Focus on what you did in the job, NOT what your job was: there's a difference.
- Include a one or two top line job description first, and then list your accomplishments.
- For each point ask yourself, 'What was the benefit of having done what I did?'
- Accomplishments should be unique to you, not just a list of what someone else did.
- Avoid using the generic descriptions of the jobs you originally applied for or held.

3. <u>Quantify Your Accomplishments</u>

Q: What's the most common resume mistake?

Making too many general claims and using too much industry jargon that does not market the candidate. A resume is a marketing document designed to sell your skills and strengths rather than just portray a bio of the candidate.

- Include and highlight specific achievements that present a comprehensive picture of your marketability.
- Quantify your achievements to ensure greater confidence in the hiring manager and thereby generate interest; use percentages, dollars, number of employees, etc.

- Work backwards to quantify your accomplishments by asking, 'If I had not done X, what could have happened?

4. Cater Your Resume for the Industry

Unlike advertising and design professionals who have greater creative license in designing their resume for those fields, the mechanical engineering industry won't be impressed and may be turned off by distinctive resume design.

- Err on the side of being conservative stylistically.
- Your accomplishments, error-free writing, grammatically-correct, clean, crisp type and paper will make the impression for you.

5. Replace your Objective" with a "Career Summary"

A Career Summary is designed to give a brief overview of who you are and what you do. Most Objectives sound similar: Seeking a challenging, interesting position in X where I can use my skills of X, Y, and Z to contribute to the bottom line. Not telling at all.

- Grab a hiring manager's attention right from the beginning, remembering you have only 25 few seconds to make a good impression.
- Spend time developing a summary that immediately gets their attention, and accurately and powerfully describes you as a solution to their problems.

6. Network. Network. Network.

For unemployed candidates, handing out resumes should be a full-time job. The majority of mid-to senior-level positions are filled through networking, so contact absolutely everyone you know in addition to recruiters who are in a position to hire you or share insights. Networking can include

Personal business contacts, people you've worked for or who worked for you.
Vendors and sales representatives you've dealt with in the past five years.
People listed in the alumni directory of your alma mater.

Questions 15-21

Use **NOT MORE THAN ONE WORD** from the text above to fill in the blanks.

15. If your resume is not written poorly, and you follow the guidelines given in this article, you will be able to get called for more ....
16. Using different .... helps to guide the reader on to specific parts of the resume.
17. Candidates who can solve problems are sought after in the .... field.
18. A resume is not just a list of positions held; it should be written such that it helps to .... the candidate.
19. All organizations have challenges, and they look for people who are a .... to these problems.
20. If your resume is well written, without spelling mistakes, mistakes of tenses or usage of verbs, and punctuated correctly, it will make a good ....
21. It is important to .... all those you have worked in the past as part of your net-working effort in your search for a job.

Read the text below and answer Questions 22 – 27

ALL ABOUT BEARS

Understanding bear behaviour is an essential part of creating safe environments for both bears and people. More often than not, bear behaviour is misinterpreted. To truly understand bear behaviour, you must interpret bear postures and vocalizations in terms of what the bear fears.

The more you can learn about bears and how they behave, the less likely you will be to have a negative encounter or misinterpret interactions. Bears are predictable. In fact, bears are usually more predictable than people. If you learn more about bears and how to interpret their behaviour, you will be able to react appropriately if you bump into them and avoid a negative encounter.

Bears, like humans and other animals, have a "critical space" – an area around them that they may defend. Once you have entered a bear's critical space, you have forced the bear to act – either to run away or be aggressive. The size of the critical or personal space is different for every bear and every situation.

Although black bears and grizzly bears do share some common traits, it's important to understand the difference in the way they react to perceived threats. Each species has evolved different strategies for survival. Black bears, for instance, are usually less aggressive and more tolerant of people. They often live near human settlements, whereas grizzly bears prefer to stay away from human settlements and are often extirpated from heavily used or populated areas.

When a black bear is threatened he usually runs from the perceived threat or goes up a tree. With cubs out of danger, female black bears don't have to make vigorous defences that risk potential injury. Brown (or grizzly) bears tend to live in coastal or mountain forests, but they evolved in treeless habitat that influenced their behavioural response to perceived threats. As such, they are not good tree climbers, though it is important to note they can climb trees. A black bear's first line of defence is retreat, but grizzlies, especially sows with cubs, can be very aggressive towards other bears and people they perceive as threats.

Bears are often described as asocial when compared to wolves, chimps or lions, but to use the term "asocial" to describe bears is incorrect. While bears do not live in extended family groups or join in hunts, they can co-exist in very close proximity to each other and in fact form alliances and friendships.

Bears live in a dominance hierarchy based on age, size and temperament. Mature males are at the top of the hierarchy, and sub-adults and cubs at the bottom. Bears establish and maintain their social position and place in the hierarchy by posturing or acting aggressively. Single females and sub-adults are almost always submissive to mature males but have a loose hierarchy within their own group.

Bears are not always aware. Bears, particularly adult brown bears, are not always aware of what is going on around them. A bear following a trail doesn't always look ahead. He may be distracted by a yummy food source or may not be able to hear over the loud sounds of rushing water or blowing wind. A bear can literally blunder into an unsuspecting person.

Questions 22-27
Choose the correct letter, A, B or C:

22. If you are familiar with how bears behave:
a) More often than not, you will misinterpret their behaviour.
b) You are less likely to have a bad experience if you come across a bear.
c) You can avoid bumping into them.

23. Bears are
a) Fond of retiring early.
b) Wary of the critical space around them
c) Very shy and will not react under provocation.

24. Under threat, the most likely action of a bear is:
a) Run away.
b) A grizzly bear may climb a tree.
c) A black bear will opt to back-off.

25. As far as social interactions of bears are concerned
a) They are not as social as wolves or lions.
b) They form alliances when they go hunting together.
c) Bears of a region are usually familiar with each other, while those from different regions are not.

26. Single female bears are
a) Subservient to grown up male bears.
b) Are equal in hierarchy to sub-adult bears.
c) Act aggressively to maintain their position in the hierarchy.

27. When walking down a track in the forest

a) A bear may not be conscious of his surroundings

b) A bear does not look straight ahead

c) A bear is unable to hear clearly.

SECTION 3

Read the text below and answer questions 28 – 40

Questions 28 -35

The text has 8 SECTIONS, marked A to H. Choose the correct heading for each paragraph from the list of headings below.

i. Investigation & analysis
ii. The gastronomic challenge
iii. Raising them at home
iv. The challenge of keeping them healthy
v. The relevance of zoos in our world
vi. Swap and barter
vii. Summers and winters co-exist here
viii. How it all began

28. Paragraph A ....
29. Paragraph B ....
30. Paragraph C ....
31. Paragraph D ....
32. Paragraph E ....
33. Paragraph F ....
34. Paragraph G ....
35. Paragraph H ....

ALL ABOUT ZOOS

A. Keeping wild animals in zoos is an old practice. But today zoos seem more popular than ever. Each year more people in North America go to zoos than to all the professional baseball, football, and basketball games combined.

Why are zoos so popular? One reason may be that more people now live in cities and towns, where they see little wildlife. They seek places where they can have some contact with nature. In many zoos, you can see more kinds of animals in a day than you might see in weeks of travel to faraway places.

Zoos teach people about the importance of nature. They provide scientists with opportunities to study wild animals. And they are also important because thousands of species of wild animals are in danger of dying out. Saving these endangered species is one of the many purposes of modern zoos.

B. Traditional zoo exhibits include mammals, birds, reptiles, and amphibians from all over the world. The animals may be grouped according to type--a building for monkeys or reptiles, for example. Some zoos group their exhibits according to the continents or geographic regions of the earth. This is called zoogeographic exhibition.

Natural Habitat exhibits show animals in settings that mimic their natural homes. For example, a zoo may feature an African grasslands exhibit, in which zebras, giraffes and ostriches roam about in open spaces with grass, a water hole, and perhaps some trees. Ducks, turtles, and otters may be shown in a wetlands exhibit that contains a pond or a marsh. In many zoos, you can visit polar ice caps, blistering deserts, and steamy jungles—all in a day.

Nocturnal displays are featured at some zoos. Some zoos are using special lights to reverse the animals' sleeping patterns. Bright lights are kept on at night, so that the animals sleep. In daytime, the exhibit is lit by red light that the animals can barely detect. The animals behave as if it was night, and zoo visitors can see them.

C. Breeding wild animals can be difficult. Some kinds of animals, such as wild sheep and even tigers, breed readily in zoos. But others require special attention. Monkeys and apes, for example, often have strong preferences for mates of the right appearance and personality. Sometimes female monkeys need to observe breeding and infant care when they are young, so that they can behave naturally as mates and parents when they become adults.

Zoos often study the natural habits of animals to breed them successfully. For example, research has helped zoos breed cheetahs, which are slender, graceful spotted cats from Africa. Zoos previously kept male and female cheetahs in pairs for years without breeding taking place. But scientists studied cheetah behavior and learned that females need to come in contact with several males during the breeding season. Males, it seems, are also more successful breeders if they have to compete to mate with a female.

D. When zoos are successful in breeding animals, they often sell animals to other zoos or exchange them with one another. Every year thousands of animals, such as snow leopards, antelopes, penguins, and monkeys, are exchanged. Loans between zoos for breeding purposes are another way in which zoos obtain animals. These loans are important because they permit zoos to find unrelated animals for mating.

Breeding, exchanges, and loans demonstrate one of the ways that zoos take part in wildlife conservation. These activities can make collecting wild animals unnecessary.

E. More kinds of food are probably served in a zoo than in most restaurants. To feed their livestock, zoos are always buying large quantities of grain, fruit, vegetables, meat, fish, and other foods. Zoos often announce the feeding times for such animals as big cats, sea lions, eagles, and crocodiles because these animals are fed on regular schedules

Many zoo animals, especially those that eat a wide variety of foods in nature, are fairly easy to feed in captivity because they thrive on a diet that is easy to obtain. Raccoons, for example, eat familiar foods such as apples, carrots, grapes, bananas, hard-boiled eggs, and fish, as well as commercial livestock feed.

Some animals, like Australia's koala, are picky eaters in nature and need special diets. It eats only fresh leaves of eucalyptus trees from its native land. Diet plays an important part in keeping animals healthy, and zoo diets are constantly being improved as scientists learn more about the nutritional needs of animals in zoos. Zoos often add vitamin and mineral supplements to the food to prevent the problems that can arise if these substances are lacking.

F. Years ago, most veterinary treatments for zoo animals were based on knowledge of dogs, cats, and other domestic animals. Today research is advancing knowledge of wild animal medicine all the time.

Most big zoos have a full-time staff of animal health professionals, including veterinarians and animal health technicians. But even when a zoo has a full-time veterinarian, it may occasionally need the assistance of a specialist, such as a veterinary dentist, bacteriologist, or surgeon.

Even in zoos with the best animal health programs, animals occasionally get hurt and need emergency treatment. In these cases, it is often necessary to restrain the animal--wild animals do not sit still for the veterinarian. If the animal cannot be held still, the veterinarian uses a tranquilizing drug or even a general anesthetic. This can be risky because the proper doses for different sizes and species of animals are not always known.

G. Research is an important goal of the modern zoo, although many zoo visitors are not aware of these activities.

Zoo research usually falls into three categories: breeding biology, veterinary medicine, and nutrition. Research into breeding biology is important to conservation, especially in efforts to breed endangered species. Research into veterinary care and nutrition is essential to improving wild animal care. At the Bronx Zoo, for example, a professional nutritionist has conducted studies that have helped the zoo formulate better diets for leaf-eating monkeys. At some zoos, research into animal behavior is also becoming common, as curators seek to understand how animals use natural habitat exhibits.

H. Throughout history, people have had various reasons for keeping collections of wild animals. In ancient times, rulers kept wild animals to show off their wealth, entertain their subjects, or present as gifts to other kings and queens. The first step toward the modern zoo may have been taken 3,000 years ago, when a Chinese emperor developed a collection of animals for study rather than amusement. There were public zoos in Europe as early as the AD 900's, but they were mostly small. In the 1700's, however, zoos expanded their collections and began to be involved in research. In recent years the goals of conservation, education, and research have become more important to zoos, leading to many changes in the way zoos work.

Questions 36 – 40

Fill in the blanks with NOT MORE THAN ONE WORD from the text above.

36. Zoos are not just for the entertainment of human beings, they have several other ……………………

37. When animals from the same part of the world are kept together in a zoo, the layout is called ……………………

38. Zoos may loan their animals to other zoos to enable …………………… and thus increase their animal head count.

39. Many animals which eat a wide variety of foods are not ……………… eaters.

40. …………………… into their food and how to take care of the animals is very important; it helps to look after them better.

GT READING TEST 11

SECTION 1

Questions 1-14

Read the text below and answer Questions 1 – 7

ALL ABOUT COBRAS

Nearly everyone recognizes a cobra. This is primarily due to the fact that cobras display one of the most iconic snake poses: the rearing, hooded display. For proof of this, look no further than ancient Egypt. In ancient Egyptian culture, a hooded cobra symbol known as Uraeus was used to represent sovereignty, royalty, deity, or divine authority. This article provides a brief introduction to several cobra species.

A. **King Cobra:** The King Cobra may live up to 25 years and is a very large snake. Despite their size, king cobras are extremely fast and agile, and have inspired many myths and legends. Unlike other cobras, it has a proclivity for ingesting other snakes. The king cobra has a larger head and narrower hood compared to other cobra species.
In spite of its fearsome reputation, the king cobra is generally a shy snake, avoiding confrontation with humans as much as possible. Its bite is considered more serious than those from other cobra species because a greater volume of venom is injected, as well as a more rapid onset of neurotoxic symptoms. That said, bites from king cobras are rare.

B. **Monocled Cobra:** The Monocled Cobra is one of the most readily recognized cobra species because of the unique, O-shaped pattern on its dorsal hood. It is found in several Asian countries including Thailand, where it is responsible for the greatest number of human fatalities resulting from snake bites. Often, they are found in agricultural zones such as rice paddies. The Monocled Cobra exhibits bio-geographical variation between their venoms, and it has been documented that different toxicities exist between Malaysian, Thai and Vietnamese monocled cobras. They live in small rodent burrows and feed on small mammals, rodents, snakes and amphibians.

C. **Indian Cobra:** The Indian Cobra is one of the most dangerous cobra species in India. They are found in Pakistan, India, Sri Lanka and Malaysia. They have a very distinct dorsal hood pattern, and most have a v-shaped "spectacle" marking on the back of the hood. Adults feed primarily on rodents and are often encountered in villages because of the availability of abundant prey, although the cobra's natural habitat includes open fields, forest edges, agricultural land and wetlands. The Indian cobra is the species typically used by snake charmers in India.

D. **Forest Cobra:** The forest cobra is considered the largest true cobra species. It lives primarily in forest or woodlands, and it is the only cobra species found in such areas in Africa. Due to its ecological niche, humans do not often encounter forest cobras, and the species is one of the least frequent causes of snakebites suffered by humans in Africa.

E. **Spitting Cobras:** Spitting cobras have evolved the ability to project venom from their fangs. The venom is generally aimed at the eyes of the target, and if even a small quantity of venom contacts the eye, it produces intense pain, disruption of the cornea, and swelling of the eyes. These snakes are very unlikely to bite as a defensive behaviour. When interacting with any spitting species of cobras, it is imperative to wear protective eye gear, or even an entire face shield, to prevent any venom from entering your eyes if the animal decides to spit venom.

Questions 1 – 7

Do the following statements agree with the information given in the text? In boxes on your answer sheet, write

TRUE	if the statement agrees with the information
FALSE	if the statement contradicts the information
NOT GIVEN	if there is no information on this.

1. The authority of the state in ancient Egypt was represented using a symbol known as Uraeus.
2. The King Cobra is disinclined to eat other snakes.
3. King Cobras are the fastest and most agile of all cobras.
4. Monocled cobras are responsible for the largest number of deaths from snake bites in Asia.
5. Indian cobras are found near villages because farm animals are available in abundance in these places.
6. Forest cobras hardly bite human beings because they hardly come across each other often.
7. If threatened, spitting cobras are likely to spout rather than bite.

Read the text below and answer Questions 8 – 14

PLAYS RUNNING AT WEST END

The West End of London refers to a distinct region of Central London, in which many of the city's theatres are located. A snapshot of plays running in the West End theaters:

A. The Price: David Suchet delivers a comic tour de force as a silver-tongued 90 year old furniture dealer in Arthur Miller's masterpiece, 'The Price'. Two brothers, Victor and Walter Franz, one a New York cop and the other a successful surgeon, meet for the first time in sixteen years to sell their family furniture. Revelation follows stunning revelation as each brother realises the price they have paid for heart breaking decisions made decades earlier.

B. The Night of the Iguana: Globe-winner Clive Owen returns to the West End for the first time in 18 years to play Rev. T. Lawrence Shannon in 'The Night of the Iguana', a new production directed by James Macdonald. Set in the strange limbo of 1940, in a hot and humid Mexico, a group of travellers meet at the run-down Costa Verde Hotel, which brings them together in an epic battle between flesh and spirit, captivity and freedom, art and faith, heightened by a tropical rain-storm.

C. Admissions: Alex Kingston stars in this award-winning and bitingly funny new comedy. Sherri is the Head of Admissions at a private school, fighting to diversify the student intake and she wants you to know about it. When her son is deferred from his university of choice, and his best friend - who 'ticks more boxes' – makes it, Sherri's personal ambition collides with her progressive values. Piercing and provocative, 'Admissions' dares to question whether the race to the top is ever simply black and white.

D. The Mousetrap: Agatha Christie's legendary whodunit, The Mousetrap, is still thriving after over 60 years in the West End. The world's longest-running play, this masterpiece goes from strength to strength as a new generation of theatregoers are tricked and teased at St. Martin's Theatre. Experience this cracking yarn today - an irresistible treat for amateur sleuths everywhere!

E. Cyprus Avenue: David Ireland's black comedy Cyprus Avenue returns to West End for a limited four-week run. Eric Miller is a Belfast Loyalist. He believes his five-week old granddaughter is Gerry Adams. His family keep telling him to stop living in the past and fighting old battles that nobody cares about anymore but his cultural heritage is under siege. He must act. This is the story of one man struggling with the past and terrified of the future.

F. The Toast: Following a phenomenal sell-out run at the Traverse part of the Edinburgh Fringe Festival Toast now makes its West End debut. Nigel Slater's Toast is a new play based on his award-winning autobiography. Vividly recreating suburban England in the 1960s Nigel Slater's childhood is told through the tastes and smells he grew up with. From making the perfect sherry trifle, waging war over cakes through to the playground politics of sweets and the rigid rules of restaurant dining, this is a moving and evocative tale of love, loss and...toast.

G. Strange Fruits: Alvin and Errol are young, black and living in England in the 1980s, with an entire country and political system set against them. They focus firmly on their past – the sunny Caribbean and heroic father they left behind when their mother brought them to England twenty years ago. But when Alvin returns home from his grandfather's funeral a new version of their past emerges and the two brothers are caught in a desperate struggle to unearth the truth about their existence.

Questions 8 – 14

Identify the play from the following hints. Write your answers A-G on questions 8-14 of your answer sheet.

8. This play will be staged in West End for the first time.
9. The place where the actors meet is not very well maintained
10. This play is a mystery story.
11. One of the actors speaks very persuasively.
12. New facts come to light after a death in the family.
13. It is a story where one's personal values come into conflict with what the actor wants in real life.
14. This play looks at the funny side of things usually considered very serious.

SECTION 2

Read the text below and answer Questions 15 – 27

Questions 15 – 21

WHY DO PEOPLE CHANGE JOBS

People change jobs every day. In fact, somebody probably just made a decision to change their job right now, while you were reading this sentence. But why do people make that decision? What's behind their decision?

Is it money? Benefits? Better health insurance? More compensation overall? Do people really chase more money in the quest for greater career satisfaction? According to LinkedIn's recent "Why & How People Change Jobs" reports, the answer to all of these questions would appear to be "No."

LinkedIn released two reports, one globally and one for North America. Since we're in North America, we'll primarily concern ourselves with the results of that report. Of particular interest are the top reasons that people gave for accepting a company's offer of employment and starting work for them. Those reasons are as follows:

- Stronger career path/more opportunity—63%
- Better compensation/benefits—60%
- Better fit for my skills and interests—50%
- More ability to make an impact—46%
- The work sounded more challenging—45%
- I believed in the company's overall direction—45%

However, those are the top reasons why a person accepted an offer from another company. When it came to reasons why they decided to actually leave their current organization and seek another employment opportunity, compensation and benefits fell even further down the list.

When asked what contributed to their decision to leave, 48% of respondents in North America chose "I was concerned about the lack of opportunities for advancement" as their answer. Compensation slipped down to #3.

So—what can we deduce from the data contained in this report?

Without a doubt, greater opportunity is the #1 reason why people change their job.

However, it goes beyond that. A perceived lack of opportunity is what prompts a person to consider leaving their current job in the first place. Then, an attractive opportunity is the main reason that the person accepts an offer from another organization.

Clearly, people believe that greater opportunity leads to greater satisfaction in their career. Yes, money plays a role, but when it comes to spurring people to action, opportunity is king. Not only that, but things like challenging work, the company's direction, and company culture are also major parts of the decision-making process.

When was the last time you conducted an "audit" of your career? Which opportunities exist at your current employer? What kind of opportunities do you want to pursue? How would you answer the questions posed in the LinkedIn report?

Figure out where you want to go and how you're going to get there. Create a plan and then execute it. These are the steps that lead you to career growth and satisfaction.

Questions 15 – 21

Complete the sentences below using not more than 3 words from the text.

15. This article looks into what lies .... when people make up their minds to change their employer.
16. In looking for greater contentment from their jobs, do people really................ a higher level of pecuniary benefits?
17. One of the top reasons why people took up work in a new organization was that the new job was more in sync with their....................
18. While more money is the second most important reason why people take up a new job, ... does not retain its rank among the reasons people gave for deciding to leave their current job.
19. When people feel that there is a...................... in their current jobs, it triggers the desire to start looking for another job.
20. While there are many reasons why people change their jobs, including higher compensation, among all the reasons, ...
21. When changing one's job, apart from opportunity and compensation, consideration of the other factors mentioned here is part of the......................

Read the text below and answer Questions 22 – 27

THE DODO BIRD: EXTINCT

The dodo bird inhabited the island of Mauritius in the Indian Ocean, where it lived undisturbed for so long that it lost its need and ability to fly. It lived and nested on the ground and ate fruits that had fallen from trees. There were no mammals on the island and a high diversity of bird species lived in the dense forests.

In 1505, the Portuguese became the first humans to set foot on Mauritius. The island quickly became a stopover for ships on the high seas engaged in the spice trade. Weighing up to 50 pounds, the dodos were a welcome source of fresh meat for the sailors. Large numbers of dodo birds were killed for food. Later, when the Dutch used the island as a penal colony, pigs and monkeys were brought to the island along with the convicts. Many of the ships that came to Mauritius also had uninvited rats aboard, some of which escaped onto the island.

Before humans and other mammals appeared on the scene, the dodo bird had little to fear from predators. The rats, pigs and monkeys made short work of vulnerable dodo bird eggs in the ground nests. The combination of human exploitation and introduced species significantly reduced dodo bird populations. Within 100 years of the arrival of humans on Mauritius, the once abundant dodo bird was a rare bird.

Although the tale of the dodo bird's demise is well documented, no complete specimens of the bird were preserved; there are only fragments and sketches. The dodo bird is just one of the bird species driven to extinction on Mauritius. Many others were lost in the 19th century when the dense Mauritian forests were converted into tea and sugar plantations.

Although the dodo bird became extinct in 1681, its story is not over. We are just beginning to understand the effects of its extinction on the ecosystem. Recently a scientist noticed that a certain species of tree was becoming quite rare on Mauritius. In fact, he noticed that all 13 of the remaining trees of this species were about 300 years old. No new trees had germinated since the late 1600s.

Since the average life span of this tree was about 300 years, the last members of the species were extremely old. They would soon die, and the species would be extinct. Was it just a coincidence that the tree had stopped reproducing 300 years ago and that the dodo bird had become extinct 300 years ago? No. It turns out that the dodo bird ate the fruit of this tree, and it was only by passing through the dodo's digestive system that the seeds became active and could grow. Now, more than 300 years after one species became extinct, another was to follow as a direct consequence. Will more follow?

Luckily, some creative people discovered that domestic turkey gullets sufficiently mimic the action of the dodo bird's digestive system. They have used turkeys to begin a new generation of the tree, which is now called the dodo tree. If these seedlings survive to produce their own seeds, the species will be saved.

Questions 22 – 27

Use the words/phrases given in the box below to complete the following sentences.

22. Since the dodo bird could get its food requirements from fruits that had fallen from trees, it did not have the .... to fly.
23. The dodos faced an unwelcome intrusion into their lives from sailors plying the ....
24. Since the Dutch used Mauritius as a penal colony, they brought .... to the island.
25. The species of .... birds became extinct when tea and sugar plantations came up in Mauritius.
26. It was observed that a certain kind of tree was becoming quite .... in Mauritius.
27. The digestive system of the .... is similar to that of the dodo.

Need	Turkey	Fresh Meat	Dodo
Rare	Many	Ability	Extinct
Monkeys	Gullet	High Seas	Convicts

SECTION 3

Read the text below and answer questions 28 – 40

Questions 28 -35

The text has 8 SECTIONS, marked A to H. Choose the correct heading for each paragraph from the list of headings below.

i. Feel free to indulge your sweet tooth
ii. Succour for the skeletal structure
iii. Plan correctly to ensure adequate nutrients
iv. Eat smartly to get the vegan advantage
v. Eyeing a new wardrobe? Go vegan!
vi. Of matters cardiac
vii. Get over your tummy travails
viii. Bye bye big C
ix. Of bacteria in meat
x. Go vegan to control cholesterol

28. Paragraph A ....
29. Paragraph B ....
30. Paragraph C ....
31. Paragraph D ....
32. Paragraph E ....
33. Paragraph F ....
34. Paragraph G ....
35. Paragraph H ....

BEING VEGAN

A. One million people are vegan in the United States. People choose to go vegan for many different reasons, whether it's because they advocate for ethical treatment of animals or because they're hoping to reap the health benefits of a vegan diet. It's no secret that boosting your fruit and vegetable intake has major health perks, but that's only if you do it the right way. Experts say the benefits of a healthy vegan diet come from a balance of foods, conscientious eating, and smart meal plans.

B. If you switch to a vegan diet, you'll eliminate meat and animal products. In the case of a whole-foods vegan diet, replacements take the form of whole grains, fruits, vegetables, beans, peas, nuts and seeds. Since these foods make up a larger proportion of a vegan diet, they can contribute to a higher daily intake of certain beneficial nutrients. For instance, several studies have reported that vegan diets tend to provide more fiber, antioxidants and beneficial plant compounds. They also appear to be richer in potassium, magnesium, folate and vitamins A, C and E.

However, poorly planned vegan diets may provide insufficient amounts of essential fatty acids, vitamin B12, iron, calcium, iodine or zinc. That's why it's important to stay away from nutrient-poor, fast-food vegan options. Instead, plan your diet around nutrient-rich whole plants and fortified foods. You may also want to consider supplements like vitamin B12.

C. An increasing number of people are turning to plant-based diets in the hope of shedding excess weight. Many observational studies show that vegans tend to be thinner and have lower body mass indexes (BMIs) than non-vegans. In addition, several randomized controlled studies report that vegan diets are more effective for weight loss than the diets they are compared to.

In one study, a vegan diet helped participants lose 4.2 kg more than a control diet over an 18-week study period. Interestingly, participants on the vegan diet lost more weight than those who followed calorie-restricted diets, even when the vegan groups were allowed to eat until they felt full. What's more, a recent small study comparing the weight loss effects of five different diets concluded that vegetarian and vegan diets were just as well-accepted as semi-vegetarian and standard Western diets.

Vegan diets have a natural tendency to reduce your calorie intake. This makes them effective at promoting weight loss without the need to actively focus on cutting calories.

D. Going vegan may also have benefits for Type 2 diabetes and declining kidney function. Indeed, vegans tend to have lower blood sugar levels, higher and up to a 50–78% lower risk of developing type 2 diabetes. Studies even report that vegan diets lower blood sugar levels in diabetics more than the diets from the American Diabetes Association (ADA), American Heart Association (AHA) and National Cholesterol Education Program (NCEP).

In one study, 43% of participants following a vegan diet were able to reduce their dosage of blood-sugar-lowering medication, compared to only 26% in the group that followed an ADA-recommended diet. Other studies report that diabetics who substitute meat for plant protein may reduce their risk of poor kidney function. Several studies report that a vegan diet may be able to provide complete relief of systemic distal polyneuropathy symptoms — a condition in diabetics that causes sharp, burning pain. Vegan diets are also particularly effective at reducing blood sugar levels and may help prevent further medical issues from developing.

E. According to the World Health Organization, about one-third of all cancers can be prevented by factors within your control, including diet. For instance, eating legumes regularly may reduce your risk of colorectal cancer by about 9–18%. Research also suggests that eating at least seven portions of fresh fruits and vegetables per day may lower your risk of dying from cancer by up to 15%.

Vegans generally eat considerably more legumes, fruit and vegetables than non-vegans. This may explain why a recent review of 96 studies found that vegans may benefit from a 15% lower risk of developing or dying from cancer. What's more, vegan diets generally contain more soy products, which may offer some protection against breast cancer. Avoiding certain animal products may also help reduce the risk of prostate, breast and colon cancers.

It's important to note that these studies are observational in nature. However, until researchers know more, it seems wise to focus on increasing the amount of fresh fruits, vegetables and legumes you eat each day while limiting your consumption of processed, smoked and overcooked meat.

F. Eating fresh fruits, vegetables, legumes and fiber are linked to a lower risk of heart disease. All of these are generally eaten in large amounts in well-planned vegan diets. Observational studies comparing vegans to vegetarians and the general population report that vegans may benefit from up to a 75% lower risk of developing high blood pressure. Vegans may also have up to a 42% lower risk of dying from heart disease.

What's more, several randomized controlled studies report that vegan diets are much more effective at reducing blood sugar, LDL cholesterol and total cholesterol than the diets they are compared to.

This may be particularly beneficial to heart health since reducing high blood pressure, cholesterol and blood sugar levels may reduce the risk of heart disease by as much as 46%.

Compared to the general population, vegans also tend to consume more whole grains and nuts, both of which are good for your heart.

G. A few studies have reported that a vegan diet has positive effects in people with different types of arthritis. One study randomly assigned 40 arthritic participants to either continue eating their omnivorous diet or switch to a whole-food, plant-based vegan diet for 6 weeks. Those on the vegan diet reported higher energy levels and better general functioning than those who didn't change their diet.

Two other studies reported that participants in the vegan group experienced a greater improvement in symptoms such as pain, joint swelling and morning stiffness. The bottom line is that vegan diets based on probiotic-rich whole foods can significantly decrease symptoms of osteoarthritis and rheumatoid arthritis.

H. Some studies show that your diet can give your intestines a micro biome makeover quite rapidly. A small study discovered an increase in B.wadsworthia, a bacterial microbe linked to inflammation in the bowel, inside the stomachs of the people who ate animal foods. People who ate meat also had more faecal bile acid in their guts, which can cause gastrointestinal infections.

A vegan diet helps grow more good bacteria in our gut, which positively influences our digestive system as well as absorption of nutrients.

Take Home Message: Vegan diets may provide an array of health benefits. That said, until further research emerges, it can only benefit you to increase the amount of nutrient-rich, whole plant foods in your diet.

Questions 36 – 40

Choose ONE WORD from the text to complete the following sentences:

36. Some people want to be humane to .... and hence go vegan.
37. Vegan diets provide more beneficial plant compounds as has been mentioned in a number of...................
38. It has been noticed that vegans are generally .... as compared to non-vegans.
39. When it comes to succumbing to an ailment of the heart, vegans are not at as much of a.................. as non-vegans.
40. As per a study, non-vegetarian foods are linked to .... in the digestive system.

GT READING TEST 12

SECTION 1

Questions 1-14

Read the text below and answer Questions 1 – 7

DISNEYLAND ATTRACTIONS IN PARIS

Some of the attractions in Disneyland, Paris are described below.

A. **Mickey's PhilharMagic**:

There is no height restriction for guests; suitable for all age groups.

Disney magic meets Disney music in this spectacular 4D fantasy adventure starring Donald Duck. Join Donald Duck on a whirlwind tour of some of the most memorable songs in Disney animation history.

B. **It's a small world:**

There is no height restriction for guests; suitable for all age groups.

Dolls from all over the globe sing and dance to the tune of 'it's a small world'. Sing along to the classic anthem of world peace during a delightful musical boat tour hosted by the children of the world. Set sail along the Seven Seaways Waterway on a 10-minute journey. Travel to all 7 continents and, by journey's end, see for yourself that it truly is a small world after all.

C. **Big Thunder Mountain:**

Guests must be a minimum of 1.02 meters tall; suitable for kids, tweens, teens and adults.

You board a mysterious train deep in the heart of a legendary mountain for a thrilling journey of dips and sharp turns beneath the Rivers of the Far West and around a ghostly mining town. As you plummet through the darkness along a dynamite-littered track, a huge explosion shakes the cavern. The train hurtles onwards amid the rumbling sounds of a falling mineshaft. Bats swoop. The tracks shake. A river rages above. Will you make it out alive?

D. **Crush's Coaster**

Guests must be a minimum of 1.07 meters tall; suitable for kids, tweens, teens and adults.

Sit tight in your turtle shell as it dives into the ocean and begins its incredible journey, plunging to the deepest darkest depths, where a sunken submarine sits surrounded by voracious glow-fish, jellyfish and sharks. At Crush's Coaster danger lurks. However, just in the nick of time, the strong East Australian Current churns you up and sends you spiralling back to Sydney Harbour to a rousing reception.

E. **Indiana Jones™ and the Temple of Peril**

Guests must be a minimum of 1.40 meters tall; suitable for tweens, teens and adults.

You soon discover something is far from normal in the Temple of Peril. The base camp is deserted of people yet full of their clothes, food and equipment. Above the canopies stands a temple ruin, below your feet is a well-trodden path. You board a railed vehicle to find them, and the rickety cart climbs a chain lift to the top of the excavation site. You look for signs of life, but a mysterious force sends the cart into an out-of-control spiral of twists and turns through the darkest corners of this cursed ruin.

F. Star Wars Hyperspace Mountain

Guests must be a minimum of 1.20 meters tall; suitable for tweens, teens and adults.

Launch yourself into Star Wars Hyperspace Mountain for a thrilling takeover of a classic space attraction. Enlist in the Rebel Alliance and attend a briefing from Admiral Ackbar. Your mission – to spy on an Imperial Star Destroyer. However, the Empire is expecting you, welcoming your arrival from hyperspace with open armaments. It's down to you to blast through a swarm of deadly TIE fighters and blow up a menacing Star Destroyer. Will the Force be strong with you?

G. Toy Soldiers Parachute Drop

Guests must be a minimum of 1.02 meters tall; suitable for kids, tweens, teens and adults.

Sarge has enlisted you to his little green regiment. But first you need to learn to parachute. So buckle up recruit, follow your orders and brace yourself for a thrilling 82-foot drop above an army base full of lookout towers and over-sized green toy soldiers. It's as if you're part of one big play set!

Questions 1 – 7

Which attraction fits into each of the descriptions given below? Write A – G against questions 1-8 in your answer sheet. You may use any letter more than once.

1. Am afraid my kid is not tall enough for this one; he is so fond of aquatic animals, he would have really enjoyed the ride.
2. I will take my teenaged son along; it will be fun to be a secret agent for once.
3. I must check my son's height to go for this tour; if we do go, I will hold on to him so that he does not feel scared when our train plunges down in the dark.
4. I sure will love this one; I have always wanted to have a bird's eye view of the ground below.
5. We will try and find where all the missing people have gone.
6. I can take my little girl with me, and we can sing along.
7. Wow! We will have Donald Duck for company!

Read the text below and answer Questions 8 – 14

FOODS YOU SHOULD NEVER BUY AT THE AIRPORT

Soft pretzels

A big old soft pretzel is not a meal. Those fluffy carbs might smell enticing, but carbo-loading before a long flight will leave your tummy rumbling again by take-off. Look for something with protein and fibre that will keep you satisfied until you land, or better yet, pack a meal from home. Making a sandwich at home to save money or packing leftovers like pasta salad or grilled chicken in an old, washed plastic container, such as a cottage cheese tub, is recommended.

Guilty pleasures

Try not to lump your waiting time at the airport with the "treat mentality" of the rest of your vacation. Even though it might be the kick-off to a vacation, you want to save those calories for something unique when you arrive. Skip the specialty coffee drink and stick with plain coffee if you need a caffeine fix, or leave room for ice cream at the beach instead of gobbling a bag of cookies at the airport.

Yogurt based Dessert

You've seen yogurt touted time and time again as one of the healthiest snacks you can get, thanks to its satiating protein. But that fruit and yogurt dessert isn't the healthy and fresh choice that it seems. Yogurt has a halo over it as a healthy food, and obviously it is, but in context of what additives are in it. By the time you turn plain yogurt into a sugary flavoured yogurt topped with granola and fruit (which, unlike fresh berries, is full of added sugar), it isn't a healthy choice anymore.

Granola bars

Granola bars are often designed to look like a smart choice, but there's more than meets the eye. Granola bars can be packed with added sugar, high-fructose corn syrup, and other decidedly unhealthy ingredients, especially if they're covered in a waxy coating. That said, a shelf-stable, portable snack is convenient when you need to take the hunger off during your travels, so hunt down an option with 12 or fewer grams of sugar.

Glass of Wine

While a glass of wine as you wait for your flight won't do much harm for most people, you'll want to keep your drinking to a minimum. Not only could it dehydrate you before an already dehydrating plane ride, but alcohol isn't good for deep sleep. You might crash quickly, but the alcohol will wake you up and keep you out of deep REM sleep as your liver works it out.

Water bottles

Because hydration is important, especially when you're stuck in a dry plane cabin, we recommend sipping extra water the night and morning before your flight so you aren't dehydrated when you board. Especially if your flight is longer than a couple of hours; however, though, don't ignore your thirst in the name of avoiding the bathroom.

Anything your stomach isn't used to

When you're about to sit in close quarters for hours on end, you'll want to avoid foods that don't tend to sit well with your digestive system. Steer clear of foods that normally might upset your stomach, such as certain types of fibre or greasy foods. A hamburger and French fries or fried chicken before you get on a plane might not be the best idea.

Questions 8 – 14

Do the following statements agree with the information given in the text? Write:

TRUE	If the statement agrees with the information
FALSE	If the statement contradicts the information
NOT GIVEN	If there is no information on this.

8. Rather than buying a soft pretzel, buy something with protein and fibre, it is even better than your home made sandwich.
9. When you arrive at the airport, you can have an ice cream to kick off your vacation.
10. Yogurt without additives is a healthy food.
11. If granola bars have a waxy coating they are likely to have add-ons that are not healthy.
12. Alcohol will help you to go to sleep quickly.
13. Do not avoid drinking water if you are thirsty just because it may make you go to the bathroom.
14. You can eat whatever you want as long as your stomach is used to it.

SECTION 2

Questions 15 - 28

Read the text below and answer Questions 15 – 21

Distilled water has many varied uses: in lead acid batteries, in the medical industry, in CPAP machines, for jal neti in yoga practice and so on. The process to make distilled water is simple: water is heated and the water vapour, which is free of any impurity, is collected and then condensed, giving us pure H2O, that is water.

Water has to be heated upto its boiling point using a gas burner or an electric heater; any container such as a conical flask, a rectangular jar or a round flask can be used. The container is held in place with a clamp. The mouth of the container has to be sealed so that the water vapour does not escape. A thermometer may be inserted to track the temperature. The water vapour has to be channelised using a connecting tube into a device like a condenser to cool it down. Cold water is passed through the outer shell of this device to facilitate the cooling process. As the water vapor condenses, the resultant distilled water is collected in another container.

Questions 15 – 21

Based on the description above, label the diagram given below, using not more than two words taken from the text for each label.

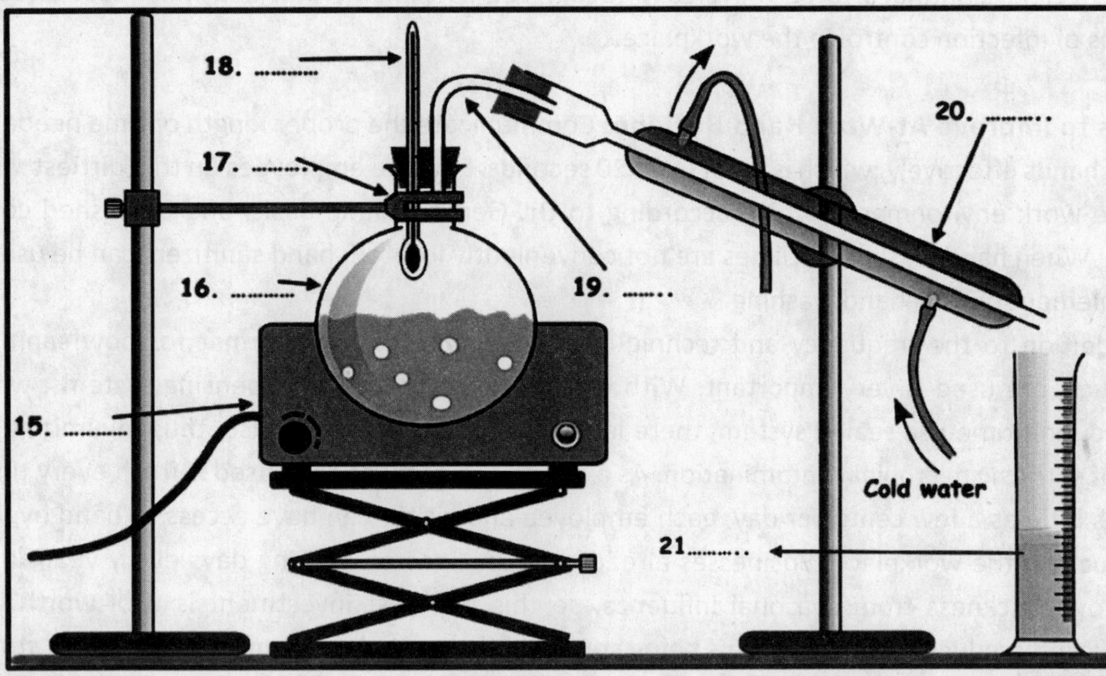

Read the text below and answer Questions 22 – 28

INFECTION PREVENTION: WHY IT MATTERS IN THE WORKPLACE

Whether you are in a workplace, public facility, leisure environment or educational facility, germs are spread from person-to-person and by touching everyday surfaces. In fact, according to a recent presentation by Dr. Charles Gerba, a microbiologist from the University of Arizona, "we share more common surfaces, with more people than ever before in history."

Enclosed environments—like the workplace—where people are working or interacting in close proximity with one another are particularly at a higher risk for the spread of germs. Poor hygiene will lead to increased illness and can result in disruption cost, lost productivity, reduced employee efficiency through illness at work, and lower morale.

Skin Hygiene Facts: Hands are the single most effective method of spreading germs, yet over half of all workers do not know the basics of hand washing. At least 40 percent of workers do not wash their hands often, or long enough, to protect against the spread of germs. Approximately 65% of maintenance and construction workers and 47% of office workers wash their hands less than five times a day. The average hand wash misses vital areas where germs are commonly found, e.g., under fingernails and on the backs of hands.

Since our hands are responsible for the spread of 80% of common infectious diseases, effective hand hygiene continues to be universally recognized as the smartest and most cost effective means of infection control in the workplace.

Ways to Improve At-Work Hand Hygiene: Communicate the proper length of time needed to wash hands effectively, which is for at least 20 seconds. Educate employees on the 'dirtiest' areas of the work environment—which according to Dr. Gerba include desks and unwashed coffee cups. When hand washing facilities are not conveniently located, hand sanitizers can be used to complement normal hand washing.

In addition to the frequency and technique of hand washing, the format for how sanitizing products are used is very important. With wall-mounted cartridge dispensing systems, with a closed, one-time-use sealed system, there is no entrance of air during use, thus minimizing any risk of extrinsic microbial contamination. As a result, the product dispensed is fresh every time.

For as little as a few cents per day, each employee and visitor can have access to hand hygiene products in the workplace. Businesses already lose millions of working days every year due to employee sickness from seasonal influenza, so this low cost investment is well worth it to significantly reduce the risk of germs being spread in the workplace. Numerous separate studies show that good hand hygiene practices can reduce employee illness, absence and associated cost on an average by around 40%.

It can be easy for businesses to think of skin care as a trivial issue and a commodity buy, or for it to fall off their radar screens completely. However, encouraging proper hand hygiene through a structured skin care system helps to protect your employees' health, as well as the operational health of your company.

Questions 22 – 28

Complete the summary below. Use ONE WORD from the above text to fill in the blanks below:

Establishments where people work are generally covered from all sides and full of surfaces that people touch. This enables the spread of germs; coupled with inadequate (22).............., this leads to increased incidence of illnesses and thus a loss of productivity. Our hands are the single most effective means of spreading germs. Almost half of all workers do not wash their hands often enough; many of them do not do so (23)................ times a day. Also, generally when hands are washed, the places where (24) .... abide are missed out. Employees have to be told about how much time is (25) .... to ensure that their hands are washed in an efficacious manner. One should ensure that an appropriate hand washing cleanser is used and the dispensing mechanism is such that the cleanser that each user gets to use is (26)................ every time. Hand hygiene products do not (27).............. much and can help reduce the costs associated with employee illness and absence by around 40%. Taking care of one's skin is not a (28).............. issue and making sure of good hand hygiene can help to protect the health of employees.

SECTION 3

Read the text below and answer questions 29 – 40

Questions 29 -36

The text has 8 SECTIONS, marked A to H. Choose the correct heading for each paragraph from the list of headings below.

i. Strategy to enable women to reach their full potential
ii. Strategize to target distinct areas
iii. In search of the answer to why
iv. World attitude to gender equality is changing
v. Financial well-being is transformative
vi. It has to be sooner than later
vii. What we hope to achieve
viii. Planning for the future
ix. Transformative results to be achieved by doubling commitment
x. How soon is soon enough

29. Paragraph A ....
30. Paragraph B ....
31. Paragraph C ....
32. Paragraph D ....
33. Paragraph E ....
34. Paragraph F ....
35. Paragraph G ....
36. Paragraph H ....

WHAT IF GENDER EQUALITY COULD CHANGE THE FACE OF POVERTY?

A. Asking questions and diving into the data are a large part of my job. The questions that keep me up at night usually begin with Why. Why are women more likely to be poor than men? Why hasn't progress in health and economies benefited both men and women equally?
Research over the years has shown that poverty and inequality are deeply intertwined. Especially in the developing world, women still earn less, learn less, own less, and wield much less social and economic power than their brothers and husbands. This leads to negative consequences that affect women's health, schooling, job prospects, and even the control women have — or lack — over their own lives and choices.

B. But the world has more appetite than ever before to advance gender equality. The leaders of 193 nations have pledged to end gender inequality by 2030. Women are raising their collective voices, and the world is listening. I remain particularly inspired by the expanding global momentum to tackle not just the symptoms, but the drivers of inequality.

So what if we flip the narrative? What if the barriers that perpetuate inequality were removed, and women and girls had the same opportunity as men and boys to earn a fair income, have a voice in their families and communities, and dictate the course of their own lives? What if gender equality could change the face of poverty? The world today realizes that the results would be transformative for women, girls, their families, and their communities.

C. For the first time, the Bill & Melinda Gates Foundation is launching a program strategy dedicated specifically to gender equality. The focus of our strategy is to transform the way women participate in economies — because we believe that taking charge of your economic future is one of the most profound ways to exercise power over your life. We know that women and girls need to be empowered economically if they are to act and engage as equals in society. And we know that we can't achieve a healthier, greater world for everyone if women and girls are still being left behind.

Gender equality has always been at the heart of our work, through initiatives on nutrition, health, and family planning. But in looking at the ways that women and girls' lives are differentially impacted by poverty across all our program areas, we realized it was necessary to develop an overarching strategy that aims to systematically tackle the barriers that hold women and girls back from living to their full potential.

D. During the past year, we conducted rigorous research and analysis in nearly 100 countries to explore what tangible steps it would take to achieve gender equality. We know there is no silver bullet to solving this challenge. But in looking at developing countries that are making significant progress toward equality, we see that economic power emerges as a consistent thread across women's stories of transformation.

In India, growth in the Business Process Outsourcing industry created an opportunity for rural women to work outside of the home. As women became employed and were able to earn a wage, the economic prospects for their daughters also changed as child marriage and early child-bearing declined and adolescent girls stayed in school longer. In Nepal, women who opened their own bank account had more decision-making control over household spending, which they then put towards their children's education and the purchase of meat and fish for her family.

E. Stories like these show that economic opportunities for women lead to other gains at home, at work and in society at large. Economic empowerment holds potential to transform the lives of both women and their daughters and others in their communities.

But we also know that poor women and girls don't always benefit when economies grow. Indeed we have learned that a rising tide does not lift all boats. Economies aren't automatically inclusive, and we need deliberate tactics to ensure women aren't left fighting the current. That's why our strategy is focusing on specific areas where the Gates Foundation and our partners can make a measurable impact toward equality.

F. For the next four years, in collaboration with partners close to the ground and embedded in the issues, we will help connect more women with mobile bank accounts so they have the opportunity to receive government transfer payments, and to decide where and how to spend their money. We will connect women to economic markets, especially in agriculture, to expand their profits and income. We will invest in self-help groups that can support women to build up their economic power and voice; and we will expand a new generation of self-help groups to empower women and adolescent girls with the skills and opportunities to control their lives, leveraging lessons learned and the power of digital technology. We will also support research that helps us better understand how productive assets can enhance women's economic options. We also are continuing the foundation's ongoing work to close gender data gaps, and strengthen the grassroots movements that build women's collective power to shape the systems and structures that exclude them. Our women's economic empowerment strategy builds off lessons learned from our previous investments and will help us strengthen the data and evidence, and hopefully garner more momentum, to tackle gender inequality.

G. With this strategy, we will help more than 63 million women not just open bank accounts but make their own decisions about spending, saving, and building their own financial futures. We will have richer data and evidence to identify the most effective ways to ensure that low income women can participate more fully in the economy. We will expand what works among "self-help groups" to empower women, including younger segments of women, in India and Africa, to chart a better future for themselves and their families. And we will have a deeper understanding of how economic assets can increase women's opportunity to find work off of her farm and outside of the home.

H. Transforming poor women's economic opportunities will really empower them to stand equally with those in their communities and in the world. In truth, it's no longer a hypothetic question of What if? But rather a practical one: How soon? And that question of how soon can only be answered by the communities of the world, both men and women; for men to work shoulder to shoulder with their women-folk in bringing about this long overdue change, and for women themselves to believe, believe in the power of collective action, believe in the strength of collaboration and most of all, believe in their own abilities and the immense possibilities of those capabilities. Regardless of how soon, it is quite clear that the time is here and now, whenever we do achieve these goals, it cannot be soon enough.

(Adapted from an article by Sarah Hendricks, the Director of Gender Equity, Bill and Melinda Gates Foundation.)

Questions 37 - 40

Fill in the blanks using **NO MORE THAN TWO WORDS** from the text.

37. In countries which are not developed, it is most likely that................ will not earn as much as their male relatives.

38. All over the globe, people nowadays understand that gender equality would lead to............................ results not only for women but also for the social circles they live in.

39. One common theme in the anecdotes of women in developing countries which have taken significant steps to remove gender inequalities is.......................

40. Actually, rather than have any doubt if gender equality will be achieved or not, one should think of .... we will achieve it.

GT READING TEST 13

SECTION 1

Questions 1 – 14

Read the text below and answer Questions 1 – 7

NEW SEVEN WONDERS OF THE WORLD

A. Great Wall of China: The Great Wall of China is a stone-and-earth fortification created to protect the borders of the Chinese Empire from invading Mongols. The Great Wall is actually a succession of multiple walls spanning approximately 4,000 miles, making it the world's longest manmade structure.

B. Christ the Redeemer Statue (Rio de Janeiro): This statue has been looming over the citizen of Rio de Janerio from upon Corcovado Mountain in an awe-inspiring state of eternal blessing since 1931. The 130-foot reinforced concrete-and-soapstone statue was designed by Heitor da Silva Costa and cost approximately $250,000 to build.

C. Machu Picchu (Peru): Machu Picchu, an Incan city of sparkling granite is thought by scholars to have been a sacred archaeological center for the nearby Incan capital of Cusco. Built at the peak of the Incan Empire in the mid-1400s, this mountain citadel was later abandoned by the Incas. The site remained unknown except to locals until 1911, when it was rediscovered by archaeologist Hiram Bingham.

D. Chichen Itza (Yucatan Peninsula, Mexico): The genius and adaptability of Mayan culture can be seen in the splendid ruins of Chichen Itza. This powerful city, a trading center for cloth, slaves, honey and salt, flourished from approximately AD 800 to 1200, and acted as the political and economic hub of the Mayan civilization.

E. The Roman Colosseum (Rome): Rome's, if not Italy's, most enduring icon is undoubtedly its Colosseum. Built between A.D. 70 and 80 A.D., the elliptical structure sat nearly 50,000 spectators, who gathered to watch gladiatorial events as well as other public spectacles, including battle re-enactments, animal hunts and executions. Earthquakes and stone-robbers have left the Colosseum in a state of ruin.

F. Taj Mahal (Agra, India): A mausoleum commissioned for the wife of Mughal Emperor Shah Jahan, the Taj Mahal was built between 1632 and 1648. Considered the most perfect specimen of Muslim art in India, the white marble structure actually represents a number of architectural styles, including Persian, Islamic, Turkish and Indian. The Taj Mahal also encompasses formal gardens of raised pathways, sunken flower beds and a linear reflecting pool.

G. Petra (Jordan): Petra was the capital of the Nabataean empire of King Aretas IV, and likely existed in its prime from 9 B.C. to A.D. 40. The members of this civilization proved to be early experts in manipulating water technology, constructing intricate tunnels and water chambers. A number of incredible structures carved into stone, a 4,000-seat amphitheater and the El-Deir monastery have also helped the site earn its fame.

Questions 1 – 7

Look at the descriptions of the Seven Wonders of the World. For which wonders are the following statements true? Write A – G against each statement.

1. It has for long been a symbol of not only the city, but also the country where it is located.
2. For a few hundred years, this city was a great commercial hub.
3. This defensive structure protected a country's borders.
4. This structure encompasses several different styles of construction.
5. This wonder arouses a sense of reverence and seems to be showering its blessings upon the city.
6. This fortress had been deserted by its inhabitants.
7. The capital of an ancient empire, this site has a number of unbelievable structures.

Read the text below and answer Questions 8 – 14

THE HISTORY OF WIMBLEDON TENNIS

It all began with an announcement in the leisure magazine, 'The Field', on 9 June 1877 that "The All England Croquet and Lawn Tennis Club, Wimbledon, proposes to hold a lawn tennis meeting, open to all amateurs, on Monday July 9th and following days". A total of 22 players stumped up the 1 Pound and 1 Shilling entrance fee, being warned to bring their own rackets and "shoes without heels" but that balls would be provided by the club gardener.

The All England Club had been founded solely for the purpose of croquet in 1869 on four acres of rented meadowland at Worple Road, Wimbledon, but croquet was rapidly overtaken by the new pastime of tennis. Conditions were primitive. A temporary three-plank stand offered seats for 30 people, the total attendance for the final was 200, the rackets resembled snowshoes in shape and weight and the balls had hand-sewn flannel outer casings.

It wasn't until 1884 that the All England Club agreed to open the Championships up to both sexes and Lottie Dodd, from Cheshire, made her mark on Wimbledon a few years later as youngest woman to win the title at the age of 15. By the 1900s, the Championships at Wimbledon had become an international affair and in 1905 May Sutton from the United States became the first overseas champion when she won the Ladies' Singles title. In 1908, Wimbledon hosted the Olympic tennis tournament at its Worple Road base and in 1922 the Championships moved to its current home on Church Road.

The Championships at Wimbledon have long attracted a royal following and have even seen a royal take to the court. In 1926 the Duke of York, who later became King George VI, competed in the men's doubles. His match formed part of the Jubilee Championships where King George V and Queen Mary presented the commemorative medals. Unfortunately he and his partner lost in straight sets.

Long-standing British favourite Fred Perry grabbed the nation's attention when he won the Championships in three consecutive years from 1936, and until Andy Murray's victory in 2013 he was the last British man to win Wimbledon.

In 1937 live sports coverage was added to the bill and the Wimbledon Championships were broadcast to those within a 40-mile radius of the BBC transmitters in north London.

Today Wimbledon demands huge viewing figures and attracts hundreds of thousands of visitors – many of them queuing for days to secure one of the much-coveted Centre Court tickets.

Matches take place across several Courts, which include the Centre Court, plus courts 1-19 – there is no court 13, which is deemed unlucky.

Questions 8 – 14

Do the following statements agree with the information given in the text?
In boxes on your answer sheet, write

TRUE	if the statement agrees with the information
FALSE	if the statement contradicts the information
NOT GIVEN	if there is no information on this.

8. Worple Road is the current home of Wimbledon Tennis.
9. A total of twenty-two men and women participated in the first tournament in 1877.
10. May Sutton from the USA was the first Women's Champion at Wimbledon.
11. The Olympic Tennis Tournament has been hosted at Wimbledon.
12. The Duke of York lost his match without winning a set.
13. Andy Murray was the last British national to win the Wimbledon Championship.
14. There are 20 courts in all at Wimbledon.

SECTION 2

Read the text below and answer Questions 15 – 27

Questions 15 – 21

THE GREATEST RISKS IN CLIMBING MOUNT EVEREST

What are the Difficulties in Climbing Mount Everest?

Altitude Sickness: This is the biggest risk to Mt. Everest climbers. It will affect many aspects of their health. The higher they get, the less oxygen there is in the air. Their body can slowly adapt to this but only up to a point. Even with the comparatively lengthy period required to climb this high, they are unlikely to ever feel quite themselves above base camp, and in the Death Zone above 8,000m they are beyond the limit of their ability to adapt to the altitude.

Temperature: Air temperature drops by roughly 0.65 degrees Centigrade per 100 meters of height gained. That means at 8,800m they can expect the temperature to be about 57 degrees Centigrade less than at sea level. That's a gross simplification ignoring many other factors but you get the idea: it is cold up there. It does not help that climbers switch from lying still in the darkness at night to slogging up-hill with the heat of the sun bearing down from above and reflecting up from the snow.

Weather: The window of opportunity for summiting will be dictated by a good weather forecast but many are the climbers who have been caught out by storms, holding out a little too long on summit day. They can't control the weather gods but they can get a good forecast, listen to their instincts and not ignore the early warning signs.

Falls: One of the highest direct causes of death on Everest is falls. These can happen both when actually climbing, particularly on the high ridges, and also in careless moments at the higher camps. Stepping out of the tent for a wee at night onto ground covered in ice being a particular example. Maintaining vigilance with their footwork, double checking knots and karabiners, and a good amount of prior experience on snow and ice are prudent steps for reducing this risk.

Avalanche: Twice as likely as falls to cause accidents are avalanches. There tend to be specific areas in which the likelihood of their occurrence is higher. In addition to falling snow, falling ice and rocks are yet other hazards they can face.

Crevasses: These are great cracks that appear in glacial ice which threaten to swallow careless or unfortunate climbers. To aid safe travel across glaciers, teams tie ropes between each of their members so they can drag out anyone unlucky enough to take a fall.

Summit Fever: Easily said but near impossible to avoid entirely, the temptation to push on for "just another ten minutes" is strong in all of us. But combine it with the intoxication of so much effort and the mind-altering effects of altitude on the danger-ridden slopes of Mount Everest and you have a recipe for disaster.

The practical advice is to have a set "turn-around time" at which point you head back down regardless of where you are. Something else worth doing is taking the time to go through your motivation for being on the mountain. If you keep the summit in perspective with the rest of the challenge it may help stop you from getting carried away.

Questions 15-21

Do the following statements agree with the information given in the passage?

Write

YES	if the statement reflects the claims of the writer
NO	if the statement contradicts the claims of the writer
NOT GIVEN	if it is impossible to say what the writer thinks about this.

15. The human body does not have unlimited ability to adapt itself to the adverse effects of high altitude.
16. It is not advisable to switch from lying still in the darkness at night to slog up-hill with the heat of the sun bearing down from above and reflecting up from the snow.
17. Pay attention to the weather forecast to help decide when to climb the summit.
18. One should avoid stepping out of the tent at night.
19. Avalanches are likely to cause more accidents than falls.
20. High altitudes impact your thought process.
21. In the final run, one has to push on regardless if one has to reach the summit.

Read the text below and answer Questions 22 – 27

PROS AND CONS OF WORKING FROM HOME

More and more Americans are working from home, thanks to technological advances that make communication and collaboration over the miles easier. But before you take the plunge into a work-from-home situation, consider the pros and cons of this option...

Working from Home Pros:

1. Offers greater flexibility for moms. If you work from home, you are likely to have more control over the hours you work, and can carve out time for doctor's appointments, attending the school party, or dropping off and picking up your kids from school. However, some employers want their work-from-home staff to be available at all times during standard office hours, so make sure you're clear about expectations.
2. Cuts out commute time. Some parents sacrifice an hour or more on each end of the work day just getting to and from the office. When working from home, it's like adding another two hours back to your day—time that can be invested in the kids, exercise, or preparing a family meal.
3. Every day is a Casual Friday. Working from home cuts out the need for so many work-appropriate clothes, and gives you a break on the budget in this area. It's also just nice to be able to spend a rainy work day in your favorite cozy sweater and yoga pants, rather than tromping down the sidewalk to the office in heels.
4. Savings on lunch and gas. Unless you're disciplined enough to pack a lunch every day, working away from home will cause you to dine out for lunch pretty frequently. Work-from-home types can just cruise into the kitchen and heat up last night's lasagna, saving major dollars. Ditto for saving on transportation costs from eliminating that commute.

Working from Home Cons:

1. Isolation. If you thrive on the social interaction and collaboration that comes with an office environment, working from home might feel isolated and lonely to you.
2. Distractions at home. Working from home requires a different level of self-discipline. After all—there's no one around to know if you're on task all day, and you have no accountability outside of your own integrity. If you work for an employer, you have to find a way to create a work environment at home that keeps you focused and putting in the hours each day that you'd devote to your job in the office. If you're self-employed, you still need boundaries to make sure that things get done, or your productivity—and income—will suffer.
3. Cost of setting up a home office. To work from home, you'll have to make an initial investment in basic equipment for production and communication with your employer and/or clients. A computer, printer, fast internet service, and conferencing accessibility are important to making yourself efficient and available.

4. Corporate disconnect. Remember the water cooler, where you learned about that coveted positions that were opening up in your department, or those lay-offs were coming and you'd better be on your toes? Working from home cuts you off from some of this type of important info. You'll have to be more proactive about networking and staying in the loop with your co-workers and bosses.
5. Keeping work and family separate. When you're working at home, you have to be careful that your work doesn't spill into family time. Just because you can work from home doesn't mean you should be available 24/7. When you're off-duty, be sure you switch your focus to family.

Questions 22-27

Fill in the blanks below by choosing not more than two words from the text.

22. You should have no doubts about the .... of your employer as regards your hours of work.
23. The time spent on travelling to your workplace and back is no longer required, so this saved time can be .... in different ways.
24. When you work from home, you can dress any which way you want; you do not need to stock up on .... clothes.
25. Since you do not have co-workers around, there is a sense of .... when you work from home.
26. There are many .... at home, so you need to impose some self-discipline.
27. When you work from home, there is a .... from information about what is going on in the company you work for, which means you are not up-to-date with all the details of what is happening at your work-place.

SECTION 3

Read the text below and answer questions 28 – 40

Questions 28 -35

The text has 8 SECTIONS, marked A to H. Choose the correct heading for each paragraph from the list of headings below.

i. Of matters inter-personal
ii. A dent in your self-confidence
iii. An all pervading presence in our lives
iv. Tension and pressure on the psyche
v. Good bye sweet dreams
vi. Looking ahead
vii. Loneliness and feelings of exclusion
viii. Despondency and dejection
ix. Facebook makes you feel inadequate

28. Paragraph A ....
29. Paragraph B ....
30. Paragraph C ....
31. Paragraph D ....
32. Paragraph E ....
33. Paragraph F ....
34. Paragraph G ....
35. Paragraph H ....

THE IMPACT OF SOCIAL MEDIA ON OUR LIVES

A. Three billion people, around 40% of the world's population, use online social media – and we're spending an average of two hours every day, sharing, liking, tweeting and updating on these platforms, according to some reports. That breaks down to around half a million tweets and Snapchat photos shared every minute.

With social media playing such a big part in our lives, could we be sacrificing our mental health and well-being as well as our time? What does the evidence actually suggest?
Since social media is relatively new to us, conclusive findings are limited. The research that does exist mainly relies on self-reporting, which can often be flawed, and the majority of studies focus on Facebook. That said, this is a fast-growing area of research, and clues are beginning to emerge. BBC Future reviewed the findings of some of the science so far.

B. People use social media to vent about everything from customer service to politics, but the downside to this is that our feeds often resemble an endless stream of stress. In 2015, researchers at the Pew Research Center based in Washington DC sought to find out if social media induces more stress than it relieves.

In the survey of 1,800 people, women reported being more stressed than men. Twitter was found to be a "significant contributor" because it increased their awareness of other people's stress.

But Twitter also acted as a coping mechanism – and the more women used it, the less stressed they were. The same effect wasn't found for men, whom the researchers said had a more distant relationship with social media. Overall, the researchers concluded that social media use was linked to "modestly lower levels" of stress.

C. Some studies have found a link between depression and social media use. Two studies involving more than 700 students found that depressive symptoms, such as low mood and feelings of worthlessness and hopelessness, were linked to the quality of online interactions. Researchers found higher levels of depressive symptoms among those who reported having more negative interactions.

However, scientists are also looking at how social media can be used to diagnose depression, which could help people receive treatment earlier. Researchers for Microsoft surveyed 476 people and analyzed their Twitter profiles for depressive language, linguistic style, engagement and emotion. From this, they developed a classifier that can accurately predict depression before it causes symptoms in seven out of 10 cases.

D. Humans used to spend their evenings in darkness, but now we're surrounded by artificial lighting all day and night. Research has found that this can inhibit the body's production of the hormone melatonin, which facilitates sleep – and blue light, which is emitted by smartphone and laptop screens, is said to be the worst culprit. In other words, if you lie on the pillow at night checking Facebook and Twitter, you're headed for restless slumber.

Last year, researchers from the University of Pittsburgh asked 1,700 18- to 30-year-olds about their social media and sleeping habits. They found a link with sleep disturbances – and concluded blue light had a part to play. How often they logged on, rather than time spent on social media sites, was a higher predictor of disturbed sleep.
The researchers say this could be caused by physiological arousal before sleep, and the bright lights of our devices can delay circadian rhythms.

E. Social media sites make more than half of users feel inadequate, according to a survey of 1,500 people by disability charity Scope, and half of 18- to 34-year-olds say it makes them feel unattractive.

A 2016 study by researchers at Penn State University suggested that viewing other people's selfies lowered self-esteem, because users compare themselves to photos of people looking their happiest. But it's not just selfies that have the potential to dent self-esteem. A study of 1,000 Swedish Facebook users found that women who spent more time on Facebook reported feeling less happy and confident. The researchers concluded: "When Facebook users compare their own lives with others' seemingly more successful careers and happy relationships, they may feel that their own lives are less successful in comparison."

F. Even the mere presence of a phone can interfere with our interactions, particularly when we're talking about something meaningful, according to one small study. Researchers writing in the Journal of Social and Personal Relationships tasked 34 pairs of strangers with having a 10-minute conversation about an interesting event that had happened to them recently. Each pair sat in private booths, and half had a mobile phone on the top of their table.

Those with a phone in eyeshot were less positive when recalling their interaction afterwards, had less meaningful conversations and reported feeling less close to their partner than the others, who had a notebook on top of the table instead.
Romantic relationships aren't immune, either. Researchers at the University of Guelph in Canada surveyed 300 people aged 17-24 in 2009 about any jealousy they felt when on Facebook, asking questions such as, 'How likely are you to become jealous after your partner has added an unknown member of the opposite sex?'.
Women spent much more time on Facebook than men, and experienced significantly more jealousy when doing so. The researchers concluded they "felt the Facebook environment created these feelings and enhanced concerns about the quality of their relationship".

G. A study published in the American Journal of Preventive Medicine last year surveyed 7,000 19- to 32-year-olds and found that those who spend the most time on social media were twice as likely to report experiencing social isolation, which can include a lack of a sense of social belonging, engagement with others and fulfilling relationships.
Spending more time on social media, the researchers said, could displace face-to-face interaction, and can also make people feel excluded.
"Exposure to such highly idealized representations of peers' lives may elicit feelings of envy and the distorted belief that others lead happier and more successful lives, which may increase perceived social isolation."

H. It's clear that in many areas, not enough is known yet to draw many strong conclusions. However, the evidence does point one way: social media affects people differently, depending on pre-existing conditions and personality traits.

As with food, gambling and many other temptations of the modern age, excessive use for some individuals is probably inadvisable. But at the same time, it would be wrong to say social media is a universally bad thing, because clearly it brings myriad benefits to our lives. Going ahead, we will explore these aspects more and more, and hopefully provide solutions that could help us all live a happier, healthier digital life.

Questions 36 – 40

Complete the following sentences using **NO MORE THAN TWO WORDS** from the text above.

36. .... is relatively recent and therefore it is not easy to be definite about the research-based findings.
37. Interestingly, while .... was found to be a cause of this emotional tension, its use was also effective in dealing with it, especially among women.
38. While social media does cause this psychological condition, it may also be used to..................... this condition, which could enable affected people to receive necessary remedial measures earlier.
39. People who spend a lot of time on social media have double the chances of a having a feeling of.......................
40. Although excessive use of social media is not good, it surely does bring.................. to our daily lives.

GT READING TEST 14

SECTION 1

Questions 1-14

Read the text below and answer Questions 1 – 7

10 CELL PHONE ETIQUETTE RULES YOU SHOULD BE FOLLOWING—BUT AREN'T

1. Put your phone away at the dinner table: This phone etiquette rule may seem obvious because, hello, it's rude, but being courteous in public to both your dining partner and other diners is important, says Amy Rice, Gadget Expert for Gazelle. Parenting, etiquette, and financial expert Brett Graff adds, "If it rings, and you must answer it, explain to your dining companions that your child is home by him or herself or that you're waiting for a huge business deal to close. Otherwise, ignore it," she says.

2. End phone conversations when paying for purchases: Just because you may not know the cashier doesn't mean you can keep chatting away while they're helping you. Unless it's an emergency, it's just rude to stay on the phone right in their face. These are the most annoying coffee shop habits, according to Starbucks baristas.

3. Never shout when talking on the phone: Can you hear me now? If they can't, maybe you should call them back later. When in public, it's a good phone etiquette practice to try not to raise your voice while on the phone. No one else needs to be privy to your conversations—or your arguments.

4. Never text or talk and drive: This is an obvious one. Many states have laws in place regarding texting and talking on the phone while driving. Hint: It's a big no-no. These are the warning signs that you could be a cell phone addict.

5. Avoid texting in work meetings: You don't want your boss looking up and seeing you texting away and completely ignoring what's going on. Plus, if you're the boss, it's setting a bad example for your workers.

6. Turn off the phone in places such as a church, temple, or theatre: There are no exceptions to this rule. There are just certain places where cell phones should be and often are off-limits. And remember, checking your phone and having it light up in a dark theatre—even if you don't talk, text, or Tweet—is just as rude.

7. Avoid talking on the phone in a waiting room, but if you must, leave the area first: Waiting rooms can be crowded and noisy—not exactly conducive to a phone call. If you must talk on the phone, Rice suggests leaving the area so as not to disturb your fellow waiting room occupants.

8. Avoid using a phone on public transportation: On public transportation, people are often stressed, rushing, or exhausted. All they want to do is get where they're going, not listen to your conversation about your cousin's new boyfriend's sister. "Be courteous when you are in public, enjoy the moment and your friends, but above all be smart about your smartphone manners," says Rice.

9. Lower your voice when using your phone in public: This phone etiquette guideline is a continuation of never shouting in public. Not only should you not shout, but you should automatically lower your voice. If you don't want to hear other people's phone conversations, they definitely don't want to hear yours either.

10. Don't take a call in the middle of a face-to-face conversation: "Cell phones can destroy all your interpersonal dealings," says Graff. "You should not even give the screen a glance while you're speaking to someone at a party or a dinner." Sometimes it's best to think of how would you feel if that happened to you? If it would bother you, then you probably shouldn't do it to someone else.

Questions 1 – 7

Do the following statements agree with the information given in the passage?

Write

YES	if the statement reflects the claims of the writer
NO	if the statement contradicts the claims of the writer
NOT GIVEN	if it is impossible to say what the writer thinks about this.

1. You are having dinner with your friends. The phone rings. It is okay to answer it, since friends will not mind.
2. Not only in front of a Starbucks cashier, but also at any other store, you should not use the phone while checking out.
3. If you have to text while driving, pull over and text instead of texting while driving.
4. If you do not mind listening to other people's conversation, it is okay that others can hear yours: it works both ways.
5. When in a place of worship, you can keep your phone on silent mode.
6. You are waiting your turn to see the doctor at his clinic. You get call from your office. It is an urgent call regarding a matter important to you. It is okay to talk softly from where you are sitting so that others are not disturbed.
7. If you are having a face to face conversation with someone, place your phone with the screen facing downwards so that you will not glance at it out of habit.

Read the text below and answer Questions 8 – 14

SOME WELL KNOWN PUBLIC SCHOOLS OF INDIA

A. Bishop Cotton School, Shimla, is the one of the oldest boarding schools in Asia, having been founded on 28th July, 1859, by Bishop George Edward Lynch Cotton, son of an Army Captain. A scholar of Westminster and a graduate of Cambridge, he was appointed Assistant Master at Rugby by Doctor Thomas Arnold, one of the founders of the British Public School system. It was the young Mr. Cotton who is spoken of as the "the model young master" in Thomas Hughes' famous book "Tom Brown's School Days" which gives an insight to school life at Rugby.

B. In 1957, an ageing English lady, Miss H. S. Oliphant, fired by the desire to create an equal educational platform for young Indian women in independent India, acquired a small estate from a Nawab in Dehradun to give shape to her dream. There were no funds, no staff, no school buildings and no students but a vision and an indomitable spirit. Under Miss Linnell's guidance 'Welham', named after a Welsh village, progressed rapidly and soon came to symbolize the qualities of independence, high scholastic standards and a progressive attitude, rooted in Indian tradition and culture.

C. Colonel Browns Cambridge School was founded in March 1926, by Col. and Mrs. Brown. It attracts students not only from all parts of India, but also from parents living abroad. An Irish man of repute, with an enviable record of distinguished service both in the sphere of education and the British Army, Col. William Brown retired from the Army but did not want to leave India, the country he had adopted, served and grown to love passionately.

D. The Lawrence School - Sanawar, established in 1847, situated at a height of 1750 meters and spread over an area of 139 acres, heavily forested with pine, deodar and other conifer trees, is the fruit of the vision of Sir Henry Lawrence, and his wife Honoria. Sanawar is a co-educational boarding school, affiliated to CBSE and has students of varying backgrounds from different parts of the sub-continent.

E. In November 1843, a fire broke out in a theatre at No. 10, Park Street, Kolkata. The fire that destroyed the theatre on that day rekindled another fire- the fire of education. Eventually that burnt out theatre became the home of an institution that redefined modern education. A small band of Belgium Jesuits opened their hearts and the doors of their abode at 10 Park Street on 16th January, 1860, to become what today stands as a symbol of quality education in the country, St, Xavier's School, Kolkata.

F. The Doon School specializes in all boys' boarding education for pupils aged 12 – 18. The school is probably the only 'All India 'school with applications from almost every state each year, as well as from Indian families overseas. Established in 1935, The Doon School is one of India's finest schools, with a strong intellectual heart-beat. The Doon School is a full boarding school and not simply a school which welcomes boarders.

G. It was more than a century ago that the Sisters of Charity of Jesus and Mary decided to start a boarding school at Dalhousie. History tell us that the choice of Dalhousie, a small hill station endowed with exquisite scenic beauty but remote and accessible only through narrow, dangerous hill roads by tonga and doli, was a daring adventure. As the years rolled on, the school expanded physically – the campus was enlarged, new buildings were erected, games fields were created and gardens laid out. The present extensive and attractive complex of the Sacred Heart School atop Potreyn hill is a living witness to its growth over the years.

Questions 8-14

Look at the following statements and the different schools below.
Match each statement with the correct section, A-G.
NB: You may use any letter more than once.

8. All she had was a dogged passion for her dream.
9. This boarding school does not take in girls.
10. This co-ed school in the hills has a lot of trees on its campus.
11. The character in a well-known book is based upon the founder of this school.
12. The founder of this school did not want to leave his adopted country.
13. This school started out in the ruins of a theatre.
14. When first established, the route to this school was not easy.

SECTION 2

Read the text below and answer 15– 27

Questions 15 – 21

A MUSEUM OF FAILED ROMANCE

A. I recently popped in to visit the Museum of Broken Relationships in Zagreb, Croatia. It was a pilgrimage of sorts, as I'd been intrigued by rave reviews of the museum and the fact that in 2011 it won the Kenneth Hudson European Museum of the Year award for "the most unusual, daring and, perhaps, controversial achievement that challenges common perceptions of the role of the museums in society." Friends found it strange that I went with my husband, Jim, but I think he enjoyed it too. And we are still together.

B. The inspiration for the museum came from two artists who began the museum after their own relationship unravelled. They're fascinated by the role that things, the ordinary stuff of life, play in a relationship—and when that relationship ends. Each of the objects are mute witnesses to better and happier times, silent, but loaded with meaning. Even the most banal object has a story to tell.

C. The objects in the museum, sent in by ex-lovers around the world, are definitely banal, including a garden gnome, a prosthetic leg, and lots of stuffed toys, a few clocks, a hand axe, deodorant, and pink fluffy handcuffs. And yet, disparate as the articles are, what unites them is the power of a story. We should never forget that people are at the centre of all museums, from the visitors to the people who made, used, cherished, or discarded the objects we show. These things, then, are always loaded with meaning—with a narrative—and each object in the Museum of Broken Relationships tell a story of pleasure and pain through the narrative of romance.

D. I wasn't prepared for what a cathartic place it is. The act of releasing a memento to the museum seems to be the final step in dispatching a terminated relationship. The labels, written by the donors, are sometimes long and introspective—meditations on romantic meltdowns. Others are delightfully direct: "A gift from S.K. from 1987. She loved antiquities—as long as things were old and didn't work. That is precisely the reason why we're not together anymore." Another favourite: "The prosthesis endured longer than our love. It was made of sturdier material!"

E. The visit made me recall the old vacuum cleaner in my closet. It is all I have left from a fiancé of more than 20 years ago and represents a moment of triumph for me since he really coveted that vacuum cleaner—but I took it with me when I left.

Questions 15-17

Match each statement with the correct paragraph, A to E. You may mention a paragraph more than once or not at all.

15. The items in the museum may be dissimilar, but conjoined by a common theme.
16. The author did not expect that the visit would give her a sense of release from her past.
17. Every object in the museum had seen their owners in more convivial times.

Questions 18-21

Fill up the blanks below using **NOT MORE THAN ONE WORD** from the text:

18. This museum was very different from other museums. It questioned what we generally understood to be the purpose of museums; hence it .... me.
19. Even the most .... item in the museum had a story.
20. Museums may display all kinds of things, be it paintings or sculptures or anything else, but each of these exhibits has a .... behind them.
21. If I were to send an item to this museum, it would be an item lying in my..................

Read the text below and answer Questions 22 – 27

FOUR WAYS TO MANAGE A DIFFICULT BOSS

You've heard it time and time again. People don't leave a company — they leave their immediate superior in the hierarchy. According to one Gallup study 50% of employees left their job "to get away from their manager to improve their overall life at some point in their career". Fifty percent! But what if you aren't ready to leave your job just yet? There are ways to manage a difficult boss; just tread carefully.

As a career coach, I advise my clients to keep their emotions in check when dealing with their manager. Normally I'm an advocate for speaking up, but in this situation, please proceed with caution. You don't want to burn any bridges. Not only do you need to deal with this person on a near daily basis, you may need the reference down the road.

If you aren't ready to leave your current job just yet, there are ways to make your work life more tolerable. Whatever your reason for sticking around (for now), here are four ways to manage a difficult boss.

1. **Practice mindfulness**. Incorporating mindfulness at work can be a game changer. It drastically lowers stress levels, which is critical when dealing with a difficult boss. Practice focusing on the present moment. This means not dwelling on what your boss said to you yesterday, or worrying about what she might say tomorrow. Another mindfulness tip is to focus on your breathing. The next time your boss says something that is about to throw you into a tailspin, sit and practice deep breathing. Inhale through your nose, hold briefly, and exhale out your mouth. Repeat until you feel calmer. Simple exercises like these will help you keep your cool and allow you to look at things with a clearer head.

2. **Empathy and Sympathy.** While this step may feel difficult, try to be the bigger person and reflect on what your boss might be going through. Is she dealing with a difficult manager or under extreme stress, or not being shown compassion for a difficult situation at home? Perhaps there's something going on in her personal life that is affecting how she handles things at work. Practicing empathy can help you understand her perspective and perhaps even realize that her behaviour towards you isn't personal.

3. **Take responsibility.** Is your boss bringing everyone else on the team down, or is she mainly focused on you? If you notice that you're the only person that has a negative relationship with your boss, resulting in inimical interactions all the time, take a step back and ask yourself how it got that way. Did something unfavourable happen that you can take responsibility for? If that's

the case, step up and rectify the situation right away. If it isn't the case, go ahead and vent...just don't do it inside of the office.

4. **Vent outside of the office.** It's healthy, normal, and totally necessary to process your emotions, especially when you're under constant stress. Otherwise, you may find yourself with pent-up anger, ready to blow at any moment. Release all the anxiousness caused by the feelings by talking it out with a friend or family member, and then let those feelings go. This will make you more pleasant to be around, and you'll have a greater capacity to handle whatever your boss throws your way. Whatever you do, don't unleash the drama on your colleagues; that's how rumours start.

Dealing with a difficult boss is no joke. If you've practiced these techniques and still find your boss to be intolerable, brush up your resume and consider leaving ASAP. Staying in a toxic work environment, exercising restraint all the time isn't worth it. The last thing you want to do is compromise your sanity or your health.

The next time you find yourself in a tough situation with your manager, remember that while you can't control your boss, you can control how you react.

Questions 22-27

Choose any of the words from the text given in the box below to fill in the blanks.

22. There are several ways in which you can .... a difficult boss.
23. When you are interacting with your manager, you have to keep your .... under control.
24. At times, if you think through the situation with ...., you may come to the conclusion that your boss does not have anything personal against you.
25. If you have a difficult boss, try to figure out if you are the centre of his attention and are you the sole individual with whom he has................... vibes.
26. When you have a difficult boss, it is quite natural to get emotional with all the .... of the workplace.
27. There will be times when you will be in a difficult situation vis-à-vis your immediate supervisor; while you cannot forecast what he or she will do or say, you must ensure that you maintain .... over your reactions.

sentiments	**sympathy**	**restraint**	**pressures**
intensities	**compassion**	**industry**	**contrary**
dominate	**anger**	**control**	**jaundiced**
handle	**insight**	**adverse**	**oversight**

SECTION 3

Read the text below and answer questions 28 – 40

Questions 28 - 32

The text below has 5 SECTIONS, marked A to E. Choose the correct heading for each paragraph from the list of headings below.

i. Growing their lineage
ii. Matters related to gender
iii. A normal work-day
iv. Of grey matters
v. The basics
vi. Height, weight and color
vii. Dietary habits

28. Paragraph A ....
29. Paragraph B ....
30. Paragraph C ....
31. Paragraph D ....
32. Paragraph E ....

CHIMPANZEES

A. Chimpanzees are a species of apes that are most closely related to humans. Chimpanzees inhabit tropical forests and savannahs of equatorial Africa. Individuals vary considerably in size and appearance, but chimpanzees stand approximately 1–1.7 meters tall when erect and weigh about 32–60 kg. Males tend to be larger and more robust than females. Chimpanzees are covered by a coat of brown or black hair, but their faces are bare except for a short white beard. Skin colour is generally white except for the face, hands, and feet, which are black. The faces of younger animals may be pinkish or whitish. Among older males and females, the forehead often becomes bald and the back becomes grey.

B. Chimpanzees awaken at dawn, and their day is spent both on trees and on the ground. After a lengthy midday rest, late afternoon is usually the most intensive feeding period. In the trees, where most feeding takes place, chimps use their hands and feet to move about. They also leap and swing by their arms skilfully from branch to branch. Movement over any significant distance usually takes place on the ground. Though able to walk upright, chimpanzees more often move about on all fours, leaning forward on the knuckles of their hands. Chimpanzees are unable to swim, but they will wade in water. The chimpanzee diet is primarily vegetarian and consists of mostly fruits, berries, leaves, blossoms and seeds, but also bird eggs and chicks. They also appear to use certain plants medicinally to cure diseases and expel intestinal parasites. At night they usually sleep in the trees in nests they build of branches and leaves.

C. The female chimpanzee bears a single young at any time of year after a gestation period of about eight months. The new-born weighs about 1.8 kg, is almost helpless, and clings to the fur of the mother's belly as she moves. From about 6 months to 2 years, the youngster rides on the mother's back. Weaning takes place at about 5 years. Males are considered adults at 16 years of age, and females usually begin to reproduce at about 13 years, but often only two offspring survive during her lifetime. The longevity of chimps is about 45 years in the wild and 58 in captivity; however, older individuals have been documented. For example, Cheetah the chimpanzee, an animal actor from the Tarzan movies of the 1930s and '40s, was reported to have lived approximately 80 years.

D. Chimpanzees are highly social and live in loose and flexible groups known as communities or unit groups that are based on associations between adult males within a home range, or territory. A community can number from 20 or fewer to well over 100 members. Social dominance exists, with adult males being dominant over adult females and adolescent males. Within a community, there are twice or three times as many adult females as adult males; the number of adults is about equal to the number of immature individuals. The dominance hierarchy among male chimpanzees is very fluid; individuals associate with each other and join and leave different subgroups with complete freedom. The alpha male of a group can monopolize ovulating females through possessive behaviour. On the other hand, gang attack by subordinate males can expel an alpha male. Males spend all of their lives in the community they are born in, but occasionally a juvenile male may transfer to another community with his mother. In contrast to males, most females leave their group of birth to join a neighbouring group when they mature at around age 11. Female chimpanzees spend most of their time with their young or with other females. Females have been known to form coalitions against a bullying adult male or newly immigrated female

E. Chimpanzees are highly intelligent and are able to solve many kinds of problems posed to them by human trainers and experimenters. A number of researchers have taught chimpanzees to use sign language or languages based on the display of tokens or pictorial symbols. Communication between chimps in the wild takes the form of facial expressions, gestures, and a large array of vocalizations, including screams, hoots, grunts, and roars. Males display excitement by standing erect, stamping or swaying, and letting out a chorus of screams. Chimps use louder calls and gestures for long-distance communication (such as drumming on tree buttresses) and quieter calls and facial expressions for short-distance communication. Chimpanzees "fish" for termites and ants with probes made of grass stalks, vines, branches, peeled bark, and midribs of leaves. They crack hard nuts open by using stones, roots, and wood as hammers or anvils, and they use "leafy sponges" (a handful of folded leaves or moss) to drink water. Branches and leaves are detached and displayed during courtship. Chimpanzees' intelligence, responsiveness, and exuberance have made them ideal nonhuman subjects for psychological, medical, and biological experiments. Young chimpanzees can become very attached to their human trainers, and their expressions of feeling resemble those of humans more closely than any other animal.

Questions 33 -37

Do the following statements agree with the information given in the text?

In boxes on your answer sheet, write

TRUE	if the statement agrees with the information
FALSE	if the statement contradicts the information
NOT GIVEN	if there is no information on this.

33. Chimpanzees are adept at swinging skilfully from branch to branch, and can also walk on the ground. When they have to move over long distances, they prefer the former approach.
34. Chimpanzees are pure vegetarians.
35. A baby chimpanzee starts eating food other than its mother's milk only after about 5 years.
36. Chimpanzees found in the savannahs of Equatorial Africa do not live as long as those captured or reared by humans.
37. The dominating male in a group can be ousted by other males joining forces against him.

Questions 38 -40

Complete the following sentences using **NOT MORE THAN 2 WORDS** from the text above:

38. Chimpanzees can walk on their two legs, but you are likely to find them moving around on...................... when on the ground.

39. If a female chimpanzee transfers herself from one chimpanzee group to another, her......................... son may also move with her.

40. Transmission and receipt of messages between chimpanzees take various forms, including............................

GT READING TEST 15

SECTION 1

Questions 1-14

Read the text below and answer Questions 1 – 7

GENERATING SOLAR POWER

Many power plants today use fossil fuels as a heat source to boil water. The steam from the boiling water rotates a large turbine, which activates a generator that produces electricity. However, new generations of power plants, with concentrating solar power systems, use the sun as a heat source. There are three main types of concentrating solar power systems: parabolic-trough, dish/engine, and power tower.

Parabolic-trough systems concentrate the sun's energy through long rectangular, curved (U-shaped) mirrors. These mirrors are tilted toward the sun, focusing sunlight on a pipe that runs down the centre of the trough. This heats the oil flowing through the pipe. The hot oil is then used to boil water in a conventional steam generator to produce electricity.

A dish/engine system uses a mirrored dish (similar to a very large satellite dish). The dish-shaped surface collects and concentrates the sun's heat onto a receiver, which absorbs the heat and transfers it to a fluid within the engine. The heat causes the fluid to expand against a piston or turbine to produce mechanical power. The mechanical power is then used to run a generator or alternator to produce electricity.

A power tower system uses a large field of mirrors to concentrate sunlight onto the top of a tower, where a receiver sits. This heats molten salt flowing through the receiver. Then, the salt's heat is used to generate electricity through a conventional steam generator. Molten salt retains heat efficiently, so it can be stored for days before being converted into electricity. That means electricity can be produced on cloudy days or even several hours after sunset.

Questions 1 – 7

Complete the following sentences using NOT MORE THAN ONE WORD from the text.

1. In many power plants, when water is boiled, the .... that emanates is used to move other equipment in a certain sequence to generate electricity.
2. In the generation of solar power, there are many ways of concentrating the power of the sun; this article discusses the .... most common ones.
3. When U shaped mirrors are used, the sun's rays first heats .... running in a pipe.
4. When a contraption which looks something like a .... dish is used, the heat generated by the sun's rays is concentrated on to a receptacle device.
5. If you see a lot of .... in a solar power generating system, the receiver of the sun-rays will be on top of a **6.** ....
7. Unlike the other systems, if there is a large filed of mirrors in a solar power generating system, what is heated by the sun is .... in its liquid form.

Read the text below and answer Questions 8 – 14

ABOUT DOLPHINS

Here are 10 fascinating dolphin facts that will make you love them even more.

1. Nearly 40 species of dolphins swim the waters of the world. Most live in shallow areas of tropical and temperate oceans, and five species live in rivers.
2. Dolphins are carnivores. Fish, squid and crustaceans are included in their list of prey. A 260-pound dolphin eats about 33 pounds of fish a day.
3. Known for their playful behaviour, dolphins are highly intelligent. They are as smart as apes, and the evolution of their larger brains is surprisingly similar to humans.
4. Dolphins are part of the family of whales that includes orcas and pilot whales. Killer whales are actually dolphins.
5. Dolphins are very social, living in groups that hunt and even play together. Large pods of dolphins can have 1,000 members or more.
6. Depending on the species, gestation takes nine to 17 months. After birth, dolphins are surprisingly maternal. They have been observed nestling and cuddling their young.
7. A dolphin calf nurses for up to two years. Calves stay with the mothers anywhere from three to eight years.
8. Dolphins have acute eyesight both in and out of the water. They hear frequencies 10 times the upper limit of adult humans. Their sense of touch is well-developed, but they have no sense of smell.
9. Dolphins have few natural enemies. Humans are their main threat. Pollution, fishing and hunting mean some dolphin species have an uncertain future. In 2006, the Yangtze River dolphin was named functionally extinct.
10. Because dolphins are mammals, they need to come to the surface of the water to breathe. Unlike land mammals that breathe and eat through their mouths, dolphins have separate holes for each task. Dolphins eat through their mouths and breathe through their blowholes. This prevents the dolphin from sucking up water into the lungs when hunting, reducing the risk of drowning.

Questions 8 -14

Complete the following sentences using the most appropriate words given in the box below.

8. Most dolphins live in parts of the ocean which are not very ....
9. In their eating habits, we find that dolphins do not eat ....
10. Dolphins are another kind of whales; they are very smart and very .... by nature.
11. Dolphins love to interact with one another; they live in communities, ... and frolicking around.
12. A dolphin, once ...., gives birth anywhere between 9 to17 months.
13. Dolphins have no sense of smell; as regards their ...., it is very sharp.
14. Because of the threat from humans, it is not very sure how long some species of dolphins will ....

shallow	survive	touch	mutton
feeding	subsist	bottomless	pregnant
vision	lively	foraging	intelligent
vegetables	incubated	deep	

SECTION 2

Read the text below and answer Questions 15 – 27

Questions 15 – 21

ALL ABOUT BEES

ANATOMY

The body of the bee comprises of three major sections, the head, thorax and abdomen. Bees have three pairs of legs, the forelegs, middle legs and the hind legs. Two protrusions in front of the bee's head are its antennae, which are used for touch, smell and taste. The very last tip of the abdomen is where the stinger of the bee is located.

TYPES OF BEES

BUMBLE BEES are large furry looking black and yellow bees. They are social and generally build their nests underground. Bumble bees are important pollinators of certain crops and ornamental plants. They will sting aggressively when their nest is disturbed.

EUROPEAN HONEY BEES are about one inch long and are brown with black encircling their abdomen, giving them a subtle striped appearance. Africanized honey bees are slightly smaller than European honey bees, but it's impossible to tell them apart on appearance alone.

CARPENTER BEES are often seen hovering around flowers or near buildings. Very large and black, the hovering bees are usually males, which cannot sting and are harmless. Carpenter bees build burrows in exposed dry wood but generally cause little damage.

INSECTS RESEMBLING BEES

PAPER WASPS build relatively small, umbrella-like nests under the eaves of houses, attic rafters, etc. They feed on many species of pest insects and are therefore beneficial. They will sting if provoked.

MUD DAUBERS are solitary wasps make tube-like nests out of mud, often attached to walls or overhangs. They feed on spiders and are not particularly aggressive

YELLOWJACKETS, commonly seen around picnics, build nests both above ground and in the ground. The aerial species are non-aggressive and eat many insects. The ground nesting type will attack to defend their nests.

DIGGER WASPS/SAND WASPS These non-aggressive wasps closely resemble yellow-jackets and build their nests in sandy soil. There is only one wasp per nest. They feed on beetle grubs, which are lawn pests.

Bees sting to defend their hive. Bees generally do not sting without provocation, since worker bees die after stinging. Africanized honey bees are more aggressive when defending their hive. They will sting with less provocation, in greater numbers, and are more persistent, therefore making them a greater public health concern.

FIRST AID FOR BEE STINGS

Remove stinger quickly by scraping with a fingernail or edge of a dull thin object. • Clean the sting with soap and water. • Apply an ice pack to the wound. • Monitor the sting for any unusual swelling or systemic reaction. If you are allergic to bee stings, or experience breathing difficulties, seek professional medical care immediately!

Questions 15-18

Name the body parts of a bee in the picture below:

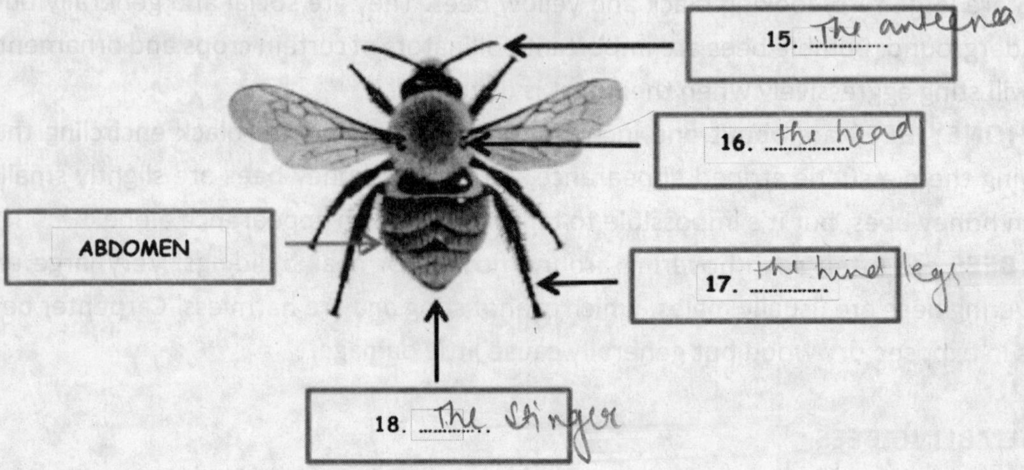

Questions 19 – 21

Do the following statements agree with the information given in the text.

Write:

TRUE	If the statement agrees with the information
FALSE	If the statement contradicts the information
NOT GIVEN	If there is no information on this.

19. A worker bee will sting repeatedly in order to protect its hive. T
20. Yellow jackets and sand wasps resemble each other. T
21. Several sand wasps will build a nest to live together. F

Read the text below and answer Questions 22 – 27

ANIMALS IN CAPTIVITY

Animals in zoos, pseudo-sanctuaries, traveling shows, and roadside displays are forced to spend their lives behind bars just to entertain the public.

Living conditions are often dismal, with animals confined to tiny, filthy, barren enclosures. Even the best artificial environments can't come close to matching the space, diversity, and freedom that animals want and need. This deprivation—combined with relentless boredom, loneliness, and sometimes even abuse from the people who are supposed to be caring for them—causes many captive animals to lose their minds. This condition, called "zoochosis" is so rampant, that some zoos administer antidepressants and antipsychotics to try to curb the abnormal behaviour.

Scam Shelters: The number of roadside zoos that have tacked on the word "sanctuary" or "rescue" to their names has skyrocketed in recent years. Kind people are naturally drawn to places that claim to rescue animals and offer them sanctuary, but many of these outfits are nothing more than breeders, dealers, and exhibitors exploiting the public's goodwill and generosity.

The fundamental purpose of any legitimate animal sanctuary is to provide animals with safe, comfortable living conditions that give them as natural an existence as captivity allows. No legitimate animal sanctuary breeds or sells animals. No reputable exotic-animal sanctuary allows any kind of "hands-on" interaction, and that includes taking photos with animals or taking them out on the road for public display.

Drive-Through Safaris: While drive-through safaris or wildlife parks may seem like a better alternative, many of these facilities breed animals continuously, because baby animals attract customers. But babies grow up quickly, and older, unwanted animals may be warehoused like inventory or quietly shipped out. Since paper trails are notoriously inaccurate and difficult to follow, it's nearly impossible to know how many "surplus" animals end up at auctions, in slaughterhouses, or on hunting ranches.

Traveling and Petting Zoos: Animals used in traveling zoos are subjected to the stresses of transport, strange and frightening environments, irregular feeding and watering, mishandling, and extensive public contact. The sheer logistics of getting from one venue to the next does not allow for much downtime to let animals rest or exercise or to enable caretakers to attend to sick or injured animals. It's impossible to know how many animals suffer and die en route, because zoo caravans are constantly on the move, and for the most part, no one is watching. The U.S.

Department of Agriculture (USDA) oversees animal displays, but with just over 100 officers responsible for inspecting more than 8,600 licensees, who are simply not enough to monitor all exhibitors adequately.

Forced to interact with crowds of people all day long, animals used in petting zoos may not get enough food, water, and rest. Some snap. Many children and adults have been seriously injured by tigers, primates, and other animals that are used as props in photo shoots.

What You Can Do: Don't pass a few hours at a place where animals will languish in misery long after you've gone home. Please don't buy a ticket. Instead, explain to your children why your family does not support cruelty to animals.
(Adapted from: https://www.peta.org/issues/animals-in-entertainment/zoos-pseudo-sanctuaries/)

Questions 22-27

Fill up the blanks in the following summary of the article above, using **ONE WORD ONLY** from the text.

Animals that are kept for the entertainment of humans live in very bleak conditions. Their living spaces are often small and dirty and do not give them the heterogeneous environment or the 22.................... they yearn for. This has an adverse psychological impact on them, and the way they behave becomes 23..................... Many of the establishments which call themselves sanctuaries and say they rescue animals, actually 24................ and exhibit animals. Open spaces, where people board a vehicle to watch animals, seem to be more animal friendly. However, since visitors prefer to see 25.................... animals, these outfits are always in a breeding mode, with the older ones being disposed of. The USDA, which oversees animal displays, does not have 26........................ manpower. What we can do is to discourage these establishments by not visiting them, and thus ensure we do not, in any way, 27....................... the ill treatment of animals.

SECTION 3
Read the text below and answer questions 28 – 40
Questions 28 - 34

The text has 7 SECTIONS, marked A to G. Choose the correct heading for each paragraph from the list of headings below.

i. Working harder won't get what you need
ii. Burnout sneaks upon you
iii. It's not selfish to be selfish
iv. First, admit to the problem
v. Therapy helps
vi. There is no permanent cure
vii. When being productive equals self-worth
viii. About my job
ix. My detailed symptoms

28. Paragraph A ....
29. Paragraph B ....
30. Paragraph C ....
31. Paragraph D ....
32. Paragraph E ....
33. Paragraph F ....
34. Paragraph G ....

I WAS A BURNED-OUT WORKAHOLIC FOR 20 YEARS—TILL THIS CHANGED EVERYTHING

I've always been a hard worker and, I admit it, an overachiever. Yet I was shocked when I was diagnosed as a workaholic. Here's how I got healthy again.

A. We live in a time where the 'go big or go home' mentality reigns, including at work. In order to feel good about yourself, you have to be constantly productive - and that was the trap I had fallen into. It leads to burnout, which clinically speaking is exhaustion, depression, and anxiety. It's a mental health problem becoming increasingly common in western countries.

B. The symptoms of burnout are incremental. They start small and are easy to ignore as just part of the normal stress that comes with modern life. But the longer you dismiss them, the worse the burnout symptoms get. For me, what started as minor headaches, irritation at inefficiency, and difficulty concentrating soon turned into sleeping only a couple hours a night, a resting heart rate of 140 (normal is between 60 and 100 beats per minute), and snap judgments about other people.

C. I spent most of my career as a government policy executive. I tried hard to be a caring boss and easy-to-work-with colleague, to go beyond what was asked, and to be as helpful as I could to everyone. But I didn't realize the sacrifices I was making in my health, happiness, and relationships to do it.
When things got tough, I just did more of what had always worked for me in the past. I worked longer and harder. But I didn't realize that this wasn't sustainable. I lost the capacity to even see that working harder was actually bringing me fewer of the emotional rewards I usually got from doing a good job.

D. When I finally went to see my doctor about my lack of energy and health issues, she diagnosed me with exhaustion, anxiety, depression, and workaholism. I now understand that what I thought was normal—the adrenaline rush from helping others and from checking something off my to-do list—are, indeed, clear indicators of workaholism. Workaholics feel inner pressure to work beyond what's reasonable, to the point where their health and relationships suffer.
At first, I followed my doctor's advice, but I didn't really take it to heart. I made some small changes and I started to feel better, and then returned to work as soon as she let me. That's when I relapsed into burnout. Unless you accept you have a situation to resolve and do the deeper, inner work to change your unhealthy patterns, you're just going to repeat them.

E. After the second burnout, I finally realized I needed to change my habits. I went on sick leave, took anti-anxiety/antidepressant medication, did kundalini yoga, and tried to recreate what had formerly been fun for me. Most importantly, I worked with a cognitive behavioural therapist to understand what motivated me to keep working regardless of how it was hurting me. Through CBT, I figured out what drives me, what my priorities are, and how it's important to say no and set boundaries in order to achieve those priorities. I now give myself credit for my achievements, big and small. I'm much better at living in the moment rather than focusing on the next items on my to-do list or dwelling on what I've just done that didn't go perfectly.

F. That was the lesson I truly needed to learn: Putting myself first. It's something you hear every time you get on a plane: Put on your own oxygen mask first, before you try to help anyone else. Basically, if you want to be good at taking care of others, you need to be happy and healthy yourself first. And you're the only person who can do that for yourself.

G. Like alcoholism, I'll always be at risk of relapsing into my workaholic ways. I still fight the "shoulds"—that I should be working or should be more productive. But I'm much more aware of my habits and choices and I now listen to what my body is telling me.
The best part is that I'm better at what I do, now when I give myself breaks. Along with deadlines and meetings, I schedule exercise and fun stuff too. With regular effort, I'm now able to stay well. I just remember the secret to being the productive, helpful, and kind person I want to be—taking care of myself first.

Questions 35 – 40

Complete the following sentences using **NOT MORE THAN ONE WORD** from the text for each answer.

35. I had be performing well all the time in order to feel good, but this ultimately led to a ....
36. When burnout happens, one feels tired and worries a lot; it actually is the .... of your mind that has been adversely affected.
37. In the initial stages, there are small, seemingly minor signs, and then, in .... steps, burnout assumes larger proportions.
38. When I started experiencing the initial, my response was to put in even more effort over more hours of work; little did I know that this was not ....
39. In order to address my situation, what I had to change were my ....
40. .... helped me to identify what motivated me and how I chose the sequence of tasks I did.

GT READING TEST 16

SECTION 1
Questions 1 – 13
Read the text below and answer Questions 1 – 6

Six Classical Dances of India

Dance is an ancient and celebrated cultural tradition in India. Folk dances abound all across the country, and huge crowds of people can be found dancing at festivals and weddings. Here are six of the most important classical dance forms of India.

Bharatanatyam: Bharatanatyam is a dance of Tamil Nadu in southern India. It traces its origins back to the Natyashastra, an ancient treatise on theatre written by the mythic priest Bharata. Originally a temple dance for women, bharatanatyam is often used to express Hindu religious stories and devotions. It was not commonly seen on the public stage until the 20th century. The dance movements are characterized by bent legs, while feet keep rhythm. Hands may be used in a series of mudras, or symbolic hand gestures, to tell a story.

Kathakali: Kathakali comes from south-western India, around the state of Kerala. Like bharatanatyam, kathakali is a religious dance. It draws inspiration from the Ramayana and stories from Shaiva traditions. Kathakali is traditionally performed by boys and men, even for female roles. The costumes and makeup are especially elaborate, with faces made to look like painted masks and enormous headdresses.

Kathak: A dance of northern India, Kathak is often a dance of love. It is performed by both men and women. The movements include intricate footwork accented by bells worn around the ankles and stylized gestures adapted from normal body language. It was originated by Kathakas, professional storytellers who used a mixture of dance, song, and drama. Like other Indian dances it began as a temple dance, but soon moved into the courts of ruling houses.

Manipuri: Manipuri comes from Manipur in north-eastern India. It has its roots in that state's folk traditions and rituals, and often depicts scenes from the life of the god Krishna. Unlike some of the other, more rhythmic dances, Manipuri is characterized by smooth and graceful movements. Female roles are especially fluid in the arms and hands, while male roles tend to have more forceful movements. The dance may be accompanied by narrative chanting and choral singing.

Kuchipudi: Unlike the other styles mentioned, kuchipudi requires talent in both dancing and singing. This dance, from the state of Andhra Pradesh in south-eastern India, is highly ritualized, with a formalized song-and-dance introduction, sprinkling of holy water, and burning of incense, along with invocations of goddesses. Traditionally the dance was performed by men, even the female roles, although now it is predominantly performed by women.

Odissi: Odissi is indigenous to Orissa in eastern India. It is predominantly a dance for women, with postures that replicate those found in temple sculptures. Based on archaeological findings, odissi is believed to be the oldest of the surviving Indian classical dances. Odissi is a very complex and expressive dance, with over fifty mudras (symbolic hand gestures) commonly used.

Questions 1 – 6

The six dance forms are given in the text above in bold and underlined letter. Match each statement below to the appropriate dance form. Use **ONE WORD ONLY** for each answer

1. This dance depicts incidents from the life of Krishna. ....
2. The females you see dancing are actually males. ....
3. This dance will remind you of the various poses you may have seen chiseled on the walls of temples. ....
4. This dance form is based on a discourse written by someone who may not have even existed. ....
5. To perform this dance, not only do you have to know how to dance, but also have the ability to sing. ....
6. A dance of love, performed in durbars. ....:...

Read the text below and answer Questions 7 – 13

HISTORY OF WRITING IMPLEMENTS - TOOLS FOR WRITING

Writing is one of the most important inventions of humanity. It allowed us to record our history, ideas and discoveries and spread them across the globe for all to know.

The earliest writing tools were made to be rigid so they could engrave texts into different materials. The Chinese, for instance, carved into turtle shells. Ancient Sumerians and Babylonians used a triangular stylus to write on soft clay tablets which would be later baked. Romans wrote on wax tablets with styluses which allowed them to erase written text. Clay tablets were heavy and brittle. Wax tablets were not heat resistant. Therefore, people tried to find other solutions.

Scribes of Ancient Egypt used reed pens which were made from a single reed straw, cut and shaped into a point. Papyrus was used as a surface to write with these pens. Reed pens didn't last long when used and were too stiff so they were replaced with quills. Quills are pens made from flight feathers of large birds. Different materials were used to be written on with quills, like parchment and vellum.

The popularity of quills lasted until 19th century when the first pens with metal nibs appeared. John Mitchell from Birmingham was the first to mass-produce pens with metal nibs in 1822. These had a handle and a metal point with a split that held a small amount of ink when dipped. They worked the same as quills but lasted much longer, didn't need to be sharpened and could be made to a much finer point.

Bartholomew Folsch received a patent in England for a pen with an ink reservoir in 1809. French Government patented a fountain pen in May 1827 which was an invention of Romanian Petrache Poenaru. The ballpoint pen was invented in 1888, by John J. Loud and improved by Laszlo Biro in 1938, which attained commercial success.

Slavoljub Eduard Penkala invented the mechanical pencil in 1906 and the first solid-ink fountain pen in 1907. Felt-tipped pen, which came before markers and highlighters, was an invention of Yukio Horie from Japan. Roller ball pen, which uses water-based ink, appeared in 1963, also in Japan. We still use pens and pencils today for writing and drawing as well as styluses, but those just on touch screens.

Questions 7 – 13

Do the following statements agree with the information given in the text?

In boxes on your answer sheet, write

TRUE	if the statement agrees with the information
FALSE	if the statement contradicts the information
NOT GIVEN	if there is no information on this.

7. Among writing tools, hard tools preceded other tools like quills and reed pens.
8. Wax was the best surface to write on as whatever was written could be erased.
9. Parchment, vellum and papyrus were surfaces used to write upon.
10. The first pens with metal nibs were made in 1822 by John Mitchell from Birmingham.
11. The ball point pens invented by John Loud did not sell as well as those made by Laszlo Biro.
12. The mechanical pencil and the solid ink fountain pen were invented by the same person.
13. Markers and highlighters were invented by Yukio Horie from Japan.

SECTION 2

Read the text below and answer Questions 14 – 27

Questions 14 – 20

ANT COLONIES

A. Ant hills are familiar sights. However, these mounds are not actually ant colonies. Instead, they mark the entrance and exit to the colony. These mounds are made up of the dirt, sand and other material the ants must remove as they dig the underground tunnels and chambers in which they nest. In fact, most ant colonies stretch deep underground, some even as deep as 25 feet.

B. In terms of social organization, ant colonies are typically home to three different types of ants. The queen ant is both the founder and leader of the colony. Her primary function is to populate the colony by laying thousands of eggs. The queen's chambers are located deep within the ant colony as a protection against predators. Queen ants live much longer than the drones and workers who serve her—in some species up to 30 years. They sport wings and are much larger than the average ant encountered outside the colony.

C. Drones are male ants whose only function is to mate with the queen so she can lay her eggs. Drones die as soon as they've fulfilled this function and are rarely encountered outside the colony. Most ants are females, and nearly every ant encountered outside of the nest is a female. Worker ants are females, but unlike the queen, they don't lay eggs. Instead, they're responsible for building and maintaining the nest, protecting the colony from other ants and, most importantly, feeding the colony. Workers forage for, gather and allocate food, making sure the queen's offspring will grow to fulfill their responsibilities to the colony.

D. Ant colonies generally tend to live as long as their queen, if not longer. Therefore the average lifespan of an ant colony is specific to the species of the ant. Some of the worst ant pests are fire ants and carpenter ants. Fire ants are an aggressive and invasive species that can be very harmful to livestock and even humans, especially children. Fire ant queens can live—and lay more than 1,000 eggs a day—for as long as seven years. Carpenter ants build their colonies in wooden structures and can cause significant damage to your home.

E. The average population of an ant colony also depends upon the species of ant. Fire ant colonies can be home to tens of thousands of ants. Like some other species, fire ants can even form what are called super-colonies. These are actually cooperative networks of multiple nests, queens, workers, etc. Super-colonies can cover territories spanning miles and be home to millions of ants.

F. Carpenter ant colonies tend to be somewhat smaller, and their populations grow more gradually. Also, carpenter ant colonies tend to support only a single queen. Odorous house ants, or stink ants (if stepped on or otherwise squashed release a sickly sweet smell compared to rotten coconuts) often forage for the sugary foods they prefer inside human dwellings. Like fire ants, their colonies can be home to multiple queens. These ants also move often, setting up many temporary nests that make it very difficult to estimate the exact number of ants in the colony proper.

Questions 14 - 17

Match each statement with the correct paragraph, A to F. You may mention a paragraph more than once or not at all.

14. The ant that you see walking across your bathroom floor is most likely to be a female.
15. Some ant colonies may have more than one queen.
16. Ants do not live in ant hills.
17. Mating causes death to males.

Questions 18 – 20

Complete the following sentences using one of the words given in the box below for each answer.

18. You are walking down a path and spot an ant colony. It is more than likely that this ant is much................... than the queen ant.
19. By and large, an ant colony will .... the queen.
20. The number of ants in an ant colony depends upon the .... populating the ant colony.

bigger	stronger	smaller	respect	adore
drones	species	queen	outlive	smarter

Read the text below and answer Questions 21 – 27

STEVE JOBS: A BRIEF LIFE HISTORY

In 1976, Steve Jobs and Steve Wozniak created the first Apple computer, the Apple I. The next year, they unveiled the Apple II, which went on to become the first successful mass-produced computer.

The computer's success made Jobs a millionaire by the time he was 23. By late 1980, Apple was ready to hold an initial public offering (IPO), a sale that generated more capital than any IPO since the 1956 Ford Motor Company's offering, and created roughly 300 millionaires instantly, more than any IPO in history.

In 1983, Apple had hired PepsiCo executive John Sculley as its CEO. However, Sculley and Jobs had serious differences on the direction the company should take. Those tensions came to a head in 1985, when Jobs resigned, taking a handful of Apple employees with him to create a new company, called NeXT, Inc.

Jobs invested $7 million of his own money, which the company burned through in its first year. Ross Perot stepped in as an investor, and the company released its first product, the NeXT Computer, in 1990. It was state-of-the-art, but, at $9,999, too expensive for most, especially its target customer—the education sector. By 1993, the company had only sold 50,000 machines, and decided to switch to software development. The move led to its first profit, when it netted $1 million in 1994.

At the same time, however, Jobs became involved with a venture that would go a long way toward cementing his reputation and his fortune, when he bought Lucasfilm's computer graphics division for $10 million. The standalone company was renamed Pixar and created a generation of iconic children's movies, including Toy Story, Monsters, Inc., Finding Nemo, The Incredibles and WALL-E. In 2006, The Walt Disney Company acquired Pixar for $7.4 billion in stock, making Jobs the biggest single shareholder of The Walt Disney Company.

In 2000, Jobs returned to Apple as its CEO and he began to look beyond the PC again, first with the groundbreaking iPod digital music player, which changed the way people listened to music. Prior to the iPod's launch in 2001, very few people listened to music on portable digital players. By 2012, more than 350 million devices had been sold worldwide. The iPod's sleek design and easy user interface paved the way for the company's 2007 release of the iPhone, which revolutionized cellular phone design. In 2014 alone, Apple sold roughly 170 million iPhones worldwide.

Not content to forever alter the way people used mobile phones and listened to music, Jobs launched the iPad in 2010. The very first version of the compact tablet computer sold more than 250 million units. It has been credited with singlehandedly revitalizing the previously moribund market for tablet computers.

In 2011, with Apple at the summit of not just the tech industry, but of all of American business, Jobs resigned as Apple's CEO. He was suffering from pancreatic cancer, and knew he would soon die. After his resignation, he stayed on as chairman of the board, continuing to work for Apple until the day before his death.

Questions 21 – 27

Complete the table below using NOT MORE THAN 3 WORDS AND/OR A NUMBER from the text above.

21.	Before Apple II, there had not been any	
22.	Ford Motor Company had its IPO	
23.	Before joining Apple, John Sculley was working in	
24.	The intended users of the NeXT Computer were in	
25.	Pixar helped Steve Jobs to consolidate his	
26.	Listening to music on portable digital players was not very common	
27.	Before the I-Pad, the market for tablet computers had been	

SECTION 3

Read the text below and answer questions 28 – 40

Questions 28 -35

The text has 8 SECTIONS, marked A to H. Choose the correct heading for each paragraph from the list of headings below.

i. The game starts to get organized
ii. A game of passion
iii. The genesis of the game
iv. The game takes its form
v. The first competitions
vi. What is in a name?
vii. Globalization of the game
viii. The great modern competitions
ix. Rugby and football differentiated
x. The game goes professional

28. Paragraph A ....
29. Paragraph B ....
30. Paragraph C ....
31. Paragraph D ....
32. Paragraph E ....
33. Paragraph F ....
34. Paragraph G ....
35. Paragraph H ....

THE HISTORY OF FOOTBALL

A. The first known examples of a team game involving a ball, which was made out of a rock, occurred in old Mesoamerican cultures for over 3,000 years ago. According to the sources, the ball would symbolize the sun and the captain of the losing team would be sacrificed to the gods. Other earlier variety of ball games had been known from Ancient Greece. The ball was made by shreds of leather filled with hair. The first documents of balls filled with air are from the 7th century. In the Ancient Rome, games with balls were not included in the entertainment on the big arenas, but could occur in exercises in the military. It was the Roman culture that would bring football to the British island (Britannica).

B. The most admitted story tells that the game was developed in England in the 12th century. Besides kicks, the game also involved punches of the ball with the fist. This early form of football was also much rougher and more violent than the modern way of playing. At times forbidden for its violent nature, football-like games would appear again in the streets of London in the 17th century. It would be forbidden again in 1835, but at this stage the game had been established in the public schools.
The game was often played in schools and two of the predominant schools were Rugby and Eton. At Rugby the rules included the possibility to take up the ball with the hands; at Eton on the other hand the ball was played exclusively with the feet and this game can be seen as a close predecessor to the modern football. The game in Rugby was called "the running game" while the game in Eton was called "the dribbling game".
An attempt to create proper rules for the game was done at a meeting in Cambridge in 1848, but a final solution to some questions of rules was not achieved. It was decided that carrying the ball with the hands wasn't allowed. The meeting also resulted in a standardization of the size and weight of the ball.

C. Football clubs have existed since the 15th century, but unorganized and without official status. It is therefore hard to decide which the first football club was. Some historians suggest that it was the Foot-Ball Club formed 1824 in Edinburgh. Earlier clubs were often formed by former school students and the first of this kind was formed in Sheffield in 1855. The oldest among professional football clubs is the English club Notts County, formed in 1862 and still exists today.
Initially, football was dominated by public school teams, but later, teams consisting of workers would be the majority. Another change was when some clubs became willing to pay the best players to join their team. This would be the start of a long period of transition, not without friction, in which the game would develop to a professional level.
The motivation behind paying players was not only to win more matches, but in the 1880s the interest in the game had moved ahead to a level that tickets were sold for the matches. And finally, in 1885 professional football was legalized and three years later the Football League was established. During the first season, 12 clubs joined the league, but soon more clubs became interested and the competition would consequently expand into more divisions.

D. Other milestones were now to follow. Football Association Challenge Cup (FA Cup) became the first important competition when it was run in 1871. The following year a match between two national teams was played for the first time. The match that involved England and Scotland ended 0-0 and was followed by 4,000 people. Twelve years later, in 1883, the first international tournament took place and included four national teams: England, Ireland, Scotland and Wales.

Football was for a long time a British phenomenon, but gradually spread to other European countries. The first game that took place outside Europe occurred in Argentina in 1867, but it was foreign British workers who were involved and not Argentinean citizens.
Domestic leagues occurred in many countries, the first was the English Football League which was established in 1888. In 1908 football would be, for the first time, included as an official sport in the Olympic Games. Until the first FIFA World Cup was played in 1930, the Olympic Games football tournament would rank as the most prestigious. Women's football was not added until 1996.

E. Few other sports show examples of zeal and intensity to the extent as in football. In 1894, the FA Cup final between Notts County and Bolton Wanderers was attended by 37,000 people. A milestone in football stadiums is the construction of Maracanã Stadium. In 1950 the imposing stadium in Rio de Janeiro was ready for almost 200,000 people. No other sport has seen stadiums of that capacity built to host its games.
There have been two different traditions of fan culture on the arenas: the British and the South American. The British fans adopted the tradition of singing, the repertoire were inspired from pub and working songs among other areas. The South Americans on the other hand would adopt the carnival style which includes firecrackers and fireworks.

F. No other sport event besides the Olympic Games can today measure itself with the FIFA World Cup. The first edition of the FIFA World Cup was played in 1930 in Uruguay and has since then returned every fourth year (with two exceptions due to the Second World War). In 1991 the first World Cup for women was held in China and has since then also returned every fourth year. Today the biggest global tournament for clubs is the Champions League, played since 1992.

G. In the late 19th century, only a few national football teams existed; England and Scotland had the first active teams that played games against each other in the 1870s. Today there are 211 national associations included in the Fédération Internationale de Football Association (FIFA), the world governing body of the sport. Another proof of the globalization could be seen in the increase of nations participating in World Cup qualifiers: from 32 in 1934 to over 200 in 2014.

H. In most parts of the world, football is used as the name for the "chess of the green pitch", the biggest sport in the world. In the United States and Canada, however, soccer is used instead as a distinction from American football. A more formal name sometimes used is association football, but in popular speech, it is either football or soccer.

Questions 36 – 40

Complete the following sentences using **A WORD OR A NUMBER** taken from the box below.

36 The .... that most people agree with is that the game was developed in England.

37 There have been clubs playing football since the 1400s, and it is .... to identify the first one.

38 The first football match between two national teams was played in ....

39 Citizens of the .... country were not involved in the first game of football played outside Europe.

40 European and South American spectators of the sport can be .... from the manner in which they cheer their team.

spotted	1871	host	separated	1872
conclusion	distinguished	European	impossible	tough
local	narrative	1870		

GT READING TEST 17

SECTION 1

Questions 1 – 14

Read the text below and answer Questions 1 – 7

OLDEST PUBS OF ENGLAND

A. Adam and Eve has records dating back to 1249, when workmen building the nearby Norwich Cathedral were the pub's first recorded customers as they were housed there and were paid with bread and ale. The pub's first owners were monks from the Great Hospital, which is located down the road. Adam and Eve has a reputation for being haunted by a medieval French-speaking monk, whose remains were found during a cellar excavation in the 1970s.

B. Ye Olde Trip to Jerusalem claims that the pub was established in 1189; however there are no records verifying this date. There is evidence that the earliest parts of the pub's building only date back to 1650. The pub is famous for its cave rooms, which are part of nearby Castle Rock – these caves were used as a brew house for the castle and date back to when the castle was constructed in 1068.

C. The Royal Standard of England is one of the only pubs which claims it is England's oldest, to have actual proof of its history going back to at least 1086, because its existence as an alehouse, called the Ship Inn, is documented in the Domesday Book. The pub got its name from King Charles II, who frequently met his mistresses in the rooms above the pub – he granted the pub's landlord permission to change the name from The Ship to its current name. Like several other old English buildings, The Royal Standard claims that it is haunted by various ghosts.

D. The Bingley Arms, which used to be called The Priests Inn, served as a courthouse from around AD 1000 from which offenders were taken to the pillory across the road; it was also a safe house for persecuted Catholic priests. There is evidence that suggests the pub may be even older than its known history – it may go as far back as 905 and could have been standing before nearby All Hallows Church that was built in 950.

E. The Porch House has been renovated in recent years, but it claims that parts of the building were once a hospice built by order of the Duke of Cornwall 947. In the 1970s, when the pub was receiving renovations, some of the building's timber was dated to 1000 ± 50 years, which backs up the pub's story of its history.

F. Ye Olde Fighting Cocks also claims it is England's oldest pub. According to the pub's own history, it dates back to the 18th. Century and the pub's foundations were part of the Palace of Offa, king of the Mercians, dating back to around 793. Locals believe that there are several tunnels connecting the pub's beer cellar to St Albans Cathedral, which were used by monks in the past.

G. The Old Ferry Boat Inn claims that it is England's oldest inn. According to legend, the inn has been serving alcohol on its premises since 560, which would make it the oldest pub in England. No one knows for sure if the Old Ferry Boat Inn is as old as it claims as the building's age has been hard to date. In addition to its claim as England's oldest pub and inn, it is reportedly haunted. Local legend says that a young, heartbroken girl named Juliet committed suicide near the town's church and that the inn was built over her grave.

Questions 1 – 7

Identify the pub referred to in each of the statements below. Write the correct answer A-G in questions 1-7 of your answer sheet.

1. Clerics found refuge in this pub.
2. The ghost here speaks a foreign language!
3. The place of Christian worship nearby had underground access to this pub's offerings.
4. Parts of this pub's building was earlier used to look after the old and terminally ill.
5. This pub has been witness to royal indiscretions.
6. This one has connections with caves and castles!
7. Drink to the heartbroken lover here.

Read the text below and answer Questions 8 – 14

ASHA BHOSLE LIVE

If the near capacity crowd signifies Asha Bhosle's importance, the fevered dancing and deafening screams of the fans underline it. The Indian singer's songs have appeared in more than a thousand Bollywood movies over the course of seven decades, and the audience mirrors the breadth of her career: senior citizens with walking sticks jam the aisles, moving subtly, while young children shimmy, standing on seats. During a particularly rousing rendition of Dum Maro Dum, security guards cease trying to quell the rambunctious mass dancing. Bhosle, 85, controls this show of a global farewell tour with grace: she appears when she wants, occasionally ceding the stage to Sudesh Bhosle, and to her granddaughter Zaina. Like Asha, Sudesh is a renowned mimic and playback singer – an artist who records songs that actors mime – and runs through old movie numbers. His performance, though, is lead-footed: stilted theatrics as a palate cleanser between the main event's courses.

It is Asha after all, not Sudesh that the crowd are here for. When she does sing, it is with a tight-knit band, some of whom have been with her for decades. This proves vital, as though she often displays virtuosic skill, her voice also repeatedly cracks from exhaustion. The band – a cosmopolitan blend of saxophone, trombone, dholak, tabla, trumpet, drums, guitars, keyboards and harmonium – cleverly mask this time and again.

Vocal quality is perhaps beside the point: this is a star saying goodbye to loyal fans, and during momentous songs such as Piya Tu Ab To Aaja, Bhosle defies her age, dancing and moving around the stage while powerfully belting out numbers. When in full flow, it is an intimate, bone-deep sound that's both joyful and warm, invoking a nostalgia that is inseparable from Bhosle's music. By the end of the night, the screams of the audience dissolve into tears. She's unable to stand unsupported for long periods, and it does feel as if this is the last time Asha Bhosle will perform in the UK. The audience know it – they soak up every moment she manages to give them. She has to call for extra tissues before uttering: "I love you. I cannot speak any more'', and exits one final time.

Questions 8 – 14

Do the following statements agree with the information given in the text?

In boxes on your answer sheet, write

TRUE if the statement agrees with the information

FALSE if the statement contradicts the information

NOT GIVEN if there is no information on this.

8 Sudesh Bhosle is distantly related to Asha Bhosle.

9 When Dum Maro Dum is sung, the audience starts dancing in a wildly boisterous manner.

10 Sudesh Bhosle's singing is ungainly and wooden when compared to Asha Bhosle's catchy and peppy voice.

11 Asha Bhosle's band covers up for her breaks in singing when she gets tired.

12 Asha Bhosle displays tremendous energy, standing and singing on the stage throughout the show.

13 Youngsters sway their bodies to the music at the show.

14 This is the last time the 85 year old artist will perform in the UK.

SECTION 2

Read the text below and answer Questions 15 – 27

Questions 15 – 21

GROUP DISCUSSIONS

When a particular idea or topic is debated upon by a group of people, it is called a Group Discussion (GD). GDs serve as one of the yardsticks to select candidates in management schools or for certain jobs. Here are some rules and tips to help you improve your GD skills.

A.

Speaking is a must in a group discussion, but when and how is vital. It is preferable if you are the first speaker: it proves your ability to initiate matters. Now, if you have initiated the GD, you have to be very knowledgeable and be able to respond to counter arguments. Also the middle part and conclusion are also important. Remain involved in the GD throughout.

B. Not only speaking but your listening behaviour is also tested in a group discussion. You have to prove your point with facts but at the same time you cannot force your opinion on others. Be smart and witty, and listen to what others are saying to be able to counter their specific points.

C. Involvement throughout the group discussion is a must. As mentioned earlier, you must remain engaged in the GD throughout the time it is going on. As for body language, keep it sober rather than aggressive. Pointing fingers is a strict no-no. Even when you are rebutting a point, keep your demeanor pleasant.

D. If you are speaking amongst a bunch of smart, outgoing and well-spoken management aspirants you better not fumble at any point. In this case working on your communication entails the practice of conveying ideas within a specific time frame, expressing your ideas with a perfectly agreeable body language and using the right words in their correct context.

E. Make sure you clarify your doubts regarding the topic, if any, with the moderator as soon as the topic is given to you and not later when your turn to speak comes. Topics may range from general issues like dowry, child labour, gender inequality, and price rise to current affairs like Kashmir, Coalgate, and Scams etc. If you are asked to highlight a specific facet of the topic, try to concentrate on that instead of discussing all the facets of the same.

F. Yes, always take a stand on the topic given to you. There might be a topic like- "Indian Athletes Are a No-Show at the Olympics." Convey clearly whether you agree with the topic or not and make sure that you have equally strong stats to back your claim. Don't be ambivalent. Be careful not to sound too assertive in the process. Instead, put across your point with clear arguments which will automatically reflect your point of view.

G. It might seem a little difficult to sum up all your points of argument in a well-drawn conclusion in just about 1-2 minutes. But that's the trick! Do try to master this, as it helps the speaker after you to carry on from what you said and also makes you stand out.

H. Be aware of what's happening around you. You should be well informed, both on current hot topics and also general topics of perennial interest. Your knowledge might be sourced from news headlines, newspapers, internet, books, informative TV channels etc. Avoid sources which are too promotional and give you only one side of a particular issue.

I. Carry a notebook. To start with you may make some notes of the points that you wish to cover. During the GD, write down the points already discussed made by those who oppose you, so that you may rebut them later. Try to come up with unique but sensible points to boost your argument.

Questions 15-17

Match the statements below to the paragraph where they are mentioned. Write the correct letter A-I in boxes 15-17 of your answer sheet.

15. You have to put across your point succinctly with utmost clarity.
16. You cannot have mixed feelings about the topic.
17. Remain calm and pleasant even when you are expressing disagreement.

Questions 18 – 21

Do the following statements agree with the information given in the text?

In boxes on your answer sheet, write

TRUE	if the statement agrees with the information
FALSE	if the statement contradicts the information
NOT GIVEN	if there is no information on this.

18. If you do not know the topic very well, do not initiate the discussion.
19. GDs are serious discussions aimed at making a selection of persons; displaying a sense of humour in GDs is not a good idea.
20. Unless you listen to the arguments of others you will not be able to rebut their arguments.
21. You are not allowed to seek clarifications on the topic once the GD has begun.

Read the text below and answer Questions 22 – 27

TIPS FOR GOOD ORAL HYGIENE

Your dental health is an important component of your physical health. It's a frequently underappreciated aspect that can have a profound systemic influence. In fact, thousands of studies have linked oral disease to diseases in the rest of the body.

Your mouth is like a window to your health; the soft tissues and your teeth reflect what's going on in the rest of your body. Inflammation is well-known as a ravaging and disease-causing force, and gum disease and other oral diseases produce chronic low-grade inflammation.

When the bacteria that cause tooth decay and gum disease enter into your circulatory system, it causes your liver to release C-reactive proteins, which have inflammatory effects on your entire circulatory system.

People who fail to brush their teeth twice a day may be putting themselves at risk of heart disease, and advanced gum disease can raise your risk of a fatal heart attack up to 10 times.

There's also a 700 percent higher incidence of type 2 diabetes among those with gum disease. Other health effects associated with poor oral health include an increased risk of

- Bad breath (halitosis)
- Dementia
- Pneumonia:
- Kidney disease and more

Overall, your diet is the most significant determinant of your oral and dental health, but how you clean your teeth can also make a big difference. Flossing, for example, is an important strategy, yet one-third of American adults never floss. If you're one of them, I'd encourage you to reconsider.

The Importance of Flossing

Flossing is perhaps even more important than brushing because it removes bacteria that are the precursors of plaque, which if left to fester will turn into tartar that cannot be removed by regular brushing or flossing. Most people are aware that flossing is a recommended practice for optimal oral health, yet nearly one-third of Americans never floss. Remarkably, 1 in 5 Americans also do not brush their teeth twice a day. According to a recent investigation:

32.4% of U.S. adults over the age of 30 never floss

37.3% floss, but not daily

30.3% floss on a daily basis

More women than men never floss

Low-income participants are less likely to floss than those in higher income brackets

Flossing Guidelines

Use a piece of floss that is about 15 to 18 inches long, wrapping each end around your index fingers. Slide the floss between your teeth and wrap it around the side of the tooth in the shape of a "C."

Scrub the area by moving the floss up and down, and back and forth. Make sure you scrub both sides of the adjacent teeth before moving on to the next set.

While flossing, you can get telltale signs of potential health problems. For example, bleeding gums is a warning sign that you have bacteria in your mouth causing damage, which can easily spread through your blood stream and cause chronic inflammation elsewhere in your body.

Tooth Brushing and Oil Pulling

Research suggests the ideal brushing time is two minutes, and the ideal pressure is 150 grams, which is about the weight of an orange. Brushing your teeth too hard and longer than necessary can cause more harm than good.

Oil pulling is an ancient Ayurvedic practice. When combined with the antimicrobial power of coconut oil, I believe it can be a powerful tool to improve your oral health. Oil pulling is thought to improve oral and physical health by reducing your toxic load. By swishing and "pulling" the oil between your teeth, it helps draw out micro-organisms that might otherwise migrate into other areas of your body. When done correctly, oil pulling has a significant cleansing, detoxifying and healing effect.

Questions 22-27

Do the following statements agree with the information given in the text?

In boxes on your answer sheet, write

YES	if the statement agrees with the information
NO	if the statement contradicts the information
NOT GIVEN	if there is no information on this.

22. If you have a disease in your body, it probably started with a disease in your mouth.
23. If you do not brush your teeth twice a day, you may be at a risk of contracting a heart disease.
24. The most significant impact on your dental health is made by the food you eat.
25. More than 50% Americans aged 30 or more floss their teeth.
26. If there are two persons, one with a lower income than the other, the latter is more likely to be flossing his teeth.
27. If you are oil pulling, there is no need to floss.

SECTION 3

Read the text below and answer questions 28 – 40

Questions 28 -35

The text has 8 SECTIONS, marked A to H. Choose the correct heading for each paragraph from the list of headings below.

i. Insider tips
ii. Boarding and alighting
iii. Not just a tourist attraction
iv. Pricey, but not exorbitant
v. Each route has its attractions
vi. The festive Thursday
vii. The cable car chronology
viii. Not just a tourist attraction
ix. Cable car basics
x. Cable car start and end timings

28. Paragraph A ....
29. Paragraph B ....
30. Paragraph C ....
31. Paragraph D ....
32. Paragraph E ....
33. Paragraph F ....
34. Paragraph G ....
35. Paragraph H ....

SAN FRANCISCO CABLE CARS

A. Cable cars are a historic symbol recognized around the globe and offer real working transportation up the steep hills of San Francisco. The cable cars begin their runs at 6 a.m. and continue until midnight. The cable cars generally run about every 10 minutes.
From Union Square to the crest of Nob Hill, cable cars offer a thrilling way to move within the City. A ride on San Francisco's cable cars may be the most iconic and memorable of your entire trip to California. Even people who might dismiss cable cars as a cheesy tourist attraction will admit that there is something incredibly romantic about these rides.

B. The cable car fare is $7.00 and all fares are one way. There are discounted fares for seniors during non-peak hours. If you anticipate using the cable cars more than once in a day you should get a

day pass which is $17.00. The all-day pass is also a good choice if you will be transferring from one line to another or if you will be transferring from a cable car to a MUNI bus.
Your one-way fare as well as your all-day passport can be purchased directly from the cable car operator on the car, who can make change up to $20. Alternatively you can purchase tickets at the booths that are located at the Powell/Market cable car turnaround or Hyde and Beach cable car turnaround. Unlimited cable car and bus / trolley rides together with museum passes can be purchased at a discount.

C. For the best views, you want to be on the side that faces the bay. When you exit, wait for the cable car to pass rather than crossing in front of it. The drivers are always paying attention but this is a heavy vehicle that can't swerve to miss you, so stay aware!
Cable cars are sometimes late if it's raining. It takes them longer to slow down when the tracks are wet. Even on warm days it can get chilly on the cable car as it gets moving up and down those hills. Bring a windbreaker.
Put your belongings, such as bags and backpacks, on your lap or at your feet, they shouldn't be hanging off of the car. Hang on tight. And watch your children. This is a form of transportation, not a ride, and you should treat it with that respect and safety in mind.

D. The Powell/Hyde line ends near Ghirardelli Square where you can shop or eat; or exit the cable car at Lombard Street, famous for being the world's most crooked street; else, get your camera ready because at the top of this hill you are treated to an unobstructed view of Alcatraz Island. Across the street from the end of this line is The Buena Vista Cafe, where legend has it that the Irish Coffee was born.
Powell/Mason: This cable car line drops you off in North Beach, a quick walk to Fishermen's Wharf near Pier 39. If you're hungry, head over to Kennedy's Irish Pub and Curry House, a curious mixture of an Irish bar, a game arcade, and unbelievably delicious Indian food.
California/ Van Ness: This cable car rides through the hills of the Financial District and hits the top of Nob Hill where you'll find luxury hotels and nightclubs with some of the most stunning views of the city. Make sure to check out Grace Cathedral if you like beautiful gothic architecture.

E. Most visitors will get on the cable car at the beginning or end of the line and ride it all the way to the other end to get the most bang for their buck. There is a cable car turnaround at the intersection of Powell and Market Street near Union Square. Here you can get in line to get on both the Powell/Hyde and Powell/Mason lines. Note that everyone gets in the same line. Look at the sign on the top of the cable car to see which one is about to leave.
You are allowed to get on the car at any stop along the route. The car will stop for you and you can climb on. You do not need to wave it down. You are allowed to sit in the outside seats or inside seats, stand in the inside section, stand on the back section or stand on the footstep area

on either side of the car. The most adventurous ride is in the front of the car, standing on the running board; it sure beats being cooped up inside where you won't see anything.

There are no buttons to push or bells to ring to let the driver know that you want to get off the cable car. On busy days, the cable car will stop at all of the stops along the route and you can just get off when it stops. However, if it is a slow day, you may want to let the driver or attendant know what stop you want.

F. Many people assume that the cable cars are just a ride that the tourists go on. While it is definitely one of the city's major attractions, it is also a viable form of transportation and one that people who live in the city sometimes do use, although usually only in the offseason when the cars aren't so jam-packed! This is important to know even as a visitor because there are a few rare instances in which the cable car is actually quicker and more convenient than the bus system. For example, during peak hours in low-tourism seasons it can be faster to take a cable car to Chinatown than to take a bus. Note, however, that it's also more expensive!

G. The cable car system in San Francisco was built in 1873. Local legend has it that Andrew Hallidie was inspired to build the cable car system when he witnessed some wagon- horses fall to their death due to the steepness of Jackson Street. By 1890 it had nearly two dozen lines operating to get people all around the city. However, the system was short lived because electric streetcars were developed towards the end of the nineteenth century and provided a more efficient and cost-effective system of getting around. The final nail in the original cable car system was the 1906 earthquake, which damaged much of the city's existing infrastructure.

By 1912 only three cable car lines remained. By the 1920s there were also buses as alternatives to these lines. However, some people did want to keep the historic cable cars running and there was a lot of debate about how to do so. Changes have been made to the lines over time but today the three main lines do continue to run.

H. If you're lucky enough to be visiting during the month of July then you won't want to miss the annual cable car bell ringing contests, which happen on either the second or third Thursday of the month. The contests are held in Union Square and draw thousands of spectators. Some of the men are extremely good at what they do and the applause that they receive can be thunderous with approval. Grab a hot dog and make a day of it; the event draws celebrities and local dignitaries like the Mayor of San Francisco so you know you'll be in for a wild time.

If you have your own special event in the city, you can actually charter a cable car for your group. Learn more at the website of the San Francisco Municipal Transport Agency.

Questions 36 – 40

Complete the following sentences using a word taken from the box below.

36. The conductor's .... to return your dues in change depends upon the denomination of the note you give him.

37. The cable cars running on the .... line go up a hill.

38. In the off-season, when there are not too many ...., you may tell the driver where you want to disembark.

39. Taking a bus to Chinatown is .... than the cable car.

40. If you have a special event, you can .... a cable car for your group.

ability	appropriate	hire	cheaper	Powell/Hyde
visitors	Powell/Mason	passengers	costlier	Hyde/Mason

GT READING TEST 18

SECTION 1

Questions 1 – 13

Read the text below and answer Questions 1 – 6

THE FIRST COCO COLA BOTTLE

More than 100 years ago, designers went back and forth quite a bit coming up with the perfect design for the glass Coca-Cola bottle. The only known, intact model of one of those discarded prototypes is now on the block, at Morphy Auctions in Las Vegas, Nevada, where it is expected to sell this month for at least 100,000 dollars.

The story goes all the way back to 1915, when the Coca-Cola Bottling Company of Atlanta, Georgia, solicited proposals for a bottle design, requiring all entries to include not only a description, but an actual sample bottle. According to Morphy of Morphy Auctions, a "committee of several bottlers" joined Coca-Cola's lawyers in Atlanta, in August 1915, to evaluate the eight submissions the company had received. The winning entry was by Earl R. Dean, of the Root Glass Company—but it still needed some work. Dean's design was incompatible with the machinery that the company would use to bottle its soda, it was too wide for the conveyor belt, so Mr. Root himself helped slim the design down to a version sized appropriately for the machines. As a matter of fact, Coca-Cola's iconic curved bottle wasn't introduced until 1917 when the company was desperate to come up with a design that would distinguish themselves from other soda producers.

"We need a bottle which a person can recognize as a Coca-Cola bottle when he feels it in the dark," Coca-Cola Bottling Company co-founder Benjamin Thomas said in his design brief. Designer Earl R. Dean was reportedly inspired by the shape of cacao pods, the fruit of the cacao tree which become chocolate. To keep their curvaceous scheme a secret, all of the previous prototypes were destroyed. Coca-Cola proceeded to conduct a round of testing on the refined design, producing test bottles from plants in Alabama, Georgia, and Tennessee. Though the tests were successful, the company destroyed its test bottles—all of them, apparently, except for this one. The bottle is embossed with the date November 15, 1915; the test-proof design was patented the following day.

Why just this bottle survived may forever remain a mystery of the bottling arts and sciences. People, after all, had tried to find others. In preparing this lot for auction, Morphy consulted the bottle scholar Dennis Smith, who "conducted a bottle dig" more than 40 years ago in a Birmingham, Alabama, dump where the local test plant had disposed of its samples. Despite his noble efforts, Smith came up with nothing but fragments. This bottle—along with a 1933 model—was discovered in a retired Coca-Cola employee's collection of company paraphernalia. It is the only known, unbroken survivor from that original test run.

Questions 1 – 6

Do the following statements agree with the information given in the text? Write:

TRUE	If the statement agrees with the information
FALSE	If the statement contradicts the information
NOT GIVEN	If there is no information on this.

1. Morphy was involved in the design of the Coco Cola bottle prototype.
2. The Coco Cola Company evaluated more than half a dozen designs of a glass bottle based upon a brief given by Benjamin Thomas.
3. Benjamin Thomas felt that people would prefer to drink Coco Cola in the dark and hence the bottle should be so designed that one could make out it is a Coco Cola bottle just by feeling it.
4. Designer Earl Dean made the bottle in the shape of the cacao pod.
5. The design of the bottle was patented on November 16, 1915.
6. Mr. Root was the owner of Root Glass Company.

Read the text below and answer Questions 7 – 13

RACING PIGEONS

In many cities around the world, feral pigeons are a dime a dozen. They roost on roofs, they coo from wires, and they peck outside bakeries, waiting for day-old hand-outs. Pigeons that bred for racing are birds of a fancier feather—and one buyer recently shelled out $1.4 million to add a little guy named Armando to their roster of winged competitors.

A Belgian breeder put Armando up for sale on the pigeon auction site PIPA, where several bidders scrambled to nab him. When bidding closed, Armando's price had inched above €1.2 million (more than $1.4 million, in U.S. dollars). Seven of Armando's offspring were also up for sale, and they'll fan out across Belgium, Turkey, Germany, The Netherlands, and China. Armando will head to China, too, where the sport of pigeon racing has boomed in recent years. On the mainland, where most forms of gambling are prohibited, pigeon racing gets a pass, and there are at least 100,000 pigeon breeders in Beijing alone, CNN reported.

Many wildlife groups and rehabilitators are fundamentally opposed to pigeon racing, arguing that the birds face a barrage of challenges before, during, and after the events, which sometimes span hundreds of miles. "We think this is a flawed situation right from the beginning," says Elizabeth Young, founding director of Palomacy, a pigeon rescue organization in the San Francisco Bay Area. Young's group works with domestic pigeons who find themselves in the wild, including ones that were grounded during races, often because they were struck by hawks, outmatched by the wind, or ran out of energy.

From a purchaser's perspective, this bird had several things working in his favour, says Tim Heidrich, secretary of the National Pigeon Association, a bird fanciers' group. Armando has already soared past the competition in several long-distance races, and delivered sterling performances in Belgium, Heinrich says, where competition is stiff. Selecting a racing pigeon can be similar to selecting champion dogs or thoroughbred race horses, says Deone Roberts, sport development manager at the American Racing Pigeon Union. "Pedigree can be important for the owner who may be hoping for genetic transmission of the most desired qualities," Roberts says. Armando is also young enough to be bred several times over the years, Heidrich says, "thus maximizing the investment in him."

While other top birds have sold for hundreds of thousands of dollars in the past—and despite Armando's bona fides—"I think the price got very much out of hand," Heidrich writes in an email. "You probably had a couple of billionaires bidding with their egos instead of their brains." Still, Heidrich adds, "Like a great race horse, he's worth what someone is willing to pay."

Questions 7-13

Fill in the blanks in the following sentences, using words from the box below.

7. It is very common to see hordes of .... pigeons in many cities around the world.
8. Some people .... pigeons for racing as these birds fetch very high prices.
9. Pigeon racing as a .... has greatly increased over the last few years.
10. In mainland China, many kinds of .... are not permitted.
11. The .... of a bird is seen to be important when it comes to selecting one for purchase.
12. In bidding for Armando, people were swayed more by their .... rather than logic.
13. There are several bodies that do not .... pigeon racing as a sport.

like	support	conceit	speculation	pride	track-record	gambling
racing	untamed	sport	competitions	keep	breed	
speed	lineage	domesticated				

SECTION 2

Read the text below and answer Questions 14 – 27

Questions 14 – 20

THE OUTBREAK OF WORLD WAR II

World War II was the biggest and deadliest war in history, involving more than 30 countries. Sparked by the 1939 Nazi invasion of Poland, the war dragged on for six bloody years until the Allies defeated Nazi Germany and Japan in 1945.

By the early part of 1939 the German dictator Adolf Hitler had become determined to invade and occupy Poland. Poland, for its part, had guarantees of French and British military support should it be attacked by Germany. Hitler intended to invade Poland anyway, but first he had to neutralize the possibility that the Soviet Union would resist the invasion of its western neighbour. Secret negotiations led on August 23 to the signing of the German-Soviet Non-aggression Pact in Moscow. In a secret protocol of this pact, the Germans and the Soviets agreed that Poland should be divided between them, with the western third of the country going to Germany and the eastern two-thirds being taken over by the U.S.S.R. Having achieved this cynical agreement, the other provisions of which stupefied Europe even without divulgence of the secret protocol, Hitler thought that Germany could attack Poland with no danger of Soviet or British intervention and gave orders for the invasion to start on August 26. News of the signing, on August 25, of a formal treaty of mutual assistance between Great Britain and Poland (to supersede a previous though temporary agreement) caused him to postpone the start of hostilities for a few days. He was still determined, however, to ignore the diplomatic efforts of the western powers to restrain him. Finally, at 12:40 PM on August 31, 1939, Hitler ordered hostilities against Poland to start at 4:45 the next morning. The invasion began as ordered. In response, Great Britain and France declared war on Germany on September 3, at 11:00 AM and at 5:00 PM, respectively. World War II had begun.

Questions 14 – 20

Fill in the blanks below using **NO MORE THAN TWO WORDS OR A WORD AND NUMBER** from the text:

- The Second World War lasted for 14) .... years.
- Poland had an assurance of assistance from 15) .... and 16) ....
- Germany and the Soviet Union agreed on a treaty not to attack each other on 17) ....
- As per their secret agreement, the Soviet Union and Germany would occupy Poland; the former would retain 18) .... of Polish territory.
- Although Hitler wanted to invade Poland on August 26, 1939, he delayed it because of an event that took place on 19) ....
- Hitler started the war against Poland on 20) ....

Read the text below and answer Questions 21 – 27

CLEOPATRA

More than 2,000 years after her death in 30 BCE, the Egyptian queen Cleopatra still looms large in the popular imagination. Despite what is known of her brilliance and charm, in mass media depictions what often comes to the forefront is Cleopatra as a ravishingly seductive femme-fatale. What did she really look like?

Today many historians subscribe to the theory that Cleopatra's looks were ancillary to her considerable intelligence, learning, foresight, and strategic skills. The image of her as a sultry seductress likely stems from a narrative originally pushed by Octavian to rationalize his rivalry and conflict with fellow Roman Marc Antony, who was portrayed as having been manipulated by a foreign temptress. What's more, casting Cleopatra as an evil beauty conveniently downplayed her competence and significance as a ruler.

While Roman historian Dio Cassius described Cleopatra as "a woman of surpassing beauty," a number of modern historians have characterized her as less than exceptionally attractive. Nevertheless, they have noted that her beauty was heralded and that her appearance was seductive. Greek biographer Plutarch, writing about a century after Cleopatra's death, presented a less flattering picture: "For her beauty, as we are told, was in itself neither altogether incomparable, nor such as to strike those who saw her."

All that aside, there are artefacts that attest to Cleopatra's appearance. One of the most prominent, a marble bust dating to the third quarter of the 1st century BCE, is housed in the Old Museum in Germany. This so-called Berlin Cleopatra depicts her wearing a royal diadem. Her face is framed by ringlets of curly hair, and the rest of her hair is gathered into a bun behind her head. Her eyes are almond-shaped. Although her nose is prominent, her features are softly modulated and have been described as reflecting her intelligence and charm. Cleopatra's hair is styled similarly on another marble bust, this one found in a villa on the Appian Way in 1784 and now displayed at the Vatican's Gregoriano Profano Museum. On this bust too, her features are generally soft and her lips full.

An aquiline nose is the most prominent feature of the profiles of Cleopatra on contemporary coins (issued by Cleopatra or in her name) that are widely held to give the best representation of her appearance. On some of the coins, her nose is less hooked, her cheeks are full, and her chin is small, as on the marble busts.

In Hollywood, Cleopatra has been played by an array of stunning actresses. Elizabeth Taylor who was put under the "gaze" as the "Queen of the Nile" in the best-known film version of the ruler's story, Cleopatra (1963), is a mainstay on short lists of moviedom's most attractive leading ladies. One of cinema's first sex symbols, Theda Bara, invested her Cleopatra with dark sensuality in the lost silent classic Cleopatra (1917). A scantily clad Claudette Colbert caused a sensation in Cecil B. DeMille's epic Cleopatra (1934), and Vivian Leigh was the beguiling queen in Caesar and Cleopatra (1945). But how did this image of Cleopatra come to be?

As William Shakespeare wrote in his play, Antony and Cleopatra, Age cannot wither her, nor custom stale/ Her infinite variety. Other women cloy / The appetites they feed, but she makes hungry / Where most she satisfies.

Questions 21-27

Fill in the blanks in the paragraph below, using **NO MORE THAN TWO WORDS** from the text:

Although she has been dead or more than 2000 year, Cleopatra is still remembered by a large number of people. She is generally portrayed as a 21....................... woman, and her other qualities are pushed to the background. However, chroniclers endorse the view that she had considerable mental abilities, and her countenance was only an 22.................... factor in her overall demeanour. The image of Cleopatra as a seductress was possibly promoted by the Roman rivals for her attention, Octavian and Marc Antony. Historians differ in their assessment of what she looked like; while some say she was very beautiful, some have said that her looks were not23...................... Cleopatra's busts in different museums give us an idea of what she looked like. In one, she is wearing a small jewelled crown and has 24................. eyes. On coins issued by her, the most prominent feature is her 25......................... Many movies on Cleopatra have been made, and in the most well-known movie of her life, her role has been essayed by 26. .... She has also been the subject of a play written by 27..........................., where he extols her beauty.

SECTION 3

Read the text below and answer questions 28 – 40

Questions 28 -35

The text has 8 SECTIONS, marked A to H. Choose the correct heading for each paragraph from the list of headings below.

i. Another jewel in the British crown
ii. The emergence of a modern democracy
iii. The primordial times
iv. The birth of a nation
v. The post war boom
vi. The emergence of cities
vii. Australians in global conflicts
viii. Politics over the years
ix. The oldest continuous culture on earth
x. Victorious in wars

28. Paragraph A ....
29. Paragraph B ....
30. Paragraph C ....
31. Paragraph D ....
32. Paragraph E ....
33. Paragraph F ....
34. Paragraph G ....
35. Paragraph H ....

A BRIEF HISTORY OF AUSTRALIA

A. Australia's aboriginal people have the oldest continuous culture on Earth. They are believed to have arrived here by boat at least 50,000 years ago. At the time of European settlement there were up to one million Aboriginal people living across the continent as hunters and gatherers. They were scattered in 500 different clans, or 'nations', speaking about 700 languages. Each clan had a spiritual connection with their land, but travelled widely to trade and find water and seasonal produce, as well as for ritual gatherings. Despite their homelands being very diverse – from outback deserts to tropical rainforest and snow-capped mountains – all Aboriginal people share the belief in the Dreaming, or 'Tjukurrpa'. According to Aboriginal myth, the ancestor spirits forged all aspects of life and continue to link the past, present, the people and the land. Dreaming stories describe the journeys of spiritual ancestors and are told through song, dance, painting and storytelling.

There are many opportunities to explore Australia's Indigenous culture, significantly in northern Australia, where you can take a tour through the world-famous Kakadu National Park, which is home to more than 5,000 sites of rock art dating back 20,000 years. Or join a Dreamtime walk, guided by the Kuku Yalanji people, through the lush rainforests of Mossman Gorge, 80 kilometres north of Cairns.

B. A number of European explorers sailed the coast of Australia, then known as New Holland, during the 17th century. But it wasn't until 1770 that Captain James Cook chartered the east coast and claimed it for Britain. The new outpost was put to use as a penal colony and on 26 January 1788, the First Fleet of 11 ships – carrying 1,500 people, half of them convicts – arrived in Sydney Harbour. When penal transportation ended in 1868, more than 160,000 men and women had come to Australia as convicts.

While free settlers began to flow in from the early 1790s, life for prisoners was harsh. Male re-offenders were brutally flogged and could be hanged for crimes as petty as stealing. Women were outnumbered five to one and lived under constant threat of sexual exploitation.

The colonization of Australia had a devastating impact on the Aboriginal people, with dispossession of their land, illness and death from introduced diseases and huge disruption of their traditional lifestyles and practices.

C. By the 1820s, many soldiers, officers and emancipated convicts had turned land they received from the government into flourishing farms. News of Australia's cheap land and bountiful work was bringing more and more boatloads of migrants from Britain. Settlers, or 'squatters', began to move deeper into Aboriginal territories – often armed – in search of pasture and water for their stock.

In 1825, a party of soldiers and convicts settled in the territory of the Yuggera people, close to modern-day Brisbane. Perth was settled by English gentlemen in 1829, and in 1835 a squatter sailed to Port Phillip Bay and chose the location for Melbourne. At the same time a private British company, proud to have no convict links, settled Adelaide in South Australia.

D. Gold was discovered in New South Wales and Central Victoria in 1851, luring thousands of hopefuls from the other states. They were joined by boatloads of prospectors from China and a chaotic carnival of entertainers, publicans, illicit liquor-sellers, and quacks from across the world. In Victoria, the British governor imposed mining licenses on goldfield workers, which led to the violent, anti-authoritarian struggle of the Eureka Stockade in 1854. The miners lost the battle, but were granted more rights and in 1854 a bill were passed, giving the right to vote and stand for parliament to any digger who owned a miner's licence.

Many historians regard this as the beginning of Australian democracy. Australia's six states became a nation under a single constitution on 1 January 1901. Today people from more than 200 countries make up the Australian community, and more than 300 languages are spoken in Australian homes.

E. The First World War had a devastating effect on Australia. There were less than three million men in 1914, and around 420,000 of them volunteered for service in the war. An estimated 60,000 died and tens of thousands were wounded in action. In response, the Australian Government established the 'Soldier Settler Scheme', providing farmland and funds to returning soldiers.

The end of war heralded the 'Roaring Twenties' and a whirlwind of new cars, American jazz and movies as well as fervour for the British Empire. When the Great Depression hit in 1929, social and economic divisions widened and many Australian financial institutions collapsed. Sport was the national distraction and sporting heroes, such as racehorse champion Phar Lap and cricketer Donald Bradman, gained near-mythical status.

During the Second World War, Australian forces made a significant contribution to the Allied victory in Europe, Asia and the Pacific. In February of 1942, the largest single attack ever conducted by a foreign military power on Australia took place in Darwin. The Bombing of Darwin involved 260 enemy aircraft and targetted the town, port and airfields. The generation that fought in the war and survived came out of it with a sense of pride.

F. During the war many new occupations opened to women, and the number of women employed grew quickly. When WWII ended in 1945, hundreds of thousands of migrants from across Europe and the Middle East arrived in Australia, many finding jobs in the rapidly growing manufacturing sector. Australia's economy flourished throughout the 1950s with major nation-building projects such as the Snowy Mountains Hydroelectric Scheme and the Sydney Opera House. International demand grew for Australia's major exports of metals, wools, meat and wheat and suburban Australia also prospered. The rate of home ownership rose dramatically from barely 40 per cent in 1947 to more than 70 per cent by the 1960s.

G. Australians were swept up in the revolutionary atmosphere of the 1960s. Australia's new ethnic diversity, increasing independence from Britain and popular resistance to the Vietnam War all contributed to an atmosphere of political, economic and social change.

In 1967, Australians voted overwhelmingly 'yes' in a national referendum to let the federal government make laws on behalf of Aboriginal Australians and include them in future censuses. The result was the culmination of a strong reform campaign by both Aboriginal and white Australians.

In 1972, the Australian Labour Party under the idealistic leadership of Gough Whitlam was elected to power, ending the post-war domination of the Liberal and Country Party coalition. Over the next three years, his new government ended conscription, abolished university fees, introduced free universal health care, abandoned the White Australia policy, embraced multiculturalism and introduced no-fault divorce and equal pay for women.

H. Between 1983 and 1996, the Hawke–Keating Labour governments introduced a number of economic reforms, such as deregulating the banking system and floating the Australian dollar. In 1996 a Coalition Government led by John Howard won the general election and was re-elected in 1998, 2001 and 2004. The Liberal–National Coalition Government enacted several reforms, including changes in the taxation and industrial relations systems.

In 2007 the Labour Party, led by Kevin Rudd, was elected with an agenda to reform Australia's industrial relations system, cut greenhouse emissions and implement a national curriculum in education. Three years later, Rudd was challenged by Julia Gillard who was to become the first female Prime Minister of Australia. In 2013 the new Coalition government was sworn in, led by Tony Abbott. In September 2015 Abbott was defeated in a leadership ballot by Malcolm Turnbull, who was re-elected in a general election in July 2016. In August of 2018, Scott Morrison of the Liberal Party was sworn in as Prime Minister of Australia.

Questions 36 – 40

Fill in the blanks in the sentences below using **ONE WORD ONLY** for each answer from the text.

36. Aboriginal people all believed in the Dreaming, although the places where they lived all over Australia were very .... in terms of the flora, fauna, climate etc.
37. At first, the British colony was used to house ....
38. There were winds of .... in the country during the 1960s.
39. Following a .... by both the original people and settlers who came later, Australians approved that the govt. make laws on behalf of the former.
40. Following the war, several major projects were undertaken, which ensured that the .... prospered.

GT READING TEST 19

SECTION 1

Questions 1 – 14

Read the text below and answer Questions 1 – 7

TEN GREATEST OSCAR WINNERS FOR BEST PICTURE

The ten best movie Oscar award winners of all time are:

10. Gone with the Wind (1939)

Historically, it's a mess. Civil war explanations are muddy and the film completely sidesteps the issue of slavery. (Mammy and Big Sam seem like O'Hara family friends.) Despite its flaws, this is one of the best examples of big-scale Hollywood storytelling, funny, sad and always involving. As a bonus, Vivien Leigh offers one of the screen's great performances as the self-centred, steely Scarlett O'Hara. W

9. All About Eve (1950)

Along with "Casablanca" and "The Wizard of Oz," this film may have the most quotable lines of dialogue in movie history. The plot is a rare Hollywood look at professional rivalries, and it is non-stop witty; there are numerous great performances under writer-director Joseph L Mankiewicz. Along with "Titanic" and "La La Land," it holds the Oscar record for nominations, with each earning 14; "Eve" won six.

8. The Hurt Locket (2008)

Director Kathryn Bigelow and screenwriter Mark Boal succeeded where many previous filmmakers failed: They made a movie that gave the Iraq War an immediacy and made the actions there seem both terrifying and heroic. Both won Academy Awards for their work, and Bigelow so far remains the only woman director to win an award.

7. The Titanic (1997)

Rich girl, poor boy, a doomed love affair – the film walks a fine line between corny and classic, but it works like gang busters. James Cameroon had epic ambitions and makes everything work, with ground-breaking contributions behind the camera plus Leonardo DiCaprio and Kate Winslett portraying one of the great screen romances.

6. 12 Years a Slave (2013)

The Steve McQueen-directed film meets the criterion of greatness: It makes audiences see things in a new way. The film upends many preconceptions about slavery, 19th century life, and about human nature. John Ridley scripted from Solomon Northup's memoirs, resulting in a powerful experience.

5. The Lord of the Rings: The Return of the King (2003)

J.R.R. Tolkien invented an entire universe with his trilogy of books. Many filmmakers tried to adapt them with no success, until New Zealand's Peter Jackson came along in one of film history's greatest gambles, by filming three epics simultaneously. Jackson reinvented film language with new technology and he kept the multiple narratives always clear and exciting.

4. The Best Years of Our Lives (1946)

In 1946, producer Samuel Goldwyn wanted to do a film about WWII veterans re-adjusting to life back home, long before anyone knew the term PTSD. Most people thought it was too soon. But director William Wyler and writer Robert Sherwood (adapting MacKinlay Kantor's novel) pulled it off. The film is still devastating and the performance of first-time actor Harold Russell; he won two Oscars for this one performance.

3. Casablanca (1942)

The major-studios in the 1930s and '40s cranked out many forgettable films. But magic happens. This film, set in World War 2, has been a fan favourite for 75 years, thanks to the work of producer Hal Wallis, writers Howard Koch and the Epstein brothers (Julius and Philip), director Michael Curtiz and stars Humphrey Bogart and Ingrid Bergman.

2. Lawrence of Arabia (1962)

Scripted by Robert Bolt and Michael Wilson, and directed by David Lean, this is one of the most physically beautiful films ever made. The WWI-set saga, which mixes world politics with a deeply complex character, will work in home viewing. But for full impact, it should be seen on the big screen

1. The Godfather (1972)

Hollywood has made hundreds of gangster films, but Francis Ford Coppola's direction and script (with novelist Mario Puzo) take the genre to a whole other level. The Corleone saga, rich in detail and characters, succeeds as a mob film, a family drama and as a metaphor for big business.

Questions 1 – 7

Match the descriptions given below to one of the movies in the text above. Write the correct number next to the questions 1-7 in your answer sheet.

1. A novice won an Oscar in this movie.
2. The director of this movie was the first woman to be awarded for her craft.
3. This is indeed a jocular film.
4. This movie is based in a setting that does not exist in real life.
5. This is a movie about those who do not abide by the law.
6. This movie changes ones perceptions of what a life of subjugated servility was like centuries ago.
7. A movie with a memorable performance by an actress in a role where she is portrayed as a strong woman who cares only about herself.

Read the text below and answer Questions 8 – 14

THE PENNY THAT SAVED A LIFE

Of the three Trickett brothers who left their home in Lincolnshire to fight for the United Kingdom in the First World War, only John would survive. Horace and Billy were among the more than eight million soldiers killed in the Great War, which saw casualties on an unprecedented scale due to the advent of new, more advanced weapons. John, however, was saved by the most ordinary and rudimentary equipment on the entire battlefield: a penny in his breast pocket that deflected a bullet intended for his heart.

The penny, issued in 1889 (10 years before John was born) and severely bent from the bullet's impact, was sold on March 22, 2019, in Hansons Auctioneers' Medals and Militaria Auction. Initially, the highest bid was £1,700, vastly exceeding Hansons' initial estimate of between £100 and £200. Ultimately, it sold for £4500. The lot included a British victory medal as well as Trickett's 1918 discharge certificate, among other items.

Six phone bidders as well as internet bidders battled to own the collection but it was sold to a buyer in the room – Mr. Nigel Trickett, 55, of Owston Ferry, near Doncaster. Mr. Trickett, owner of a carpet business, said: "Private Trickett was my grand-dad and we wanted to keep the medals and penny in the family. It will be handed down. It's where it belongs and we'll take a lot of pride in showing it to family members.

"When the story went viral it brought 50 members of the family together – we all got in touch with each other. My grand-dad's story is very interesting and true. Everything wouldn't have happened in our family the way it has without that penny.

While we don't know precisely when and where Private Trickett had his brush with death, Adrian Stevenson, Hansons' military expert, says that the incident occurred in 1917, on the war's Western Front. The bullet, fired by a German soldier, ricocheted off Trickett's penny and traveled up through Trickett's nose, exiting through his left ear. Trickett lost hearing in that ear for the rest of his life, his granddaughter Maureen Coulson told Hansons. Trickett received an honorable discharge from the military in September 1918. After coming home, he got married, had eight children, and worked as a postmaster and switchboard operator.

Coulson answered a Hanson's advertisement for a routine valuation event, bringing the penny and Trickett's other effects to Stevenson. Ironically, the coin was "one of those real impossible things to value," says Stevenson, who eventually settled on a relatively low estimate for the item due to the "very modest" value of the metal itself. It's not the first time in Stevenson's career that he's heard of an everyday item blocking a bullet and making the difference between life and death. Bibles, shaving mirrors, and cigarette cases, he says, have all done the same—and during the war, some manufacturers even began advertising thicker mirrors, explicitly pitching their life-saving potential.

"It's strange to think," said Coulson, "that, but for that penny, [Trickett's] children would not have been born and I wouldn't be here." There could be many more families throughout the world who could say the same about other objects: Since Coulson delivered the coin to Hansons, the auction house has also acquired a shrapnel-damaged flask and belt buckle that may have saved their carriers.

"I was born after my grand-dad died but I remember seeing the penny when I was seven. We plan to visit my grand-dad's grave in Bolton upon Dearne, Yorkshire, on the way home."
The medal was sold by Private Trickett's grand-daughter Mrs. Maureen Coulson, 63, from Duffield, Derbyshire, who plans to give some of the proceeds to charity.

Questions 8 – 14

Do the following statements agree with the information given in the text?

In boxes on your answer sheet, write

TRUE	if the statement agrees with the information
FALSE	if the statement contradicts the information
NOT GIVEN	if there is no information on this.

8. The penny was a piece of equipment issued to all soldiers.
9. The penny that saved Trickett's life was bought by his grand-son.
10. John Trickett served in the British Army till 1918.
11. The auction house set a low initial price for the penny because it was made of a metal which was not very expensive.
12. But for the penny, there would have been no Mr. Coulson.
13. Thicker shaving mirrors helped to save lives during the war.
14. The auction house had acquired a shrapnel damaged flask that helped save the life of its owner.

SECTION 2

Read the text below and answer Questions 15 – 27

Questions 15 – 21

Given below is a map of a downtown area. Based upon the conversation given below, name the alphabet depicting the location of the following:

15. Walmart: ....
16. Farmer's market: ....
17. Main market street: ....
18. Parking lot: ....
19. All about eve: ....
20. The night crawler: ....
21. Coffee & beans: ....

THE DOWNTOWN AREA

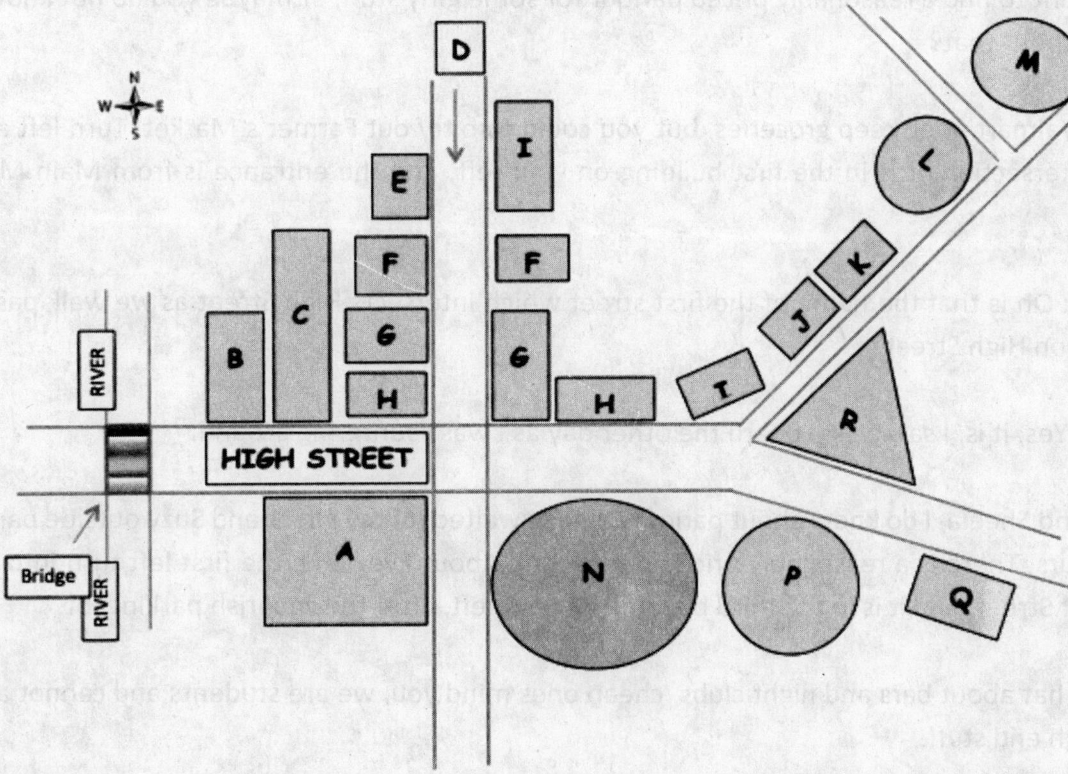

Dan: Hi, I am Dan. I have not seen you around before, are you new to this college? What is your name?

Harry: Hi Dan, I am Harry. I have just joined this semester and am new to this town. Meet my friend, Sheela; she has also joined with me. Boy, are we glad to have met you, we were hoping to get some directions around town.

Dan: Sure, it would be a pleasure, shoot, what do you want to know?

Harry: First off, I am looking for some part time work. Where do you think I can find some?

Dan: Well, that is a tough one, but you could try Walmart.

Sheela: Walmart? They really do not pay so well, but all the same, where is it?

Dan: See, we are standing on the bridge here. If you walk down High Street, you will come to a fork on the road. Go South-east, and the first building on the right is Walmart.

Sheela: Oh great, we will go there later today. Meanwhile, where can I pick up some groceries? I also want to find a reasonably priced parlour for some girly stuff, or maybe you do not know too much about that?

Dan: Walmart does keep groceries, but you could also try out Farmer's Market. Turn left at the first intersection, it is in the first building on your left, and the entrance is from Main Market Street.

Sheela: Oh is that the name of the first street which intersects High Street as we walk past the bridge on High Street?

Harry: Yes, it is, I saw a sign board the other day as I was sauntering around.

Dan: And Sheela, I do know about parlours, I have waited for my girl-friend Suzy outside parlours for hours. There is a reasonably priced parlour, All About Eve. Take the first left turn into Main Market Street, and it is in the third building on your left, after the squarish parking lot.

Dan, what about bars and night clubs, cheap ones mind you, we are students and cannot afford the high end stuff.

Dan: But of course. So, there is The Night Crawler. You walk down High Street, and go north-east at the fork. Keep walking, and you will find a road branching off to your left. Just after this road, there is a circular building inside which this pub is located. It is by far the most popular bar in town. There is another one, closer, in the building just after Walmart. It is called The Bar Above.
Sheela: Well, while Harry sorts out his night life, Dan, I would like to go to a coffee shop once in a while and use their free Wi-Fi to catch upon my work. Can you suggest me some place suitable?

Dan: My favourite place is Coffee and Beans. They have a small outlet in the building next to Farmer's Market as you walk down High Street.

Harry: Thank you, Dan, you have been a great help.

Sheela: Oh yes, we now feel we know our way about town.

Dan: You are welcome guys!

Questions 22-27

Read the following job ads and answer the questions at the end.

A. A multi-product firm selling domestic appliances with branches across the country is looking for a marketing manager. The job entails interaction with distributors and dealers and extensive travel to meet them and understand and address their issues. A post graduate qualification in marketing and experience of at least 5 years in a similar role or profile is essential.

B. We are in the business of making your homes cooler in summers and warmer in winters with appropriate appliances. For our regional office, we need a marketing co-ordinator. The role includes interaction with dealers and a good knowledge of marketing essentials. Please apply if you have an MBA in marketing coupled with appropriate experience.

C. To promote our newly launched range of home air purifiers, Breathe Easy, we are creating teams of promoters who would demonstrate these products at places with a high foot fall, such as malls, or in high end housing societies and clubs. Female candidates with a pleasing personality and excellent communication skills are encouraged to apply. The job would require travelling within the city where you will be located.

D. We are an established firm dealing in industrial detergents and market our products through a network of dealers. In order to further our reach in the market, we need a marketing director, who will spearhead our efforts in doubling our market-share in the next three years. Young and ambitious marketing professionals with similar prior experience may apply.

E. We are a leading recruitment consulting company, providing our services to a wide variety of clients across different market segments. We specialize in marketing opportunities and have a large number of currently available openings for which we are sourcing suitable candidates on behalf of our clients. A formal qualification in marketing is always as asset and looked upon favourably. Send us your resume with details of your qualification and experience and let us take your career to the next level!

F. We are the country's leading service provider in the care and maintenance of domestic appliances. We not only provide warranty maintenance services, but also contractual services for maintenance contracts and one-off paid services. In order to address a critical need, we wish to appoint a marketing head expeditiously. He will work intimately with our existing client base and also our alliance partners, whose products we service. He will also need to increase the alliance partners so as to increase the product portfolio. Revenue and bottom line growth will be the key parameters. Candidates with suitable experience may apply.

G. We are a multi-level marketing firm, with a wide range of household products in our portfolio. We are looking for sales promoters who will in turn form their own teams from among their social circles to grow and expand their business and earnings. We are looking for outgoing individuals with good social skills, and a burning desire to excel will do well.

Questions 22-27

Which paragraph contains the answer to the following questions. Write the correct alphabet A-G in boxes 22-27 of your answer sheet.

22. Which company sells products that are not used at home?
23. Which ad is not for a job opening?
24. Which job opening ad is from a company which does not sell a product?
25. If you do not have an MBA in marketing, do not apply for this job.
26. Which company has given the name of its product in the ad?
27. Which job opening can be applied for by a person with no prior job experience?

SECTION 3

Read the text below and answer questions 28 – 40

Questions 28 - 34

The text has 7 SECTIONS, marked A to G. Choose the correct heading for each paragraph from the list of headings below.

i. The largest of them all
ii. It all began at saqqara
iii. A mythological creature immortalized
iv. A peek into a majestic, gone-by era
v. The end of the pyramid era
vi. The pyramids remain magical
vii. A haven for ka
viii. Honoring Osiris, the God of the dead
ix. The third and fourth dynasties

28. Paragraph A ....
29. Paragraph B ....
30. Paragraph C ....
31. Paragraph D ....
32. Paragraph E ....
33. Paragraph F ....
34. Paragraph G ....

THE PYRAMIDS

A. Built during a time when Egypt was one of the richest and most powerful civilizations in the world, the pyramids—especially the Great Pyramids of Giza—are some of the most magnificent man-made structures in history. Their massive scale reflects the unique role that the pharaoh (king) played in ancient Egyptian society. Though pyramids were built from the beginning of the Old Kingdom to the close of the Ptolemaic period in the fourth century A.D., the peak of pyramid building began with the late third dynasty and continued until roughly the sixth (c. 2325 B.C.). More than 4,000 years later, the Egyptian pyramids still retain much of their majesty, providing a glimpse into the country's rich and glorious past.

B. During the third and fourth dynasties of the Old Kingdom, Egypt enjoyed tremendous economic prosperity and stability. Somewhere in between human and divine, pharaohs were believed to have been chosen by the gods to serve as mediators between them and the people on earth.

Because of this, it was in everyone's interest to keep the king's majesty intact even after his death, when he was believed to become Osiris, god of the dead. The new pharaoh, in turn, became Horus, the falcon-god who served as protector of the sun-god, Ra.

Ancient Egyptians believed that when the king died, part of his spirit, known as "ka", remained with his body. To properly care for his spirit, the corpse was mummified, and everything the king would need in the afterlife was buried with him, including gold vessels, food, furniture and other offerings. The pyramids became the focus of a cult of the dead king that was supposed to continue well after his death. Their riches would provide not only for him, but also for the relatives, officials and priests who were buried near him.

C. From the beginning of the Dynastic Era (2950 B.C.), royal tombs were carved into rock and covered with flat-roofed rectangular structures known as "mastabas," which were precursors to the pyramids. The oldest known pyramid in Egypt was built around 2630 B.C. at Saqqara, for the third dynasty's King Djoser. Known as the Step Pyramid, it began as a traditional mastaba but grew into something much more ambitious. As the story goes, the pyramid's architect was Imhotep, a priest and healer who some 1,400 years later would be deified as the patron saint of scribes and physicians. Over the course of Djoser's nearly 20-year reign, pyramid builders assembled six stepped layers of stone (as opposed to mud-brick, like most earlier tombs) that eventually reached a height of 204 feet (62 meters); it was the tallest building of its time.

After Djoser, the stepped pyramid became the norm for royal burials, although none of those planned by his dynastic successors were completed (probably due to their relatively short reigns). The earliest tomb constructed as a "true" (smooth-sided, not stepped) pyramid was the Red Pyramid at Dahshur, one of three burial structures built for the first king of the fourth dynasty, Sneferu (2613-2589 B.C.) It was named for the color of the limestone blocks used to construct the pyramid's core.

D. No pyramids are more celebrated than the Great Pyramids of Giza, located on a plateau on the west bank of the Nile River, on the outskirts of modern-day Cairo. The oldest and largest of the three pyramids at Giza, known as the Great Pyramid, is the only surviving structure out of the famed seven wonders of the ancient world. It was built for Khufu (Cheops, in Greek), Sneferu's successor and the second of the eight kings of the fourth dynasty. Though Khufu reigned for 23 years (2589-2566 B.C.), relatively little is known of his reign beyond the grandeur of his pyramid. The sides of the pyramid's base average 755.75 feet (230 meters), and its original height was 481.4 feet (147 meters), making it the largest pyramid in the world.

Approximately 2.3 million blocks of stone, averaging about 2.5 tons each had to be cut, transported and assembled to build Khufu's Great Pyramid. Though some popular versions of history held that the pyramids were built by slaves or foreigners forced into labor, skeletons excavated from the area show that the workers were probably native Egyptian agricultural laborers who worked on the pyramids during the time of year when the Nile River flooded much of the land nearby.

E. The middle pyramid at Giza was built for Khufu's son Khafre (2558-2532 B.C). A unique feature built inside Khafre's pyramid complex was the Great Sphinx, a guardian statue carved in limestone with the head of a man and the body of a lion. It was the largest statue in the ancient world, measuring 240 feet long and 66 feet high. Its face seems to bear a resemblance to Khafre's, and the royal headdress that it wears is particular to pharaohs.
The Sphinx is a mythological creature and is said to have terrorized the people by demanding the answer to a riddle: What is it that has one voice and yet becomes four-footed and two-footed and three-footed? Eventually Oedipus gave the proper answer: man, who crawls on all fours in infancy, walks on two feet when grown, and leans on a staff in old age. The sphinx thereupon killed herself. From this tale apparently grew the legend that the sphinx was omniscient and even today the wisdom of the sphinx is proverbial.

F. Pyramids continued to be built throughout the fifth and sixth dynasties, but the general quality and scale of their construction declined over this period, along with the power and wealth of the kings themselves. The last of the great pyramid builders was Pepy II (2278-2184 B.C.), who came to power as a young boy and supposedly ruled for 94 years. By the time of his rule, Old Kingdom prosperity was dwindling, and the pharaoh had lost some of his quasi-divine status as the power of non-royal administrative officials grew. Pepy II's pyramid, built at Saqqara was much shorter (172 feet) than others of the Old Kingdom. With Pepy's death, the kingdom and strong central government virtually collapsed. Later kings, of the 12th dynasty, would return to pyramid building during the so-called Middle Kingdom phase, but it was never on the same scale as the Great Pyramids.

G. Tomb robbers and other vandals in both ancient and modern times have removed most of the bodies and funeral goods from Egypt's pyramids and plundered their exteriors as well. Stripped of most of their smooth white limestone coverings, the Great Pyramids no longer reach their original heights; Khufu's, for example, measures only 451 feet high.
Nonetheless, millions of people continue to visit the pyramids each year, drawn by their towering grandeur and the enduring allure of Egypt's rich and glorious past. Today, they continue to work their magic on all who visit. No trip to Egypt is complete without time spent here at one of the world's most recognizable tourist attractions. Towering incongruously over the edge of Cairo's suburban sprawl, these mighty monuments are a tribute to the power and ambition of Egypt's Pharaonic rulers.

Questions 35 – 40

Complete the following sentences using **NO MORE THAN ONE WORD** from the text:

35. The humongous effort that went into building the pyramids is indicative of the very special position of the ....

36. It was believed that the kings were supposed to be a kind of a bridge or a ...., between their subjects and the gods.

37. Before the pyramids came into being, the royal tombs were shaped differently, and called ....

38. The mastaba that grew into a pyramid was built by ....

39. Contrary to other accounts, the Great Pyramid was built by Egyptians, and not by forced ....

40. Although they have been vandalised, the Pyramids continue to.................. visitors in large numbers.

GT READING TEST 20

SECTION 1

Questions 1 – 14

Read the text below and answer Questions 1 – 7

AFRICAN DESERTS

Deserts– barren areas that receive little rain and offer harsh living conditions– are not the first landscapes that spring to mind for most people considering where to go on vacation. But there are 33 major deserts, from subtropical and cool coastal to cold winter deserts, and most are sparsely populated. So, for those hoping to "get away from it all," here's a look at three of largest deserts in the Africa, with compelling reasons why you should add some to your bucket list.

SAHARA DESERT: With a total area of over 3.5 million square miles, the third biggest desert in the world covers approximately 31% of the African continent. It spans twelve different North African countries, from Mauritania and Morocco in the west over to Egypt and Sudan in the east. The Sahara is the largest hot subtropical desert in the world: Only the Arctic and Antarctica are bigger. Its low latitude location makes it extremely hot and dry, with virtually no rainfall whatsoever. Yet still it boasts a surprisingly diverse array of flora and fauna, including around 2800 species of plants. Humans have lived here for at least 10,000 years, with some 30,000 petroglyphs remaining as evidence.

In terms of wildlife, the region is home to three species of Fox, numerous Gazelles and Antelopes, two endangered subspecies of Cheetah, African Wild Dogs, Monitor Lizards, Hyrax, North African Ostrich, Desert Crocodiles, and numerous other animals. In terms of domesticated species, Camels and Goats are by far the most common.

KALAHARI DESERT: Covering approximately 360,000 square miles, the world's sixth biggest desert is in central Southern Africa. It ranges from Angola down through Botswana and Namibia to South Africa. The hunter-gatherer San people have inhabited this area for over 20,000 years. The Kalahari is what's known as a semi-desert, receiving around 5 to 10 inches of rain each year on average. It has vast expanses of arid land, including salt pans such as Namibi's Etosha Pan and Botswana's Makgadikgadi Pan (one of the largest in the world). But it's also home to Okavango River, which flows into the world-renowned delta of the same name. So, depending on where you go, you may see wildlife such as African Wild Dogs, Cheetahs, Giraffes, Leopards, Lions, Spotted Hyenas, and countless other species.

If you're interested in taking a wildlife safari, the Kalahari has several amazing destinations that have yet to see the overcrowding that comes with mass tourism. The most noteworthy are Kgalagadi Trans-frontier Park, Central Kalahari Game Reserve, the world's second largest wildlife park, and Tswalu Kalahari, Southern Africa's largest private game reserve.

NAMIB DESERT: Encompassing 31,000 square miles, the Namib Desert is by far the smallest on this list. But if you talk to anyone who's traveled there, they'll probably tell you it's the desert most worth visiting, containing some of Namibia's most incredible ecotourism attractions.
Though sparsely populated, there are rich indigenous cultures there, such as the Himba and Herero people. There's the Skeleton Coast, which is littered with more than 1,000 shipwrecks due to the dense fog there. There are massive Fur Seal colonies, not to mention the Lions that often prey on them.
In terms of other wildlife, the region is home to numerous weird animals that have adapted to the arid climate. These include Desert Elephants and a Darkling Beetle that can catch and drink moisture from fog using bumps and troughs on its back. But the region's #1 attraction is Namib-Naukluft National Park, one of the largest in the world. The park is home to iconic sites such as the striking red dunes of Sossusvlei, the skeleton trees of Deadvlei, and Sesriem Canyon, a 98-foot deep canyon that's often overlooked by tourists.

Questions 1 – 7

Do the following statements agree with the information given in the text?

In boxes on your answer sheet, write

TRUE	if the statement agrees with the information
FALSE	if the statement contradicts the information
NOT GIVEN	if there is no information on this.

1. Deserts the world over experience very high temperatures.
2. The Sahara is the largest desert in Africa.
3. While one finds domesticated animals like camels in the Sahara desert, wild animals are conspicuous by their absence.
4. Kalahari is the only desert which has a river running through it.
5. The number of tourists visiting the wildlife safaris at the Kalahari is lesser as compared to other safari locations
6. The Namib Desert adjoins a coastal area.
7. Tourists at the Namibian National Park often look into the 98 ft. deep canyon, the Sesriem Canyon.

Read the text below and answer Questions 8 – 14

THE JAPANESE TEA CEREMONY

The Japanese tea ceremony is a tradition steeped in history. It is a ceremonial way of preparing and drinking green tea typically in a traditional tearoom. Beyond just serving and receiving tea, one of the main purposes of the tea ceremony is for the guests to enjoy the hospitality of the host in an atmosphere distinct from the fast pace of everyday life.

Historical background: Tea was introduced to Japan in the 8th. century from China and was drunk as a medicinal beverage mainly amongst priests and the upper class. Among the affluent members of society, tea drinking parties became popular. Around the same time, a more refined version of tea parties developed with Zen inspired simplicity and a greater emphasis on spirituality. It is from these gatherings that the tea ceremony has its origins.

Tea ceremony procedure: A formal tea ceremony is a multi-hour event that starts with a meal, followed by a bowl of thick tea and ends with a bowl of thin tea. However, most tea ceremonies these days are much abbreviated events that are limited to the enjoyment of a bowl of thin tea. The protocol of a tea ceremony is defined down to exact hand movements. In most cases, regular tourists are not expected to know the rules in detail, but knowledge of the basic points can help make the event a more dignified affair.

Dress code: Avoid gaudy fashion and fragrance that distracts from the tea experience. Wear modest clothes, remove jewelry that may damage the tea equipment and avoid strong perfumes.

Garden: The traditional tea ceremony venue is surrounded by a garden, although many modern venues lack a garden. The garden is deliberately kept tranquil and simple to encourage a calm spirit. Stones of varying shapes and sizes make up the path that leads to the teahouse. A stone lantern is placed close to a stone basin near the entrance where visitors wash their hands before entering the tearoom.

The Ceremony: The ceremony is traditionally held in a tatami room. The entrance for guests is kept low so that entering guests have to bend over, symbolizing humility. Decorative elements in the tea-room include an alcove where a scroll or seasonal flowers are displayed. After a bow, the head guest enters the room and takes the seat closest to the alcove, followed by the other guests. Once guests have taken their positions, it is customary to bow once more before observing the decorations which were carefully selected for the occasion.

The tea bowl is placed onto the tatami mat in front of you, with its front facing you. Pick it up with your right hand and place it on your left palm. With your right hand, turn it clockwise by around 90 degrees so that its front is not facing you anymore. Drink the tea in a few sips and place it back onto the tatami. Bow and express gratitude after receiving and finishing your tea.

Towards the end of the ceremony, there will be time to inspect and appreciate the tea bowl by lifting it. Once finished, turn the bowl so that the front now faces the host. The host may ask if guests would like another round of tea, and if not, the tea ceremony is over when the host washes the tea utensils and returns the equipment to where they were before starting.

Questions 8 – 14

Fill in the blanks using words from the box given below:

8. The tea ceremony in Japan is no ordinary event; it is very traditional and is .... with a historical legacy.
9. Tea was introduced from China and in Japan; it became popular among the .... members of society.
10. The exact .... of activities to be followed in a tea ceremony is laid down in great detail.
11. The attire worn for the tea ceremony should be such that it does not .... from the objective of the occasion.
12. While these days it is not always the case, the .... tea ceremony venue is usually in the middle of a garden.
13. It is an indication of ...., when one has to bend to go past the low entrance to the room where the tea ceremony is held.
14. When you drink the tea, the front of the bowl should face .... from you.

soaked	**successful**	**diverts**	**humbleness**	**side-track**
befuddle	**detract**	**imbued**	**conventional**	**sequence**
fashionable	**prosperous**	**away**	**opposite**	**towards**

SECTION 2

Read the text below and answer Questions 15 – 29

Questions 15 – 21

The following are a collection of advertisements. Read them and answer the questions at the end.

A. **Windy Bays** is the resort to be in when you visit Goa. A 10 minute walk from the beach, you are away from the noise and hustle and bustle, and at the same time, within easy reach of the beach. Buffet breakfast is complimentary, as is an airport pick-up and drop. Book your rooms early to avail of the best rates.

B. **The Shanty Shacks** are exactly what the beach-bummers look for when in Goa. Walk out of your room and feel the fine white sands crunching between your toes; and even before you have got over this delightfully exhilarating experience you will find yourself in the warm and welcoming waters of the Arabian Sea. You can choose to share a room and thus save on costs and also make new friends. Restaurants are plentiful on the beach, so all your meals are just a holler away.

C. One block from the beach, **The Mandarin** is a premium property in Goa, redefining luxury for the discerning tourist. Tastefully appointed en suite rooms and suites, three in-house restaurants serving Chinese, Italian and Indian cuisines, an Olympic sized swimming pool, a well-equipped gym and en-suite bathrooms complete the Mandarin experience.

D. **The Sea King Hotel** has been a favourite of travellers on business and leisure for a long long time. A well-equipped conference-cum-banquet hall with in-built audio-visual equipment, attentive service staff, and group discount for corporates, along with a resto-bar with live music on weekends; add to it the swimming pool, gym and billiards room, shuttles to and from the beach every 15 minutes during peak hours, the Sea King is the King of hotels in Goa.

E. **The House on the Mandovi River** is beautifully located property, with a view of the hills adjacent to Panjim on one side and serenely flowing river on the other. Wake up to the chirping of birds, revel in the beauties of nature and relax and refresh yourself, away from the hustle and bustle of your daily grind. Join our daily Yoga classes or walk across to the spa for a rejuvenating session with our experts. Airport pick-up and drop is available on request.

F. **Mystical Chimes** is the place to be come to when in Goa. Our in-house band is the most well known in these parts and with Arushi, the award winning Deejay at the turn-table, our evenings are jam-packed with the young at heart wanting to shake a leg. Your cover includes a buffet dinner, and you can bring your alcohol, what else would you want? We place a limit on the number of guests, so dial in now and make a booking!

G. **The Hermitage** is one of Goa's best known hotels for exotic views, where every room is tastefully done up with its own private balcony over-looking the ocean, which is just around the corner of the street. Add to it the Oriental restaurant where we serve delicious cuisines including vegan choices, 24 hrs. room service and a travel desk to take care of all your local travel needs including air-port pick-up and drop, ours is a hard choice to beat.

Questions 15-21

Which paragraph contains the answer to the following questions. Write the correct alphabet A-G in boxes 15-21 of your answer sheet.

15. Which is the hotel closest to the beach?
16. You do not take dairy products. Which hotel would you go to for a meal?
17. You would like to get a massage every other day, which hotel would you choose?
18. Which is not a hotel ad?
19. Which hotel has advertised that its rooms have an attached bathroom and toilet?
20. Which hotel offers a free airport pick up and drop?
21. Which hotel would you choose to organize a board meeting?

Read the text below and answer Questions 22 – 29

THE RIGHT EXTINGUISHER FOR THE RIGHT KIND OF FIRE

It is perhaps not quite well known that the nearest fire extinguisher may not be appropriate for the fire that just broke out. Just as there are different kinds of fires, there are different kinds of extinguishers. Let us understand the specifics.

Fires are classified into six different types, based upon what has caught fire, except for electrical fires, where the classification is based not on what is on fire, but by what has caused it, which in this case is electrical equipment.

The most basic fire, Type A, is a fire involving organic solids like wood or paper. Forest fires would fall in this category. These fires can be put out by all extinguishers except the ones using special powders or carbon di-oxide. Type B fire occurs when, let us say, an oil spill catches fire, meaning a flammable liquid is on fire. Type C fires are similar to Type B fires, except that instead of a flammable liquid, it is a flammable gas on fire. For both these kinds of fire, one should avoid using a water based extinguisher; for the former, one would use an extinguisher which uses either foam, or dry powder or carbon di-oxide; for the latter, only the dry powder based extinguisher is used.

Going on the next three kinds of fires, Class D fires are where there are burning metals; there is no Class E, but there is a Class F which signifies fires involving fats such as those used in deep fat fryers. For electric fires, there is no letter used; instead the symbol of an electric spark is used. While only a wet chemical type of an extinguisher can be used for a fire involving cooking fats, for electrical fires we can use extinguishers based either on dry powder or carbon di-oxide; and for a Class D fire, one uses a wet chemical based extinguisher. So, if you have been reading carefully, you would note that there are six kinds of fires and an equal number of extinguishers.

It is also interesting to note that each kind of extinguisher is distinguished by a unique colour combination. While extinguishers which use water as the agent to put out the fire are red in colour, all others have, in addition to the red, an add-on colour panel above the operating instructions printed on the extinguisher, to differentiate them. Thus, while a foam based unit will have a cream panel, a dry powder or a special powder type of an extinguisher will have a blue one. Finally, those using carbon dioxide to extinguish the fire will have a black panel, and ones using wet chemical will have a yellow one.

Questions 22-26

The box below has a grid with the types of fire and types of extinguishers in a tabular format.

Answer

YES if the Type of Extinguisher is appropriate to be used for the type of fire,

NO if the Type of Extinguisher is NOT appropriate to be used for the type of fire,

NA If the requisite information is not given, type

As an example, the column under a Type A Fire has been filled out.

Type of Fire → / ↓ Type of Extinguisher						
WATER	YES			22...........		
FOAM	YES				23.	
DRY POWDER	YES	24.				
SPECIAL POWDER	NO					
CARBON DIOXIDE	NO				25...........	
WET CHEMICAL	YES					26. ....

Questions 27 – 29

Do the following statements agree with the information given in the text?

In boxes on your answer sheet, write

TRUE if the statement agrees with the information

FALSE if the statement contradicts the information

NOT GIVEN if there is no information on this.

27. The Dry Powder based fire extinguisher is the most versatile extinguisher as it can be used in most kinds of fires.
28. A Class B fire can be handled with the most number of different kinds of fire extinguishers
29. No two kinds of extinguishers have the same colour of panel in addition to red on them.

SECTION 3

Read the text below and answer questions 30 – 40

Questions 30 - 36

The text has 8 SECTIONS, marked A to G. Choose the correct heading for each paragraph from the list of headings below.

i. A bed of roses life is not
ii. Umpiring perils
iii. A male preserve
iv. The divine connect
v. A matter of girth
vi. Wardrobe guidelines
vii. Rules of the game
viii. The case of the lady governor
ix. Eat and sleep ad infinitum
x. It is a very old sport

30. Paragraph A ....
31. Paragraph B ....
32. Paragraph C ....
33. Paragraph D ....
34. Paragraph E ....
35. Paragraph F ....
36. Paragraph G ....

SUMO WRESTLING

This is a write-upon sumo wrestling, the national sport of Japan.

A. Compared with most sports in the world today, sumo originated a long time ago. About 1,500 years, in fact. From the very beginning it was entwined with Shinto ritual, when it was performed at shrines to ensure a bountiful harvest and to honour the spirits – known as kami. Sumo is still very closely associated with its religious origins, and Shinto principles continue to govern the everyday life of today's sumo wrestlers. Each of the ring-entering ceremonies is a Shinto purification ritual, and every newly promoted yokozuna (the highest rank in sumo) performs his first ring-entering ceremony at the Meiji Shrine in Tokyo. The canopy that hangs over the ring is modelled after the roof of a Shinto shrine, indicating that the ring itself is a holy place.

B. A sumo match doesn't start until both wrestlers have placed both hands on the ground at the same time. This leads to quite a lot of fannying about whilst each wrestler tries to psyche the other out, pretending to put his hand down and then getting back up again.
Once they finally do begin, it is very rare for sumo bouts to last longer than a few seconds – although occasionally they can go on for a few minutes. This means that the action is very fast-paced and exciting. A match ends when one of the wrestlers is either thrown out of the ring, or if any part of his body apart from the soles of his feet touches the ground.
Interestingly, the match can also end if one of the wrestlers loses his mawashi, or loincloth – in which case the de-loin-clothed wrestler is disqualified. This outcome is very rare in sumo, but a wardrobe malfunction did occur during a match in May 2000, when the unfortunate wrestler was disqualified immediately.

C. It would be easy to assume from their famously substantial girth that wrestlers live a life of excess outside their training schedule. In reality, sumo wrestlers' lives are possibly the most rigidly regimented and disciplined of any athletes in the world, and life in a sumo stable is incredibly hard. Life is hardest for the lower ranked wrestlers, who are expected to get up earliest and cook, clean, serve food and generally wait on the higher ranked wrestlers. They even have to bathe last after training, and get last pick at dinner time – after their more senior peers have gobbled all the choice morsels!
It is a fact of sumo life that the younger, inexperienced wrestlers endure systematic hazing and physical punishment in order to toughen them up. This is part and parcel of sumo culture and something that young wrestlers know to expect, but it can sometimes go too far – resulting in injury and in very rare cases, even death.

D. In fact, it was only very recently in the history of sumo that the wrestlers developed the chubbiness they are now famous for. Since there are no weight divisions in professional sumo, every wrestler basically just wants to get as big as possible so that he can use his weight in the ring. It wasn't until well into the twentieth century that the modern image of the whale-like sumo wrestler really emerged – with earlier wrestlers typically much more wiry and muscular.
If you've ever wondered just how modern sumo wrestlers get so fat, it's all thanks to something called chanko nabe. This is a special kind of hotpot packed with meat, veggies and noodles that is specifically associated with sumo wrestlers in Japan. Wrestlers have a special routine of exercising on an empty stomach and sleeping after eating to help turn the calories they consume, purportedly up to 10,000 per day, into bulk.

E. Sumo referees, or gyoji, are as interesting as the wrestlers. Like the wrestlers, they enter the world of sumo at a young age, about sixteen, and remain in their profession until they retire. The traditional clothing they wear in the ring is strictly graded according to rank, and as they progress up the ranks they earn honorific names by which they become known. The top ranked gyoji, the equivalent of yokozuna for wrestlers, takes the name Kimura Shonosuke but, unlike the rank of yokozuna, it can only be held by one person at any one time.

Perhaps most interestingly, the gyoji also carries a sword of about six to twelve inches in length. The significance of the sword is to show that the gyoji understands the seriousness of the decisions he has to make – and is prepared to commit seppuku (ritual suicide by disembowelment) if he makes a bad decision!

Thankfully, nowadays, the gyoji usually just submits his resignation instead as a gesture of contrition. In most cases the gesture is just that, and the erring gyoji's resignation is very rarely accepted.

F. In accordance with the strict rules governing their lives, sumo wrestlers aren't allowed to choose their own clothes. As soon as they join a stable they are expected to grow their hair in order to form a topknot similar to the samurai hairstyles of the Edo Period. They are expected to wear this hairstyle and traditional dress at all times when out in public – which means that sumo wrestlers are pretty easy to spot on the subway! Not only must they wear traditional dress, but the specifics of their dress are also closely controlled. The less experienced wrestlers must wear a lower-quality, thin cotton robe and wooden sandals even in winter, whilst higher ranked wrestlers can wear increasingly swanky robes and even get to choose their own!

G. There aren't many sports from which women are actually forbidden from participating. Sumo, however, is one of them, they are not allowed to even enter the, as it is considered a violation of the purity of the ring.

This caused a bit of an issue when there was a female Governor of Osaka – Fusae Ohta, governor from 2000 – 2008. The Governor traditionally presents the Governor's Prize in the ring at the end of the tournament, but obviously this is a bit tricky when the Governor is banned from the ring. Ohta wasn't all too impressed by this ruling, and she repeatedly challenged the Sumo Association to allow her to fulfil her traditional role as Governor. She was repeatedly turned down until she eventually stepped down from office.

It wasn't always the case that sumo was so hostile to women, however, and as early as the 18th century there was a form of female sumo commonly performed in some areas of Japan. Most of the time this was just a form of entertainment, but in some areas of Japan female sumo did have a serious role in Shinto rituals. Today it is prohibited from taking place in anything but an amateur setting.

So there you have it. The next time you're tempted to laugh at a sumo wrestler's man boobs, just remember that those wobbly abs and thunder thighs conceal an incredible discipline the likes of which you or I can hardly imagine.

Questions 37 – 40

Fill in the blanks in the paragraph below using **NO MORE THAN ONE WORD** from the text.

37. Sumo wrestling originated about 1500 years ago. It is very closely interlaced with religious overtones, namely the customary norms of .... practices.
38. A sumo bout ends when one of the opponents is thrown out of the ring, or any art of his body apart from the soles of his feet touch the ground; it can also end if either wrestler's...................... comes off.
39. A sumo wrestler, especially the junior ones, lead a difficult life, and have to tolerate a lot of harassment and bodily....................
40. Their hairstyle, their clothes, the fabric that it is made of, all these are very rigorously........................

ANSWERS – INTRODUCTORY QUESTIONS

INTRODUCTION QUESTION ANSWERS
TRUE/FALSE/NOT GIVEN

1. TRUE
2. NOT GIVEN
3. FALSE
4. FALSE

SHORT ANSWER QUESTIONS

1. CONVENIENT AND INEXPENSIVE
2. BOOK EARLY
3. MAY 2017
4. RATNAGIRI AND KUDAL

MATCH THE STATEMENT TO A PART OF TEXT QUESTIONS

1. G
2. B
3. A
4. C
5. D

FILL IN THE BLANKS USING WORDS FROM THE BOX

1. SERIOUS
2. AGREEMENT
3. RAMIFICATIONS
4. YEARNING
5. DOCTRINE

DIAGRAM LABELING QUESTIONS TYPE 1

1. A. THORAX
2. B. ANTENNAE
3. C. FORE LEGS
4. E. SPIRACLES
5. F. HINDLEGS

DIAGRAM LABELLING QUESTIONS TYPE 2

1. B
2. D
3. H
4. K
5. E
6. M
7. G

COMPLETING THE SUMMARY

1. ANNIHILATE
2. 1901
3. $225 MILLION
4. WINNER
5. DISCOVERIES
6. 50 YEARS

PARAGRAPH HEADINGS QUESTIONS

1. III
2. IV
3. I
4. V
5. II
6. VIII
7. VII
8. VI

READING ANSWERS

	Reading 1	Reading 2	Reading 3	Reading 4	Reading 5
1.	C	E	NOT GIVEN	D	C
2.	B	H	TRUE,	C	G
3.	C	B	NOT GIVEN	E	A
4.	D	G	TRUE	A	F
5.	E	D	NOT GIVEN	A	D
6.	F	A	FALSE	E	B
7.	A	C	FALSE	F	E
8.	B	F	TRUE	FALSE	H
9.	TRUE	FALSE	TRUE	NOT GIVEN	NOT GIVEN
10.	FALSE	FALSE	FALSE	TRUE	TRUE
11.	TRUE	FALSE	FALSE	TRUE	TRUE
12.	TRUE	TRUE	NOT GIVEN	FALSE	TRUE
13.	NOT GIVEN	FALSE	TRUE	TRUE	FALSE
14.	FALSE	NOT GIVEN	TRUE	FALSE	NOT GIVEN
15.	RESPOND	VENOUS	FIRST	TWO	OVERLOOKE D
16.	REACT	ERECT	CUSTOMER SERVICE	HOME	DETECTORS
17.	KEY-MESSAGE	MOVEMENTS	FLEXIBILITY	CONCENTRATE	PANIC
18.	CORE	MOOD	EXPENSES	LIFELINE	PREMIUM
19.	YOU	SARVASANA	CLERICAL	BELIEVE	SAFE
20.	BREATHING	RELIEVE	MICROSOFT OFFICE	CONFIDENT	SUFFICIENT
21.	RELAX	INDIA	POPULAR	WORKING	FALSE
22.	DEADLINE	TALK	AFFORDABLE	FOG	TRUE
23.	NICETIES	VALUED	WHOLE LIFE	INTERNATIONAL CARD	NOT GIVEN
24.	LAST	CONTRIBUTIO N	CHILD PLAN	TOURIST AGENCY	TRUE
25.	CALENDAR	GIFT	RETIREMENT PLAN	POPULAR	FALSE
26.	FLEXIBILITY	SURVEYS	WHOLE LIFE	VIATOR	FALSE
27.	FRIDAY	POSITIVE	ULIP	SHOPPING TOUR	FALSE
28.	IV	IV	III	III	VIII
29.	I	I	IV	I	III
30.	II	II	I	VI	I
31.	VI	V	V	IV	V
32.	III	III	II	VII	II
33.	VII	VIII	VIII	V	VI
34.	VIII	VII	VII	VIII	IV
35.	V	VI	VI	II	VII
36.	PRODUCTION	HUMANS	SUBSISTENCE	1936	EXTERNALITIES
37.	DEFORESTATION	OIL	REMOTE	ACTRESSES	METHANE
38.	HYBRID	NILE	OIL	HIGHER	POWER
39.	SULPHUR	FIVE	LANDMARK	BRIGHTLY	DANGEROUS
40.	UNFORTUNATE	ECONOMIC	RESILIENCE	CONTINGENCY	THERMAL

	Reading 6	Reading 7	Reading 8	Reading 9	Reading 10
1.	D	FALSE	E	G	FALSE
2.	F	NOT GIVEN	C	E	TRUE
3.	A	NOT GIVEN	A	A	FALSE
4.	G	TRUE	G	D	TRUE
5.	B	TRUE	B	B	NOT GIVEN
6.	E	TRUE	H	C	NOT GIVEN
7.	C	TRUE	F	F	FALSE
8.	E	NOT GIVEN	D	H	MULTI-GUN
9.	TRUE	F	FALSE	FALSE	OBVIOUS
10.	TRUE	D	FALSE	NOT GIVEN	DIFFERENT
11.	FALSE	B	TRUE	FALSE	SCENARIO
12.	TRUE	G	NOT GIVEN	TRUE	COMBAT
13.	FALSE	A	FALSE	FALSE	PERMITTED
14.	NOT GIVEN	C	TRUE	TRUE	LEARN
15.	REVIEW	A	PERCENTAGE	FLAVOR	INTERVIEWS
16.	ABIDE	C	STRATEGY	PERFECT	TYPEFACES
17.	SATISFACTION	H	PERFORMANCE	SKIN	ENGINEERIN G
18.	ADJUST	E	HIGHER	YOUNG	MARKET
19.	DOCUMENT	B	CATEGORIES	RADISH	SOLUTION
20.	ADVANTAGEO US	F	MOTIVATED	BULK	IMPRESSION
21.	FALSE	FALSE	MERIT	ANTI-OXIDANTS	CONTACT
22.	TRUE	FALSE	D	B	B
23.	FALSE	TRUE	B	C	B
24.	FALSE	FALSE	G	B	C
25.	FALSE	FALSE	F	A	A
26.	NOT GIVEN	FALSE	E	C	A
27.	TRUE	NOT GIVEN	C	C	A
28.	IV	IV	VIII	III	V
29.	VII	VII	III	IV	VII
30.	I	I	I	V	III
31.	V	V	V	VI	VI
32.	II	II	II	VII	II
33.	VI	VI	VI	II	IV
34.	III	III	IV	VIII	I
35.	VIII	VIII	VII	I	VIII
36.	INFRASTRUCT URE	OCCUPATION	FUTURE	GUILT-RIDDEN	PURPOSES
37.	AFFORDABLE	AGRICULTURE	SATISFACTION	WELCOME	ZOOGEOGRA PHIC
38.	WORLD ECONOMY	INCREDIBLE	OBJECTIVE	MORE	BREEDING
39.	HOPELESSNES S	COLOURFUL/C OLORFUL	PRIVATE	INFLUENCED	PICKY
40.	OVERNIGHT	COLLAPSE	GRIEVANCE	EDUCATION	RESEARCH

	Reading 11	Reading 12	Reading 13	Reading 14	Reading 15
1.	TRUE	D	E	NO	STEAM
2.	FALSE	F	D	YES	THREE
3.	NOT GIVEN	C	A	NOT GIVEN	OIL
4.	FALSE	G	F	NO	SATELLITE
5.	FALSE	E	B	NO	MIRRORS
6.	TRUE	B	C	NO	TOWER
7.	TRUE	A	G	NOT GIVEN	SALT
8.	F	FALSE	FALSE	B	DEEP
9.	B	FALSE	FALSE	F	VEGETABLES
10.	D	TRUE	FALSE	D	LIVELY
11.	A	TRUE	TRUE	A	FORAGING
12.	G	TRUE	TRUE	C	PREGNANT
13.	C	TRUE	NOT GIVEN	E	VISION
14.	E	NOT GIVEN	FALSE	G	SURVIVE
15.	BEHIND THEIR DECISION	ELECTRIC HEATER	YES	C	ANTENNAE
16.	CHASE	ROUND FLASK	NOT GIVEN	D	THORAX
17.	SKILLS AND INTERESTS	CLAMP	YES	B	HIND LEGS
18.	COMPENSATION AND BENEFITS	THERMOMETER	NOT GIVEN	INTRIGUED	STINGER
19.	LACK OF OPPORTUNITY	CONNECTING TUBE	YES	BANAL	FALSE
20.	OPPORTUNITY IS KING	CONDENSER	YES	MEANING	TRUE
21.	DECISION MAKING PROCESS	DISTILLED WATER	NO	CLOSET	FALSE
22.	NEED	HYGIENE	EXPECTATIONS	HANDLE	FREEDOM
23.	HIGH SEAS	FIVE	INVESTED	SENTIMENTS	ABNORMAL
24.	CONVICTS	GERME	WORK-APPROPRIATE	COMPASSION	BREED
25.	MANY	NEEDED	ISOLATION	CONTRARY	BABY
26.	RARE	FRESH	DISTRACTIONS	PRESSURES	ENOUGH
27.	TURKEY	COST	DISCONNECT	RESTRAINT	SUPPORT
28.	IV	TRIVIAL	III	V	VII
29.	III	III	IV	III	II
30.	V	IV	VIII	I	I
31.	I	I	V	II	IV
32.	VIII	V	II	IV	V
33.	VI	II	I	FALSE	III
34.	II	VIII	VII	FALSE	VI
35.	VII	VII	VI	TRUE	BURNOUT
36.	ANIMALS	VI	SOCIAL MEDIA	TRUE	HEALTH
37.	STUDIES	WOMEN	TWITTER	TRUE	INCREMENTAL
38.	THINNER	TRANSFORMATIVE	DIAGNOSE	ALL FOURS	SUSTAINABLE
39.	RISK	ECONOMIC POWER	SOCIAL ISOLATION	JUVENILE	HABITS
40.	INFLAMMATION	HOW SOON	MYRIAD BENEFITS	FACIAL EXPRESSIONS/ GESTURES/ VOCALISATIONS	CBT

	Reading 16	Reading 17	Reading 18	Reading 19	Reading 20
1.	MANIPURI	D	FALSE	4	FALSE
2.	KATHAKALI	A	TRUE	8	TRUE
3.	ODISSI	F	NOT GIVEN	9	FALSE
4.	BHARATNATYAM	E	NOT GIVEN	5	NOT GIVEN
5.	KUCHIPUDI	C	TRUE	1	TRUE
6.	KATHAK	B	NOT GIVEN	6	TRUE
7.	TRUE	G	UNTAMED	10	NOT GIVEN
8.	NOT GIVEN	NOT GIVEN	BREED	NOT GIVEN	IMBUED
9.	TRUE	TRUE	SPORT	TRUE	PROSPEROUS
10.	FALSE	TRUE	GAMBLING	TRUE	SEQUENCE
11.	TRUE	TRUE	LINEAGE	TRUE	DETRACT
12.	TRUE	FALSE	PRIDE	FALSE	CONVENTIONA L
13.	NOT GIVEN	TRUE	SUPPORT	NOT GIVEN	HUMBLENESS
14.	C	NOT GIVEN	SIX	NOT GIVEN	AWAY
15.	F	D	BRITAIN/FRANCE	P	B
16.	A	F	FRANCE/BRITAIN	H	G
17.	C	C	AUGUST 23	D	E
18.	SMALLER	NOT GIVEN	TWO-THIRDS	F	F
19.	OUTLIVE	FALSE	AUGUST 25	E	C
20.	SPECIES	TRUE	SEPTEMBER 3	M	A
21.	SUCCESSFUL MASS-PRODUCED COMPUTER	NOT GIVEN	RAVISHINGLY SEDUCTIVE	G	D
22.	IN 1956	NOT GIVEN	ANCILLARY	D	NO
23.	PEPSICO	YES	INCOMPARABLE	E	NO
24.	THE EDUCATION SECTOR	YES	ALMOND-SHAPED	F	YES
25.	REPUTATION AND FORTUNE	YES	NOSE	B	YES
26.	PRIOR TO 2001	YES	ELIZABETH-TAYLOR	C	YES
27.	MORIBUND	NOT GIVEN	WILLIAM SHAKESPEARE	G	YES
28.	III	III	III	IV	YES
29.	IV	IV	I	VII	NO
30.	I	I	VI	II	IV
31.	V	V	IV	I	VII
32.	II	II	VII	III	I
33.	VIII	VIII	V	V	V
34.	VII	VII	II	VI	II
35.	VI	VI	VIII	PHAROAH	VI
36.	NARRATIVE	ABILITY	DIVERSE	MEDIATOR	III
37.	TOUGH	POWELL/HYD E	CONVICTS	MASTABAS	SHINTO
38.	1872	PASSENGERS	CHANGE	IMHOTEP	LOINCLOTH
39.	HOST	CHEAPER	CAMPAIGN	LABOUR	PUNISHMENT
40.	DISTINGUISHED	HIRE	ECONOMY	ALLURE	CONTROLLED

BUILD YOUR VOCABULARY

ENTHRALLING: keeping someone's interest and attention completely:
I found your book absolutely enthralling!

SPECTACULAR: very exciting to look at:
a spectacular view
He scored a spectacular goal in the second half.
There was a spectacular sunset last night.
especially great:
We've had spectacular success with the product.

REJUVENATE: to make someone look or feel young and energetic again:
She felt rejuvenated by her fortnight in the Bahamas.

to make an organization or system more effective by introducing new methods,ideas, or people:
He has decided to rejuvenate the team by bringing in a lot of new, young players.

ASPIRATIONS: something that you hope to achieve:
I've never had any political aspirations.

ATTAINABLE: possible to achieve:
We must ensure that we do not set ourselves goals that are not attainable.

PHENOMENON: something that exists and can be seen, felt, tasted, etc., especially something unusual or interesting:
Gravity is a natural phenomenon.
Do you believe in the paranormal and other psychic phenomena?
There's evidence to suggest that child abuse is not just a recent phenomenon.

ANTHROPOGENIC: caused by humans or their activities:
anthropogenic emissions of greenhouse gases

PHOTOSYNTHESIS: the process by which a plant uses the energy from the light of the sun to produce its own food
DETRIMENTAL: causing harm or damage:
These chemicals have a detrimental effect/impact on the environment.
Their decision could be detrimental to the future of the company.

HYBRID: a plant or animal that has been produced from two different types of plant or animal, especially to get better characteristics:
The garden strawberry is a large-fruited hybrid.
The animal looks like a hybrid of a zebra and a horse.

Something that is a mixture of two very different things:
His work is an interesting hybrid of popular and classical music.

PRIMATE: a member of the most developed and intelligent group of mammals, including humans, monkeys and apes.
EXACERBATED: to make something that is already bad even worse:
This attack will exacerbate the already tense relations between the two communities.

UBIQUITOUS: seeming to be everywhere:
Leather is very much in fashion this season, as is the ubiquitous denim.

INCINERATE: to burn something completely:
to incinerate waste
The spacecraft and its crew were incinerated by the billion-degree temperatures generated by the fireball.

CANNON BALL (IN THE SWIMMING POOL): A dive, in which you hold your knees to your chest and hit the water on your buttocks with as much force as possible with the purpose of creating a gigantic splash, thus soaking everyone in the near vicinity.
CORPUS: Masses and large amount of things

SUBSISTENCE: the state of having what you need in order to stay alive, but no more:
The money is intended to provide a basic subsistence and should not be paid to someone who receives other income.
The family was living at subsistence level.

enough money or food to keep yourself alive

MORATORIUM: a stopping of an activity for an agreed amount of time:
a five-year worldwide moratorium on nuclear weapons testing

ENSUING: happening after something and because of it:
An argument broke out and in the ensuing fight, a gun went off.
He lost his job and in the ensuing months became more and more depressed.

SENTIENCE: the quality of being able to experience feelings:
Why are humans not willing to accept the full sentience of other animals?
Research on animal sentience is beginning to inform approaches to animal welfare.

ECOLOGY: the relationships between the air, land, water, animals, plants, etc., usually of a particular area, or the scientific study of this:
The oil spill caused terrible damage to the fragile ecology of the coast.
She hopes to study ecology at college.

PERENNIAL: lasting a very long time, or happening repeatedly or all the time:
The film "White Christmas" is a perennial favourite.
We face the perennial problem of not having enough money.

HAMLET: a small village.

PLACID: having a calm appearance or characteristics:
a slow-moving and placid river
the placid pace of village life

TRAIT: a particular characteristic that can produce a particular type of behaviour:
His sense of humour is one of his better traits.
Arrogance is a very unattractive personality/character trait.

EMBLEMATIC: representing a particular person, group, or idea:
A sword is emblematic of power gained by violence.

RESILIENT: able to be happy, successful, etc. again after something difficult or bad has happened:
She's a resilient girl - she won't be unhappy for long.
Optimists argue that the economy may prove more resilient.

able to quickly return to its usual shape after being bent, stretched, orpressed:
This rubber ball is very resilient and immediately springs back into shape.
resilient materials

CONTINGENCY: something that might possibly happen in the future, usually causing problems or making further arrangements necessary:
You must be able to deal with all possible contingencies.
Have you made any contingency plans?

INTRICATE: having a lot of small parts that are arranged in a complicated or delicate way:
The watch mechanism is extremely intricate and very difficult to repair.
The tiled floor is installed in an intricate pattern.

with many complicated details that make something difficult to understand:
Police officers uncovered an intricate web of deceit.

SMUG: too pleased or satisfied about something you have achieved or something you know:
a smug grin
She deserved her promotion, but I wish she wasn't so smug about it.
He's been unbearably smug since he gave up smoking.